THE NEW-IDEA SUCCESS BOOK

Starting a money-making business

Al Riolo & Ellen Greenberg

D1738787

LIBERTY HOUSE®

LIBERTY HOUSE books are published by LIBERTY HOUSE, a division of TAB BOOKS Inc. Its trademark, consisting of the words "LIBERTY HOUSE" and the portrayal of Benjamin Franklin, is registered in the United States Patent and Copyright Office.

FIRST EDITION
FIRST PRINTING

Library of Congress Cataloging-in-Publication Data

Riolo, Al, 1939-
The new-idea success book : starting a money-making business / by
Al Riolo and Ellen Greenberg.
p.   cm.
Includes index.
ISBN 0-8306-3013-9 (pbk.)
1. New business enterprises. 2. Success in business.
I. Greenberg, Ellen.   II. Title.
HD62.5.R565 1988
658.1′141—dc19   88-28211
                                        CIP

TAB BOOKS Inc. offers software for
sale. For information and a catalog,
please contact TAB Software Department,
Blue Ridge Summit, PA 17294-0850.

Questions regarding the content of this book
should be addressed to:

Reader Inquiry Branch
TAB BOOKS Inc.
Blue Ridge Summit, PA 17294-0214

Contents

Introduction
Steps to Business Success

This book is about making money. With information in this one small volume, your favorite hobby, sport, pastime, or idea can be converted to extra cash or a vast fortune.

The book gives you everything you need to know in a quick and readable fashion. Its basic assumption is that your time is more valuably spent making money using the secrets in it than taking forever to read about how to do it.

At the start, this book will help you choose a winning idea that will become the basis for a business. It will show how to identify the things you do best and like to do most, and then it will help you create a business that capitalizes on these strengths.

The heart of the book is about the nuts and bolts of starting and running your own business. It will tell you about the licenses and tools you will need to get the ball rolling and describe ways you can organize your business. It will tell you how to find the product you've decided to sell, how to patent it if you're its inventor, how to manufacture it yourself, and how to locate someone else's product if you've decided that "reselling" is what you want to do. It also tells you how to start a service business from scratch.

The chapter on buying a business or franchise tells you how to go about these traditional ways of getting into business. It also describes the pitfalls and the pleasures.

Money doesn't have to be a problem. Chapter 10 gives you the lowdown on tapping your own resources—resources you might not know you have. It gives tips on how to get money from outside sources, from banks and the government, and through venture capitalists. Chapter 11 teaches you how to prepare a business plan that will impress the people who have the money.

Once you've settled on the product or service that will be your business, you're ready to meet your customers. Chapter 12 talks about setting your price; Chapter 13 about getting a ready-made sales force; and Chapter 14 discloses the secrets of mail-order selling. Chapter 15 is a primer on advertising and publicity, telemarketing, and trade shows.

Sometime along the way, you will probably be hiring employees. How to choose the right people and how to manage them once you've found them is what Chapter 16 is all about.

Accurate record keeping is a must. Just what kinds of records you should keep and some tips on ways to keep them are the crux of the next chapter. And just as important is a lesson on how to read what your records are telling you about the health of your business.

Then there are taxes; but don't despair, the government can become your partner. As you will discover, owning your own business can provide sizeable tax breaks.

This book encourages you to go into business for yourself. The 10-point success formula will set you on your way, and the success stories of those who have already made it will inspire you and tell you the secrets of success.

Proven universal success principles described here are yielding fabulous riches to others. Dedication to these methods will work for you too; you can count on it.

Now, get ready to achieve the prosperity, happiness, and success that should have been yours years ago. Read on!

1
Why Should You Be in Business?

A business of your own can provide freedom and independence; it can be a direct avenue to that extra money you want and need. Your ultimate objective may be to build a "wealth base," producing all the luxuries and comforts money can buy—a new car, glamorous vacations, a splendid new home, fine furnishings, stylish clothes, financial independence. Or, you may simply need more money to make ends meet or to provide that second income needed for an improved life style. Regardless, being in business can enable you to have the things you want.

Converting your favorite hobby, sport, pastime, or idea to a business of your own gives you all the benefits of the free enterprise system not available to those who merely work for others.

Being in business means tax breaks. Big tax advantages help get your business going. You can claim deductions from earned income for all business-related start-up costs. Many tax advantages thought to be available only to the rich, such as investment credits and advantageous depreciation formulas, can be yours. A portion of earned income can be sheltered if invested in your business. Normal telephone bills, stationery and other supplies, postage, auto and travel costs, personal computers, home shop supplies and expenses, small equipment items, day-to-day articles, and merchandise purchased in connection with the business are all tax deductible. If you are looking for tax breaks, owning a business is a solid way to get them.

Being in business provides priceless satisfaction. Joy and inspiration are the treasured fruits of your own initiative and accomplishments. A business of your own can bring satisfaction unmatched by any other human experience. Motivation, untapped energy, enthusiasm; discovery that fatigue, exhaustion, physical

1

aches and pains, and even physical handicap limitations practically disappear—these are all products of being in your own business. A business can work miracles in eradicating various frustrations, depression, fear, and loneliness.

Hope, exaltation, power, enjoying people once again, learning who you really are, firmly establishing yourself in the community, rediscovering meaning in life, even achieving worldwide acclaim and recognition—these are rewards money can't buy, but they can be yours when you are in business for yourself.

If you have ever been discouraged, if you have difficulties to surmount that seem to strike at your very soul, if you have ever tried and failed, if you have had an illness or a physical handicap, if you have suffered from discrimination, if you have had one serious setback after another, this book can lead to the fulfillment for which you've searched but that has so far eluded you.

This is the age of the entrepreneur. A plucky adventuresome spirit, fascination with a skill or hobby, fresh ideas, ingenuity, and the desire to be independent are some of the reasons that there are more business start-ups today than ever before.

Today almost 15 million Americans generate income by operating about 15 million business enterprises. Small businesses comprise 97 percent of the total private business sector, and 80 percent of these employ fewer than 10 people. On average, about 350,000 new businesses are formed each year. A great many are spawned from an intense interest in what the owner does best or to fill needs for products and services not dreamed of 10 years ago. Today, more than ever, small business is America's growth industry (TABLE 1-1).

TABLE 1-1. Fastest Growing Small Businesses.

1. Computers and related products and services
2. Recreation and amusement services
3. Home remodeling, masonry, stonework and repair
4. Credit reporting and collections
5. Outpatient health care
6. Wood products and carpentry
7. Medical and dental laboratories
8. Highway and street construction/repair
9. Management and public relations services
10. Painting, paperhanging, decorating and flooring

Source: U.S. Small Business Administration, *Small Business and the Economy of the 1980s* (January 1985).

PEOPLE LIKE YOURSELF HAVE MADE IT IN THEIR OWN BUSINESS

In America, the free enterprise system is open to everyone. It makes no difference what your age, current income, physical capacity, ethnic background, skin color, national origin, or gender, you can have the things you want in life through the vehicle of a business of your own. And what makes it even better is your business can be in the area of your life that is of greatest interest to you. Proof is all around you.

Just look at the variety of people generating income from business pursuits in your own community. What do you see? Men and women of all ages and backgrounds, from all walks of life, serving you and your neighbors and producing sizeable incomes from successful business pursuits.

Your Age Doesn't Matter

Success has no regard for age. Old and young alike have successfully turned a prized interest, talent, or skill into income.

At the high end of the age scale, recall the accomplishments of Colonel Harland Sanders of Kentucky Fried Chicken fame. At age 66 with his only income being a $105 per month social-security pension, Sanders capitalized on his favorite pastime: experimenting with new recipes. Pursuing his love of cooking, he found the combination of a unique recipe and a pressure cooker produced excellent-tasting chicken.

The Colonel launched a business by persuading restaurant owners to use his cooking technique then pay a 5-cent royalty on each chicken sold. While in his 70s, Sanders traveled the country with missionary zeal, selling his unique franchise to restaurant owners. In nine years, he signed 600 franchises. He was banking $1,000 a day when he sold the business for $2 million to John Y. Brown, Jr.

The Colonel is but one example of folks in their 60s, 70s, and 80s who are turning a favorite hobby, craft, or work experience into profitable businesses, and occasionally an immense fortune. At the lower end of the age scale, desire to strike it rich at a tender age is producing a new generation of entrepreneurs. Government figures show that the one-third of all new companies are owned by people under 30.

One of the most successful of this new breed of entrepreneurs is William H. Gates, founder of Microsoft Corporation, a computer software producer. At age 19, Gates had such a burning fascination with the enormous potential of computers that he dropped out of Harvard University where he was studying mathematics. Instead, he decided to concentrate all of his time and energy on creating his own business.

With a singleness of purpose, Gates established a goal to make Microsoft a one-stop supermarket for personal computer software. His business took off when Tandy hired him to develop some of the software for its Radio Shack TRS-80 personal computer. Gates' company got an even bigger boost when IBM Corporation selected Microsoft software to run its famous personal computer. At one point, 40 percent of all personal computers, regardless of manufacturing source, were shipped with Microsoft software.

Gates started Microsoft with private financing; but eventually the firm issued publicly traded stock, 40 percent of it retained by Gates. Prior to the stock market crash of 1987, *Forbes Magazine* designated Gates as one of the richest people in America, valuing his stock at $1.25 billion. The stock market crash reduced the value of Microsoft stock from $63.50 a share to $48.00, resulting in a paper loss of $255 million to Gates, who responded that he really couldn't be bothered with such trivialities.

Your Sex Doesn't Matter

Success doesn't care whether you are male or female. Starting a business is not the kind of activity reserved exclusively to either sex. However, more women are grabbing the lucrative opportunity today to be small-business owners. Government statistics show that over 3 million small businesses are owned by women, and the number is growing at the rate of 8 percent a year, On average, the number of self-employed women is increasing three times faster than the number of self-employed men. Bright, energetic women with the ability and willingness to apply knowledge and imagination are highly successful in business.

Joanne Marlow at age 20, with her passion for clothing design grossing $2.2 million per year, was rated among the nation's top 100 young entrepreneurs. Fascination with her pastime interest began as a mail-order crafts operation in her home in the Chicago suburb of Skokie, Illinois. Now her Joanne Marlow Designs produces women's clothing in a 7,000-square-foot factory in the neighboring suburb of Evanston.

Your Nationality or Race Doesn't Matter

Success doesn't give a hoot about your national origin. Christine Valmy, an immigrant from Rumania who refused to give up on a long-held idea, rocketed herself from a $45-a-week job to queen of the skin-care game.

Her scientific skin-cleansing business began with little more than an idea—a hobby fascination with glamour—hard work, and persistence. Now, Christine Valmy Skin Care Salons prosper in the United States, Canada, and Japan.

Realizing that people need products as well as services, she delivers both. Her scientific skin-care-treatment service consists of steaming tired faces, using a rotary brush made of pig bristles to remove dead skin cells, emulsifying pore plugs, vacuuming complexion, and stimulating revived skin electrically. Her products are equally fascinating. One favorite is a custom-prepared cream known as Dermovit S., which sells for around $90 a half-ounce. Ingredients consist of 46 plant extracts, amino acids, vitamins, and living cells from chick embryos. People said she was crazy for starting her business, that skin cleansing and treatment salons wouldn't work; but now she sits atop a mountain of money.

Success doesn't care about the color of your skin. Berry Gordy, Jr., founded Detroit's Motown Record Corporation because music was his favorite pastime. He began with a $700 investment. Eight years later, his company was grossing $30 million annually. Convinced he could match talented people in the black community with tunes, lyrics, and audio effects that would appeal to listeners of every race, he contributed to the gigantic growth of the record and tape industry that today exceeds $5.2 billion annually.

How Much Money You Have Doesn't Matter

Success doesn't care whether you have very little money to start with so long as you're willing to make up the difference with commitment, mental discipline, and knowledge.

Kenny Brown was short of cash, had no big money backing, and barely had tangible assets; but he parlayed a keen interest in motorcycles, some hand tools, and a shop rented for $125 a month into a giant business known as Ken Brown's Cycle World. Ken Brown enjoyed enormous financial rewards because of a proper mental attitude, thought, imagination, action, and persistence. Out of these, he created his huge motorcycle-mechanics training school and nationwide motorcycle-rental-franchise business.

Success cares not whether you already have an independent income. You may wonder why anybody already in possession of a comfortable income would want to go into business. The answer is easy to see and understand. You can count by the tens of thousands those who have plenty of money but who are desperate to do something more with their lives; do something that fills that craving to find self-expression and actualize their ideas and creations or to realize their full potential, talents, and skills. Within some, a thought or idea is burning so intensely, they cannot extinguish it no matter how often or how hard they try. In such instances, it is not insufficient money that keeps them from finding full satisfaction, but rather the lack of some other key element.

Perhaps you never gave serious thought to the idea that you could find fulfillment by turning an idea into a successful business. Perhaps you need a bit more direction, a key contact person, someone with specialized knowledge outside your field, or a company already in command of required machinery, employees, time, or whatever to transform your languishing ideas into a living reality. Perhaps, you need to be assured that you can be motivated to find real meaning by presenting that special creation to the public, that all your precious dreams can come true when that public demonstrates acceptance and appreciation by returning to you a monetary equivalent.

Look, for example, at the fabulous success of Dr. Maxwell Maltz. He was already a renowned plastic surgeon but felt compelled to tell others of a secret method he found to raise the personal self-image of post-surgical patients. Thus, he wrote a book titled *Psycho-Cybernetics.* Application of the book's ideas relieved stress and removed scars that were "within" so the patient could benefit from cosmetic surgery performed "outside." Now, more than 2 million copies have been sold, and Dr. Maltz knows real satisfaction from his contribution to others and in the process has rounded out his life.

YOUR 10-POINT SUCCESS FORMULA

Success cares not whether you are currently in an unfortunate mental or physical state of being; neither does success care about your physical appearance, manner of dress, hair style, where you live, finances, nor any of hundreds of other conditions that you may believe are keeping you from finding fulfillment. Rather, all who activate their minds, all who follow the program described in this book will be inspired to success. You are in possession of the most startlingly powerful plan of this century. Use it; don't just think or talk about it. Use it and you will be turning the key that unlocks the door to life's bountiful riches.

Defining a Major Purpose. Concentrate your thoughts on those activities you enjoy most. Of your hobbies, specialized knowledge, skills, talents, what do you do best? What do others consider your strengths? Which pursuits bring most pride, pleasure, or satisfaction? Do you have an idea so compelling, so powerful, its expression must be given tangible form or life will be incomplete? Identify these and you will be exercising the first universal success principle—defining a major purpose. Sustain this process and a successful idea will emerge; you cannot be denied.

Accurate or Controlled Thinking. List the five recurring ideas or activities produced after you've defined a major purpose. Prioritize the list according to the percentage of time you devote to each. If you identify an idea so motivating you cannot push it from your mind, give it a place of highest priority on your list. You are now exercising the second universal success principle.

Belief. Don't worry about how to convert these pursuits to cash; this book will provide specific instructions on how to do so. In truth, what your mind can conceive and believe, you can achieve. This is your powerful, third universal success principle.

Reinforcing Thought or Autosuggestion. Carry your list of favorite activities and ideas with you, look at it, and think about its contents repeatedly every day. Consider how your choices fit in with human wants, needs, habits, interests, and trends. This is the fourth universal success principle.

Organize Specialized Knowledge. Match your list of chosen ideas and activities to timeless human desires for recreation, security, convenience, companionship, good health, physical fitness, food, shelter, increasing wealth, beauty, sex, or saving time and effort. This is the fifth universal success principle.

Imagination. Identify something about the activity or idea that represents or defines a need—a need not now being met, but if met, one that would be useful to you and to others, and you will be fulfilling the sixth universal success principle.

Applied Faith. Allow your subconscious mind free rein to transform thoughts into a tangible product or service that can be converted to a monetary equivalent. Chapters 2 and 3 include additional mind stimulants to help you focus on a specific product or service to achieve this seventh universal success principle.

Intensifying Desire. Daily, visualize yourself being in business, filling needs with the product or service you have identified, for you truly do become what you think about. You will be exercising the eighth universal success principle.

Building Enthusiasm. Create a business image around the method you intend to use to fill an identified need. Later, this book provides specific instructions for building a business image. Now, the important thing is to picture yourself actually being in business; visualize all those things your own business can bring you. This is the ninth universal success principle.

Persistence. Follow through with the remaining steps in this book. Good intentions are not enough, you must take action. This is the tenth and last universal success principle.

2
Discovering a
Need You Can Fill

You can be in business in a month's time. All you need is a business license, fictitious name statement, state-tax resale permit, an Internal Revenue Service (IRS) employer number, a business checking account, and an idea.

With the exception of an idea, these items are merely mechanical building blocks required in the beginning to establish your business on a solid foundation. Arranging for these permits and accommodations in the early stages of your business is analogous to obtaining the necessary permits before you begin construction on a building.

Nailing down your business ideas is analogous to drafting a set of construction plans so all intentions are efficiently fulfilled when construction actually occurs. Without plans there can be no building; without an idea there can be no business.

WHAT IS YOUR FAVORITE ACTIVITY?

Every business begins with an idea, and the best ideas are inspired by the activities you enjoy most. Are you crazy about sports? What's your favorite hobby? How do you use free time? Do you fish, play golf, jog, hike, hunt, read for pleasure? Do you enjoy dancing, music, travel, skiing, sunbathing, home repair, trapshooting? Is your spare time used creating arts and crafts, repairing sporting equipment, camping? Do you enjoy tinkering with cars, doing needlepoint, gardening, barbecuing, making pottery, making gadgets, trying new recipes, watching television, using a computer, financial investing?

Before reading further, you must identify that activity or idea toward which you are most inclined. This book urges repeatedly to take this first step for it is the most essential ingredient of a successful business. Take the time now to identify that activity or idea most intriguing to you. When you do, recognize that an amazing source of power, happiness, recognition, peace of mind, and riches of all sorts will be yours.

HOW TO SPOT NEW OPPORTUNITIES

The first section of this book is (1) designed to generate thought leading to (2) an imaginative idea to be (3) converted to cash through (4) a definite plan of action to (5) offer a product or provide a service. Once you have identified the activity or idea that stimulates you most, you must determine a specific endeavor involving that activity or idea—one that can be converted readily to a useful purpose (TABLE 2-1).

TABLE 2-1. Source of Ideas for Business Start-Ups.

Source	%
Prior job	42
Personal interest	18
Family, friends, relatives	12
Chance	10
Suggestion	8
Education	6
Other	4

Source: U.S. Small Business Administration, *Small Business and the Economy of the 1980s* (January 1988).

All business enterprise centers around filling a need. There are only two ways to fill a need for profit:

■ Offer a product
■ Provide a service

Which method you choose will depend on your inclination; amount of available time, effort, and capital; and your ultimate objective.

Wealth-building ideas that generate hot new products and services occur most often from pent-up human desires or uncomfortable conditions.

Scarcity and Shortages

Anything in short supply will most certainly point to an unmet need. Fill this need and you can immediately see your income zoom.

Taking little more than a few hours and using three well-known sources, you can identify a host of products and services in short supply in your community and beyond.

Your Telephone Directory

Compare the Yellow Pages of your community telephone book with those of major cities. Telephone-company offices and major libraries retain these directories for your use. Methodical comparisons of index guides can produce a wide assortment of products and services lacking in your own community.

If you have never made such a comparison, this first step in the process of creating ideas should not be neglected. It is exactly the same source used by others who own successful businesses.

While engaged in this process, look carefully at the telephone-book advertisements. Count the number of advertisements or other entries for each business category you're interested in. Determine the ratio of this count to related business entries and compare this ratio to entries in your own community directory. This exercise will help you to spot a scarcity in a particular business category.

Consider carefully the impression you receive from these advertisements. Which, at first blush, capture your attention? Which fail to convey their intended message? Look at the size and placement of advertisements. Try to draw conclusions from this comparative review about the businesses that have placed them. Where are they located geographically? What features or services do they emphasize? What aspects do they overlook?

Remember, once in business, these telephone-book advertisements will be competing for *your* customers. What do you intend to do that's different or better? Once in business, what would be the appearance or your own advertisement relative to the competition? In short, begin now to visualize yourself in the business you've created out of your special interest. Make notes on precisely what you intend to do to capture your share of the market relative to your competition.

Newspapers

The second indicator of scarce products or services is news that a major supply source is no longer available or that rapid price increases are affecting consumers. When these signals begin to flash, you can be certain that marketing what were previously overlooked alternatives to a scarce item or service will be big money producers.

When news articles are telling you that something is in short supply or when you know from your own experience that prices for a particular product or service are escalating more rapidly than normal, you must engage your imagination to identify alternatives you can deliver.

Shortages and scarcities tell you that supply may be evaporating, and this condition provides opportunity to fill unmet demand. Use you talent, skill, or knowledge to accommodate demand and you have answered the question of how to produce income.

While studying newspapers on subjects of supply, demand, and prices, don't forget to conduct the same kind of review of advertisements mentioned in the section on telephone directories. Focus on advertisements from the perspective of someone engaged in that same business. Consider an advertisement's size, location, frequency. What does it announce, offer, or convey?

Advertisements are an expensive attempt by others in business to reach their customer markets. Are they effective? Begin to clip and save some advertisements; sketch and note changes you would make to these advertisements in order to compel attention and attract patronage to your company.

Libraries

The public library, that great repository of all human knowledge, is a source of powerful ideas. Thousands of new concepts are waiting there to be converted to cash, but you must make up your mind to seek them out and use them.

The subject index of the standard card catalog represents a tremendous collection of idea generators. Local college and university libraries, which are also available to you, often have a collection of business-related materials and idea-starters even greater than those of community libraries. As a taxpayer, your hard-earned dollars pay for these idea sources. Shouldn't you use them to your full advantage?

The ability to effectively use library resources is an acquired trait. Library staff are always available to show you where to find relevant information. With guidance and very little time, you can become proficient at using information-retrieval techniques, which, when you know and apply them, will quickly help turn your favorite hobby, sport, pastime, or idea into a cash-producing business.

Willingness to regularly use library resources is a matter of making up your mind to do so. Having confidence that libraries contain precious detailed information is a matter of directing your mental capacity and attitude to facilitate use of that resource. As you proceed according to your business plan and as you complete tasks leading to accomplishment of business goals, you will discover that the ability to control and direct, at will, your mental attitude has as much bearing on achievement as big-money financing.

You will find, in business, the frequent need to have access to additional information before making an important decision or choosing among alternative courses of action. At these times, it is common to wish you had access to those capable of providing solid answers. Yet, it is amazing how often the answers you seek are waiting to be picked up at the business section of a community or local college library. As you read this book, if you find that you need more information on any item mentioned or referenced, be assured that just such additional information is waiting for you at your library.

Throughout this book, mention is made of various reference books, guides, and periodicals—ones that will help you to locate information about the business that's right for you and to keep that business prospering. These information sources are valuable. Few can afford to buy this wealth of information, yet it is all available to you free at your local library.

MENTAL ATTITUDE—YOUR SECRET WEALTH BUILDER

An essential requirement to getting into business is that you begin moving in the right direction. Millions lead aimless, shallow, empty lives when their reachable alternative is to activate their minds with a compelling idea. In the divine unfolding of the universe, all that you achieve and all that you fail to achieve is the direct result of your thoughts and actions.

In the endeavor of starting a business, an individual's own responsibility is absolute. Recognizing that a condition or state of being is brought about by one's own habits and not by another's provides power and strength to alter and improve that condition through self-initiated action. Mastery of controlled thinking, a positive mental attitude, imagination, and persistence will lead to a business enterprise right for you. From your own experience, you know that before achieving anything, you must first apply thought and then act. This knowledge should be used to obtain from nearby sources all the information and new ideas to which you are entitled.

Of all the weaknesses in a person, there is one—lack of initiative—that can be easily remedied. It can be transformed to success overnight by the natural stimulant known as desire. Recognize the positive aspects of desire properly directed. Use initiative inspired by desire to seek information for attainment of business success. Know that answers you seek are immediately available. Overcome procrastination; plans for the achievement of success will unfold before you.

3
Business-Building Ideas

Every business begins with an idea. Business-building ideas center around human wants and needs. These wants and needs can be structured into categories. Take this opportunity to look through the categories presented in the following sections. As you do, allow your mind to imagine an important need you can fill. Read the secrets of how others have filled human wants and needs and captured awesome success.

While on this journey, understand the importance of knowledge. General knowledge is rarely of value in the pursuit of cash accumulation. On the other hand, specialized knowledge acquired for a definite purpose and applied toward a worthy idea has resulted in great fortunes.

Remember that everyone forms patterns. At times you may find yourself in a serious rut; you get so habitually regimented by daily routine that you cease to notice new, or recall forgotten avenues of importance. Nevertheless, the attainment of success or capitulation to failure is largely the result of habit. Good habits and new adventures beget success. Bad habits and sameness often lead to failure. Removing yourself from a rut and combining specialized knowledge and imagination will produce ideas. Believing in these ideas, channeling them into an organized plan of action, applying faith and persistence can yield riches.

RECREATION/SPORTS/ENTERTAINMENT

The recreation, sports, and entertainment markets are booming with thousands of new products and services available each year. The public buys these products and pays for recreation or entertainment services with cash outlays running into hundreds of billions of dollars annually.

Think about the recreation, sport, pastime, or entertainment you enjoy most. What is it about it that is in demand? What need is unfilled? What gadget, product, or service can make the sport, pastime, or entertainment more enjoyable? What equipment improvement or new technique will add to recreation satisfaction, convenience, and success? What service can you provide that will bring some form of entertainment pleasure to others?

The movie, song, and theater industries have grown to billion-dollar proportions by satisfying unending human desires for recreation and entertainment. Resolve now to identify a pent-up need and fill that need in a businesslike way; business income will most certainly be yours.

Jason Hendricks, a California fisherman, converted his pastime to earnings using this technique. Impressed with the high price of gold, he began panning in his favorite mountain stream during a fishing vacation. He was lucky; and during his seven days of combined fishing and prospecting, he stumbled across 22 ounces of gold worth more than $5,500.

Inspired by his good fortune, he began an intense study of gold-producing areas and learned that this precious metal has been found in 35 of the 50 states. He found that the U.S. Geological Survey prepared a report listing 500 of the nation's most important gold-finding areas.

He decided to market this information and produced a series of maps showing precise roads and trails leading to public-access gold location areas. He listed known closed mines and even pinpointed specific sides of mountains where runoffs had created earthslides and opened new areas containing gold. He also described all the methods that can be used to pan or mine gold.

He packaged all of this material in a sort of prospector's kit and began running mail-order advertisements in the more popular outdoor magazines. Now his combined business of prospecting and mail-order sales nets him about $82,000 each year.

Studying information sources, every bit as available to you, and applying some imagination produced a virtual gold mine for this weekend fisherman. Why not make a firm commitment to use these same two free tools—resource information and imagination—to produce your own gold mine in your chosen area of interest.

In your chosen area of interest, a valuable information resource available free at public libraries is the *Guide to American Directories* published by B. Klein Publications, Rye, New York. This priceless directory of directories lists almost 5,000 other directories containing valuable information on nearly every subject imaginable.

One such directory is the *Encyclopedia of Information Systems,* published by Anthony T. Kruzas Associates, Ann Arbor, Michigan. It lists more than 1,750 organizations providing information storage and retrieval services covering literally millions of subjects. For example, the directory lists an information source for the specific location of uranium and mineral deposits, including gold, silver, and platinum, as well as geology, extent of mineralization, ownership, and literature references.

If you have an idea for a recreation, sport, or entertainment-related product, you can determine if it is manufactured in the United States by asking your librarian for an appropriate directory. One such directory is the *Sporting Goods Trade Directory* published by the The Sporting Goods Dealer, St. Louis, Missouri. Another is the *Sporting Goods Jobbers' Register,* by the same publisher. These directories indicate what merchandise and equipment are produced or supplied by almost 5,000 sporting goods manufacturers and wholesalers.

Whatever your interest, a directory is available to help you locate what you need to turn that interest into business success.

SELF-IMPROVEMENT/HEALTH CARE/PRESCHOOL CARE

Self-improvement, health care, and preschool care are three of the hottest areas of business in America. Think about a product or service that improves personal care or a person's appearance, health, fitness, income, personality, comfort, popularity, conversational ability, or social prestige. Identify that need and you have the key to a successful cash-producing business.

There will always be product and service needs to alleviate pain and improve health. The entire array of physical maladies will continue to cry out for attention. In the past, back pain, arthritis, and injury have led to the development of special chairs, beds, and other supportive necessities. You can anticipate more of the same in the future. Right now the spread of AIDS creates other service and product demands for personal care of patients, health-worker protection, and publicly dispensed safeguards.

Care of the elderly; preschool needs of the young; and attention, treatment, and care of people in all kinds of conditions and circumstances create demand and result in business opportunities.

Self-improvement product or service demands have exploded, and there is no end in sight. Some 48 million Americans spend more than $70 billion a year on self-improvement products or services. Everything from physical fitness centers to seminars, newsletters, and personal-enhancement products and services are in demand.

It was but a few years ago that Ethel Cotton Monahan discovered that the inability of one person to talk easily with another was the single greatest hindrance to meeting new people and maintaining satisfying relationships. She filled this need by writing 12 simple lesson pamphlets on how to overcome barriers to conversation. Selling hundreds of thousands of these pamphlets, she catapulted the project into a vast fortune.

The tremendous increase in the number of singles in America looking for interesting things to do and new ways to meet people has led to a new phenomenon known as minicourses. About 80 percent of those taking minicourses are single, and there are about 21.5 million single Americans.

A minicourse is sort of a McDonald's of adult education for those wanting to learn fast and cheap. Courses generally last one to four sessions, cost $20 to $50, and offer a foothold to concrete experience in new fields. Almost half a million Americans register for minicourses each year in subjects ranging from "Investing in Deals and Steals" to "Fencing for Fitness." Minicourses offer a new opportunity to earn profits from self-improvement subjects by either opening such a school in your area or by just teaching some courses. All instructors are, of course, paid.

Companies offering minicourses are booming. New York's Network for Learning, which registered 52,000 students in one year and grossed $1.9 million, is just scratching the surface of this new market. A chief competitor in New York, The Learning Annex, enrolled 60,000 participants in one year and generated revenue of $1.1 million.

If you want inspiration for business ideas, you can even use a list of available minicourses to find out what people are most interested in today.

NEEDS OF SPECIALIZED GROUPS

New products and services that cater to specialized groups, such as senior citizens, college students, sports enthusiasts, car owners, hobbyists of various kinds, singles, and teenagers, appear daily. You are probably aware that you are a member of many of these same groups. Your task, then, is to think of a product or service that would be helpful to you, either as an individual or as part of a group. If the product or service will meet your discovered need, it will most certainly be in demand by millions more who have similar interests.

A comprehensive directory that identifies, describes, and lists 14,726 national group associations is the *Encylopedia of Associations* published by Gale Research Company, Detroit, Michigan. Available at your library, this directory will astound you with the diversity of group organizations in America. They range from the American Professional Needlework Association to the Worldwide Treasure Hunters' League and everything imaginable in between.

You don't have to be a genius or a formally educated person to harvest ideas from this directory. The truth is, you are educated if you know where to get knowledge, know how to apply knowledge when necessary, and know the wisdom of organizing that knowledge into a definite plan of action.

NEW TECHNOLOGY

Advances in new technology are occurring more rapidly than most of us can can obtain specialized knowledge about them. Getting in on the ground floor of the latest electronic and scientific developments is a sure money maker.

The personal computer has revolutionized the way we conduct our business and personal affairs. Not since the industrial revolution spawned mass-production methods has anything pervaded our lives as has the personal computer. Never before has a single technologic breakthrough created so many millionaires in such a short period of time.

Of course, there is the legendary example of Steve Jobs and Steven Wozniak who together entrepreneured Apple Computer Corporation. From humble beginnings in a garage, they went on to become millionaires many times over. It's estimated that for each of the highly publicized examples, another 150 entrepreneurs have been made almost as wealthy by businesses related to personal computers.

Cases abound of folks who parlayed $1,000 or so into millions of dollars in a few short years. Everything from the creation of computer hardware or software to a business selling used computers and printers or to their repair—the list of products and services related to the computer is limited only by your imagination and will continue to produce enormous wealth for perceptive individuals.

A book by Joe Weisbecker, *Home Computers Can Make You Rich,* published by Hayden Book Company, Rochelle Park, New Jersey, shows how fortunes have already been made and how many more will be made directly from a person's home. New computerized applications for arts and crafts, business and personal services, desktop publishing, novelties, games, gadgets, toys, a wide assortment of consumer items, and many more everyday products or services are transforming the conduct of American business. Read this book and you will have at your command a crop of new ideas to transform desire into money.

If you have the aptitude for electronics and perceive ways to produce products or services with direct applications of technologic breakthroughs, then you'll never find a more compelling time to launch a business.

Marketing High-Tech Items

Even without technology aptitude, you can generate business income with traditional marketplace practices. Consider the case of Joseph Sugarman, a college dropout, but the proud founder of J.S. & A., a firm bringing in more than $50 million a year by offering "products that think." Joe started his business in the basement of his home when he convinced some friends to chip in start-up money so he could buy and sell electronic calculators. He promised that his investor friends would double their money before he made a cent on the deal. Eight years after those humble beginnings, Sugarman was rich.

J.S. & A. doesn't manufacture anything. It is strictly a marketing organization, but the nation's leader in selling the newest electronic and other high-technology items. Sugarman's fascination with high-tech and electronic fad items galvanized his uncanny ability to choose merchandise that Americans want—robots that understand speech, toys that talk back, a television set that fits in your pocket, the list goes on and on. Sugarman's continuing ambition is to put new products on the market before they are presented to the general public by big department stores. And the space-age product revolution Sugarman is working with promises to make tomorrow's real on-the-shelf products stagger today's imagination.

A person can only rise, conquer, and achieve through the sustained application of ideas; the new technology is the result of this application. The process of generating new ideas is enhanced by clear thought and methodical planning. You have the unique ability to control and direct thought; and by doing so, you magically gain control of your affairs and mastery of your destiny. You are limited in achievement only by the narrow crevice or broad spectrum of your chosen thoughts and ideas.

There can be no progress, no achievement, no technologic advancement without thought and action; and a person's worldly success will be the measure by which ideas are created, goals are established, and plans are implemented.

Decide now to stimulate your thoughts in the area of new technology and be the active receptacle of new ideas by using sources found in this book and your own public library. When you do, tangible rewards will be the fruit of your success and enduring will be your achievements. Riches are the crown of effort and the product of thought, but they can be secured only through persistent action. Nurture your visions, cherish your possessions, sanctify your ideas, and revere your daily actions; out of these will grow the form and substance of your earthly condition. Remain true to your ideals, and you will have a lifetime of happiness and riches.

NOSTALGIA

Products and services that bring back sentiments of earlier times are in demand. Libraries are chocked full of magazines and newspapers from earlier years. Look through them with missionary zeal and controlled purpose. They will produce solid moneymaking ideas.

A husband-and-wife pair of history buffs in Texas hit upon an idea while looking at some old newspapers in their basement. They decided the way to cash in on the appeal of nostalgia was by taking return-to-history photographs. They found that, by the application of chemicals, they could tint photographs, giving an earlier-era appearance. They gathered an assortment of old-fashioned costumes and began outfitting customers at fairs and conventions in the style of Top-Hat Charlie, Matt Dillon, and Thomas Jefferson. Ladies are outfitted with hoop skirts and bustles and even old-fashioned bathing dresses. Their business grosses almost $80,000 per year.

Products exuding nostalgia are swept up as rapidly as they can be manufactured. Everything from ceiling fans, juke boxes, old-fashioned soda trays, tea kettles, and grandfather clock kits are cash generators; and if you sell these products at flea markets or by direct mail, you won't incur the cost of an expensive location.

The ability to evoke nostalgia can boost sales and attract customers by using decorative sentimental trappings for service businesses such as restaurants, beauty salons, and even grocery stores. The key is to think about products or services of a sentimental nature.

Through the faculty of your mind, you have the ability to arrange old concepts, ideas, and plans into new combinations. Your mind creates from the food of information, experience, observation, and exposure just as your body performs in direct relationship to nutrition, exercise, rest, and conditioning.

If you want your mind to evoke an original thought or successful idea, you must nurture and feed it information of substance. Stimulated by the emotion of extraordinary desire, imagination will produce the intended result.

You've begun the process of nurturing your mind by reading this book. Decide at this very moment that your journey to success will be filled with mind-building information to expand the specialized knowledge of your own interest.

LEGISLATIVE CHANGES

New laws or abandonment of previous statutes and ordinances create unending business opportunities for new products and services. Trade journals constantly report on how legislative enactments will revolutionize fields of endeavor.

You can obtain a listing of all such trade journals from *Ayer Directory of Publications,* published by N.W. Ayer & Son, Inc., Philadelphia; *Working Press of the Nation: Magazine Directory* volume II, published by National Research Bureau, Inc., Burlington, Iowa; and *Standard Rate and Data Service: Business Publications,* Wilmette, Illinois. If you find that a particular trade journal is not otherwise available, you can send a subscription information request to *National Business Publications,* 1913 I Street, N.W., Washington, DC 20006, which has access to specialized business periodicals on most every subject.

Business opportunities prompted by legislative changes are occurring all the time. For example, in prior years, it was unlawful in many localities for those under the age of 18 to use pinball machines. Now there are few such restrictions, and minors can participate in a wide assortment of video games in public locations. By the way, a wise selection and purchase of an electronic game requires an investment of about $2,000, and it commonly pays for itself in 30 days.

Legislative changes can prompt new business needs in service industries as well. Laws designed to regulate public activities have produced the need for contractor-licensing schools, among many others. Regulation clearing houses, smog device testing, air and water pollution testing services, and a host of other such services are now needed.

Your imaginative facility may already be tuned in to changing laws or ordinances. But if you've excluded these potential business builders in the past, begin now to consider them as new opportunities.

Rekindle your desire by visualizing you are already in possession of all the things you want. Use this stimulus to develop a plan of action for their attainment. If you have not already done so, begin today to reduce your plan to writing. By writing out a statement of your desires and a plan for fulfilling them, you will be taking a tangible step toward converting your ideas to reality.

FADS

The definition of a fad is an idea that captures the imagination of a large number of people in a bewilderingly short time. It is an idea that spreads through groups and picks up momentum as it travels. Then suddenly it ends, but not before it has made instant fortunes.

How do fads begin? Where do they come from? Probably no one knows for sure. However, one firm that has generated millions specializing in fads is Wham-O Manufacturing, 835 East El Monte, San Gabriel, CA 91776. Fun is their business, and if you have a novel idea, you can mail, phone, telegraph, or carry it to their threshold.

Just such initiative has resulted in large royalties for a house painter, brick-yard worker, bank president, aircraft engineer, retired clerk, upholsterer, and school kids, each of whom came to Wham-O with an idea. The company, which began by making slingshots, now produces Frisbees, Super Balls, Hula Hoops, Boomerangs, as well as many other items.

The sudden emergence of new fads continues to produce gigantic profits. Be aware, alert, and sensitive to overnight sensations, then capitalize on these compulsive money sources with a product or service variation. For example, designs and patterns on clothing such as T-shirts and jeans began as a fad but have become durable, expensive stylewear. New fads create new variations, and continuous changing of styles is not likely to terminate in our lifetime. Do you have an idea for a new variation?

Fads can require an investment in cash of only $300 to $700. The markup is generally three to six times the cost. One fad got its start from the production of three-dimensional television movies. An entertainment fan began producing paper designer 3-D glasses and, at 98 cents each, sold over $2 million of the novel items.

Such ideas are generated from thought impulses. Desire is thought impulse transformed to energy, which in turn is converted to money. Ideas, which are the product of continuous information, specialized knowledge, and imagination, are the touchstone of all fortunes. Belief in the value of the idea, faith that the idea has appeal, a sound plan of action to implement the idea, and persistence in following the plan will provide whatever riches you want life to bring.

CHANGING CUSTOMS

Our rapidly changing customs are opening enormous income-generating op-portunities. The need to develop satisfying relationships, meet new interesting people, squelch loneliness, and fill time voids with novel services and products is insatiable. Dating clubs, singles' travel clubs, newly organized group approaches that bring people together, roommate-finding services, and an endless stream of new products emanating from changing customs will continue to produce bonanzas.

An enterprising party-going man in the San Francisco area started a unique singles' club. He aimed his service at a slightly higher class of singles, those in good paying professions who were tired of the singles' bar scene. He arranged parties in mansions, lavish boat trips, dinners with tantalizing cuisines and fine wines, and an array of similar innovative monthly activities. Club membership was $300 per year, and each member paid expenses of the event at club cost.

When last consulted, this entrepreneur was on his way to a sizeable fortune by franchising his operation.

CONSERVATION/RESOURCE AND WILDLIFE PRESERVATION/POLLUTION CONTROL

The demand to carry on life in a cleaner, energy-efficient environment and the concomitant demand to preserve our natural and wildlife resources are producing exciting, new, lucrative business prospects. Since humankind is the perpetrator of abuses to nature but also the molder and maker of amenable surroundings, concentrated thought can identify many opportunities in this field.

Joseph Hrudka, a Cleveland lad, began making automobile exhaust gaskets for high-powered racing engines in his home garage. Barely making it through high school, his major recreation was tinkering with cars. Finding that stock, store-bought gaskets couldn't withstand the intense heat generated in racing, he discovered on his own that asbestos gaskets wouldn't blow out and thereby prevented exhaust from escaping.

Initially, only auto racers used the new gasket, but as sales poured in, his Mr. Gasket business began to grow. Then, when the automobile industry was forced to curb air pollution and searched out Joe's product, his business exploded. Six years after starting in his own home workshop, he sold the entire operation to W.R. Grace and Company. When Joe Hrudka turned 30, he was a 12-fold millionaire.

In the realm of conservation and pollution control, you can learn of many new technologic breakthroughs by reading the weekly *Patent Official Gazette* published by the U.S. Patent Office and available in libraries.

Trade journals are another valuable resource if you want to remain abreast of latest developments. They provide information on many conservation subjects. For example, one trade journal is the repository of all available information sources on products and treating agents to counteract water and air pollution, oil spills, pesticides, toxic industrial chemicals, and other hazardous wastes.

We all have the ability to look at our surroundings and reflect the human condition. So, too, should we search diligently for the vehicle that improves our condition, thus bringing riches.

Motivated by these rewards, spurred on by burning desire, each of us has the capacity to use tremendous energy reserves, and, with the application of intelligence, fashion a noble existence. To be successful, you must render a worthwhile service. Thought, imagination, applied faith, a sound plan of action, persistence—these are the mere tools with which you undertake any endeavor.

However, it is only when you engage these tools in that worthy pursuit of providing a useful service can you expect to earn profits and accumulate riches.

PERSONAL AND HOME SECURITY

Fear of harm, panic at the thought of a personal attack, worry that possessions are not secure—these emotions create an immense need for personal and home security products and services. Even with all the products and services already on the market, the public is demanding additional material evidence that person and possessions are secure. Alarms, whistles, spray toxins, private security services, hand lights and home lights, locks, possession marking devices, martial arms instruction are among the many means and methods to obtain peace of mind.

Witness John Mallon, a newspaper reporter, who spotted this need for personal and industrial security and founded IBI Security Services, Inc. He started with a uniformed guard service similar to others but then rapidly diversified into electronic crime prevention gadgets. Now he uses advanced equipment, two-way microwave ultrasonic communications, and a host of other electronic "thing-um-a-jigs" to avert crime.

His new-fangled sensor devices are used by such large corporations as TWA and Flying Tiger Airlines. IBI also produces plastic tags attached to expensive garments displayed in stores that flash a signal if the garments are removed from their location. IBI initiated work with RCA Communications to perfect a radio signal that will kill the ignition of a truck or auto if stolen. John Mallon's firm produces revenues in the millions.

Notice that the field of personal and home security represents an incredibly large need; think about it, use imagination, develop a realistic idea, convert that idea to a practical plan of action, so you are rendering a worthy service and a fortune can be yours.

HOME IMPROVEMENT

The burgeoning cost of new homes makes spending for home repairs a wise investment. Look objectively at your own home repair needs. What product can you devise or improve? What service can you render?

Home-improvement-business income in this nation has enjoyed an average annual growth rate of 15 percent and sees no predictable slowdown in the near future. If you enjoy tinkering in your home workshop or garage, if you spend your free time developing remarkable decorating innovations, you can capitalize on these natural inclinations. Thousands have done exactly that to produce extra money.

If your improved gadget or device is a hardware item, you have a ready-made merchandising resource known as the *Verified List of Hardware Wholesalers*, published by Hardware Age, Philadelphia, Pennsylvania. This guide lists general hardware wholesale houses, stores, and manufacturers' agents handling hardware and related lines.

If your creation is more decorative or if you want to market an already-made product, a valuable resource of merchandisers, manufacturers, and jobbers is the *Gift and Decorative Accessory Buyers Guide,* published by Geyer-McAllister Publications, New York, New York; or the *Schiffli Directory,* which lists manufacturers, merchandisers, designers, cutters, bleachers, and machine and other suppliers in the embroidery industry. It's available from Schiffli Lace and Embroidery Manufacturers Association, Inc., Union City, New Jersey. In addition, hundreds of other merchandising guides covering millions of products are available in the business section of your local library.

Anyone can wish for riches and most people do; but converting your favorite hobby, sport, pastime, or idea to cash takes greater desire and a definite plan that transcends idle wishing. You have the capacity to make this transition through your subconscious mind. By voluntarily and repetitively planting in your subconscious mind your desires, thoughts, ideas, and plans, your entire being automatically begins translating mental elements into their physical and monetary counterparts. Begin today to investigate every avenue for wealth that stimulates your interest. Start this very minute. Dedicate yourself to this mission; put aside all reservations; use autosuggestion and know that within you is the potential to acquire all that you demand.

BUILDING YOUR CONFIDENCE

In order to firmly establish a method of proceeding, go back now and read the 10-point success formula described at the end of Chapter 1. Any time you encounter an obstacle, become confused, or feel defeated, reread the formula. Place particular emphasis on the principles of reinforcing desire, sustaining faith, believing intensely, and applying persistence. Erase any doubt you may have; replace those doubts with full self-confidence that you will attain your objectives.

4
Setting Up Your Business

If you are following instructions expressed in this book and progressing according to plan, you have arrived at this key point, primarily by the vehicle of applied thought stimulated by burning desire. In essence, these are intangible forces. It is imperative that you now shift gears and begin using physical forces. You must begin *doing*. You must take action.

Whether you decide to offer merchandise or provide a service, you must have access to the items or means of filling your objective; have a merchandising or service delivery plan and have a method for collecting profits. Your inspiration for completing these tasks comes about through establishing your business image.

CREATING YOUR BUSINESS IMAGE

Your business image is established by the name you choose for your business and by the appearance of your letterhead, envelope, and business card.

Choosing a Name

The name of your business should be narrow enough to identify the field of business you are in, but broad enough to accommodate expanded future activities.

If you are selling product, establish your business name around the field rather than around the product. For example, if you like the outdoors and decide selling a hammock will fill a need, name your business "Outdoor Products Unlimited" rather then "Hammock Sales Company." If you are providing a service, for example an entertainment agency service, your business name should be "Entertainment Unlimited" rather than "Musician's Talent Agency."

Choosing an Address

You need not rent an office to establish your business address. Initially, you can use your home address or a post office box for letterhead purposes. You may also print your home telephone number on your letterhead and, by investing in an answering service or phone message recorder, easily handle all business calls regardless of whether you have a full-time job, are vacationing, or otherwise not at home.

If you choose not to use your home, most metropolitan areas have businesses specializing in renting an address, telephone service, even desk and office space, often at "prestige" locations and for reasonable hourly, weekly, monthly, or annual rates. Check your phone directory under the heading "Office and Desk Room Rental Services" to locate such a business in your area.

Designing a Letterhead

Your business image is extremely important; you must give it high recognition in everything you do, particularly in matters involving advertising. Your business letterhead is a form of advertising; therefore, don't hesitate to spend a little extra to have a speedy art graphics firm design it and set it in type.

Remember that your letterhead makes a statement about you and your business. If you have been careful to determine precisely the kind of business you are in and have created a descriptive business name, it should be your intention to live with these for some time. A little extra expense to design your letterhead so it projects a desired image is a wise investment that will pay off for several years. Also, make sure that printing, paper stock, and color of paper and ink are high quality; these, too, are part of a first impression made by you and your business. Names of speedy art outfits that design letterheads are in your phone directory under "Artists-Commercial."

If cash is extremely tight, one alternative is to use the services of a local print shop offering special rates for business start-up packages. Such packages include letterheads, envelopes, and business cards. Print shops offering these packages often have some standard, preset letterhead styles and type combinations that you can adopt. Often they are surprisingly good and inexpensive.

Another alternative, available if you know someone with a personal computer and desktop publishing software, is to do the designing yourself and then take the letterhead, envelope, and business card paste-ups to a local print shop.

If you choose pastel paper and also select a harmonious color of ink, when printed, your letterhead will have a stylish two-color effect for little more than it would cost to print in black and white. If you use pastel paper, don't forget to order a ream of the same color to use as a second page for business letters.

Generally, until your business gets moving, you won't need to order more than 100 of each item, but depending on your plans and finances, you may want to increase your initial order to 500.

If you live in a remote area, you can get inexpensive, quality printing from New England Business Services, Inc. (NEBS), 500 Main Street, Groton, MA 01471. By a simple request, they will be happy to send you a free catalog of printed products, letterheads, record-keeping items, computer forms, and a variety of other specialty printed products. Low-cost, gold-embossed print work is available from Harwood & Seye, 14705 Keswick Street, Van Nuys, CA 91405.

GETTING THE BALL ROLLING

At this point, the ball is on your side of the court. Your task is to give it direction and velocity so you can score big in the contest of business.

Obtaining a Business License

The types of business license and related permits needed for your business generally depend on local ordinances and, in some instances, state regulations. Your home address can be used as your official business address; but if you rely on patrons to use your facilities, the physical location must be a shop or facility meeting local zoning requirements. In either case, your city or county clerk or local licensing bureau will prove application forms, details, and an estimate of fees. A business license fee may be a flat rate, percentage of gross sales, or a combination of factors generally based on your estimate of receipts for the ensuing year.

Unless your business function allows no alternative to patron use of your facilities, it is advisable to conduct actual business transactions with customers away from your home. Use your home, workshop, or garage as a home base if you have a service business or otherwise are developing products, receiving or shipping merchandise, direct selling through mail order, and conducting most other aspects of your business. A great many businesses do not require a storefront location until they are generating high sales volume, if ever. Thus, you can keep overhead and operating expenses to a minimum by working from a home or apartment and having that address recorded on the business license.

When applying for a business license, if your business involves offering a product, you can show the business purpose as wholesale jobber, retail distributer, mail-order distributor, or any other suitable description of how you intend to offer the product. Along with this information, indicate the general line of merchandise you intend to handle.

If the business involves a service, identify the type of service. If you are running the business from your home, indicate that the service will be conducted so as not to infringe on any zoning requirements. Most service businesses perform a service on the customer's own premises.

A business license is the minimal legal requirement to be in business, and it is available to everyone in America. People in home-party businesses, such as Tupperware, and those in retail sales businesses, such as Amway and Avon, obtain business licenses every day and you can do the same. Most business license fees are small in relation to other business expenses; and if the estimate of first-year receipts is a small figure, which is quite likely when just starting out, then you should qualify for the minimum-fee payment.

Once obtained, the business license is generally required to be posted on the business premises for public inspection.

Obtaining A Fictitious Name Statement

Once you have a business name and a business license, you should file a fictitious name statement, also called a DBA (doing business as) statement. Most local ordinances require that such a statement be filed with the city or county clerk or local recording office within 30 days of starting a business. Generally, the first date you start business is the date you obtain a business license or actually have possession of income resulting from your business. Registering a fictitious name is as easy as completing a form and paying a fee of around $10, then publishing a standard notice in a general circulation newspaper.

Obtaining a State Tax Resale Permit

States with sales-tax laws require businesses selling goods on a retail basis (including through mail order) to register and obtain a permit number from their state tax or local board of equalization office. The other sales-tax requirements are that you maintain records of sales and post the retail-sales certificate where visible.

If you have established your business as a manufacturer of a specialized item or as a wholesaler selling only to retail outlets and not directly to retail customers, you may not need a resale certificate. By all means, verify requirements at your state or local sales-tax office; however, obtaining a resale permit number as early as possible can be beneficial in purchasing merchandise (it eliminates the need for you to pay sales tax on items you purchase to be resold in your business) and ligitimizes your business.

Opening a Business Checking Account

A business checking account is an excellent way to keep records of business income and expenses and to keep personal funds from being combined with business funds. Furthermore, the IRS, in considering whether your business is being conducted in earnest rather than just as a hobby, views a business checking account as an essential criterion. In addition, banks are careful to cash checks only for the actual party to whom the checks are written. This means that checks made out to your business cannot easily be deposited into your personal account.

You can open a business checking account by taking your business license and fictitious name statement to your bank. Having a business checking account also makes you a customer of the bank and gives you an opportunity to establish a business relationship should you later apply for a business loan.

Obtaining an IRS Employer Number

Filing for an IRS employer identification number is not mandatory to start a business unless you intend to employ workers. However, applying for an IRS employer number is another way of distinguishing your business from a hobby. Having an IRS employer number does not require you to employ workers; but you should consider applying for the number as early as possible, just in case you decide to hire employees at a later date. Visit the nearest IRS office, and they will courteously explain the procedure.

CHOOSING A FORM OF BUSINESS ORGANIZATION

In starting your business, you will need to decide on the legal structure most appropriate for it. The decision of which form of organization your business should take is largely a matter of judgment influenced by consideration of liability, amount of control you want to exercise, and taxation factors.

If your personal resources for borrowing money are not enough to fund your business, selling a participation in the business is a way of increasing your financial base. But while it is tempting to use the money of others, it is a temptation that must be carefully examined.

If you, as a sole proprietor, put up all the investment money, you will not only receive all the profit but also retain full control of the business. Should you sell an equity interest in the business, some of the control is lost, since backers will feel entitled to a say in how the business is run.

On the other hand, limited partnerships and syndications do offer a ready source of investment capital. Borrowing from a bank or similar source creates potential liability if the business fails, since loans from these sources must eventually be paid back. Partnerships do not require repayment since loss of investment is the risk the partners take as part-owners.

Following is some basic information to help you get a feel for the kinds of business structures available to you. Because of its complexity, this information is highly condensed and merely scratches the surface of the subject. You are strongly urged to consult an attorney before deciding on any one of the following forms your business may take.

Sole Proprietorship

Sole proprietorship is the simplest form a business can take. You simply go into business and place all business assets in your name. It is the most traditional form of business and places you in sole command of all day-to-day decisions. State laws don't require organization procedures, and government approval is not required, although you may need a local business license. A sole proprietorship is not regulated by restrictive laws as is a corporation and, therefore, is the most flexible form of business.

The business begins when you start it and ends when you stop it and can be dissolved at will. There is no need to register or qualify it before doing business in another state.

As sole proprietor, you are personally liable for all the obligations and debts of the business. Business profits are taxed as personal income, and losses can be deducted from other forms of your earned income. If you don't reach the maximum social-security deduction through other means of employment, you will have to pay an estimated quarterly social-security tax. Unless you hire others, a sole proprietorship is not required to make workers' compensation and disability insurance payments.

All the money invested in a sole proprietorship is considered your own, and any money needed to operate or expand the business by borrowing or purchasing on credit is evaluated on your personal ability to repay. All your personal assets may be used as collateral to protect borrowed funds or credit purchases.

In the event of your death, as sole proprietor, ownership of the business can be willed to your spouse or children or to anyone else you wish. Liabilities, however, will pass to them along with the business.

General Partnership

In a general partnership, business is conducted by you and any number of people who have equal status and authority with you. To set up a general partnership, partners contribute property, money, credit, skill, or labor; and these contributions need not be in equal portions. In total, they will make up the capital or foundation of the business.

A general partnership can be created simply by two or more people conducting a business for profit as coowners. A written agreement (articles of partnership) spelling out the rights, duties, and responsibilities of each partner should be drafted prior to or as soon as business begins in order to avoid misunderstandings down the line. Any written partnership agreement becomes effective when it's signed by the partners, but it's a private document and doesn't have to be registered with any public agency. To do business, a local business license is required, and some states require partners to file a Certificate of Conducting Business as Partners in order to identify all partners by name. Like a sole proprietorship, the partnership may do business across state lines without registering or qualifying in any way.

Although it is treated as a unit for accounting and tax purposes, American law generally does not regard the partnership an an entity but as a group of individuals. Just as a sole proprietorship, every partner is responsible, and personally liable, for all business debts and claims against the partnership. For tax purposes, a partnership return is filed purely for informational purposes and each partner then includes income or deducts losses on his or her own personal income tax return.

A partnership may find it slightly easier to raise funds and borrow money than a sole proprietorship. This is primarily the result of its ability to combine resources and put up more collateral than a single person can muster. In the case of borrowed money or credit, each partner is fully responsible and liable regardless of the amount of investment in the business.

When drawing up a partnership agreement, it's important to make sure that the business will not have to be liquidated if a partner dies or withdraws. The partnership agreement should specify that, in either event, the remaining partners will have the option to dissolve and liquidate the partnership or purchase the interest of the deceased or withdrawing partner (or to have the firm purchase it) at a fixed price to be determined by formula.

Limited Partnership

A limited partnership is a variation of a general partnership. Unlike a general partnership, its participants contribute capital to the business but avoid unlimited liability. Liability for the limited partner is no greater than the amount of money that partner has invested in the business.

This form of business organization is somewhat more difficult to set up than either a general partnership or a sole proprietorship, and procedures prescribed by law must be carefully followed.

Among other things, it's necessary to file the articles of limited partnership with the state, and this makes public the financing arrangement among the participants, together with certain other matters concerning the firm's internal affairs. Another requirement allows limited partners to invest either cash or tangible property; services cannot be contributed as an investment.

A third requirement is that, among the limited partners, at least one general partner must be designated to have responsibility for the prudent operation of the business. This can have the added advantage of giving you more control over your business. But if a limited partner takes an active part in the business, that partner loses limited liability status.

Because outside equity capital may be acquired by bringing in additional or different limited partners with greater assets, financing of a limited partnership may be easier. Also, because of this larger cash base and potential for repayment of loans, a limited partnership may get better borrowing terms than either a sole proprietorship or a general partnership.

A limited partnership may be taxed either as a partnership or as a corporation depending on (1) its management pattern, (2) whether ownership interests are transferable, and (3) whether it has continuity of existence.

Joint Stock Company

Unlike a partnership, owners in a joint stock company are issued freely transferable shares and thus have evidence of their equity basis in the firm that goes beyond the partnership agreement. A joint stock company is run by a central management group, and it is less likely to be seriously affected by the death or withdrawal of one of the participants. Articles of association, like articles of partnership, constitute a private contract and don't have to be registered with the state.

Financing and the ability to borrow funds are generally similar to those of a limited partnership. However, for tax purposes, joint stock companies are usually treated as separate entities and, in general, are subject to the same tax laws as corporations.

Corporations

A corporation is recognized by law as having an existence apart from the owners/shareholders. Thus, in the matter of rights, duties, and other legal matters, it's treated as an entity. It can engage in an unlimited variety of business transactions, sue and be sued, buy property, hire employees, engage in interstate commerce, and conduct all necessary means of business in its own right.

A clear advantage of a corporation is that owners are liable only to the extent of their investments. Also, ownership is transferable, and a corporation has a continuous life regardless of whether a shareholder withdraws, sells shares, or dies. A corporation has formal financial status and a distinct advantage in borrowing monies or obtaining financing through selling its stock, issuing bonds, or otherwise raising needed funds.

On the other hand, a corporation is highly regulated by state laws; restricted by corporate charter; and costly to form, operate, and manage. When making a profit, corporations pay high income taxes. In addition, since corporations are usually treated as taxable units separate from their owners, the same income may, in a sense, be taxed twice. The corporation pays federal and state income taxes on its income; the owners in turn pay income taxes on their income, which includes dividends received from the corporation.

Don't think that when you form a corporation all danger to your personal assets and estates ceases. Freeing yourself from business liability is not that simple. For example, statutes in most states impose personal liability on shareholders for the corporation's unpaid wage claims. Furthermore, shareholders who are also directors and officers may incur heavy liabilities in those capacities even if they are shielded from liability as shareholders.

In addition, when a small corporation borrows money, the bank usually requires the principal shareholders to endorse the corporation's note or act as sureties on the loan. In other words, lenders often force shareholders to contract away part of their limited liability by assuming responsibility for the payment of large corporate obligations.

There are many expensive and time-consuming aspects to operating and managing a corporation. However, if your business dream cannot be fulfilled unless you incorporate, you should read a book on the subject entitled *How To Form Your Own Corporation for Under $50* by Ted Nicholas, published by Enterprise Publishing Co., Wilmington, Delaware.

Subchapter S Corporations

In 1958, Congress amended the Internal Revenue Code by adding Subchapter S. It permits closely held corporations (those with 15 shareholders or less) to bypass the federal tax on corporation income. Thus, owners can avoid heavy corporate taxation, since income of the business is taxed to the owner/shareholder directly. Each owner/shareholder reports the share of the company's profit (or losses) on the form 1040 personal income tax return, just the same as if participating in a partnership.

A Final Word

Prudent selection of a form of business organization involves choosing not just from among the standard forms in their typical patterns, but from the forms that can be tailored by skillful planning and drafting. Legal help is essential.

A decision as to the legal structure of a business is never final. As changes occur in a business and in the financial and tax status of its owners, the question should be reexamined.

Comparative tax burdens of the various forms a business takes can be determined only by careful study of the individual business and of the financial status of its owners.

While you shouldn't let all this talk about formal business structures deter you from the paramount goal of earning money from business, be aware that the structure of your business can have far-reaching implications. A little planning in the early stages of your business can pay off handsomely later on.

5

Finding the Product
You've Decided to Sell

Thought, ideas, and imagination must be converted to action. Being your own boss, setting your own time schedule, reaping the full rewards of your labor, controlling your own future—these are the fruits of effort. The amount of money you produce will be in direct proportion to the demand for your product or service and the amount of effort you put forth to locate and satisfy your customers.

Once you have created your business image and obtained the necessary licenses and permits, you can begin doing business. If you have decided to sell a product, next you must locate or develop a source of merchandise.

MARKETING READY-MADE PRODUCTS

What are the sources of products? Who are the suppliers, manufacturers, wholesalers, importers, and producers of products?

If you have decided to offer a product as the expression of your own business, you will have to search these out with vigor. But quite frankly, once suppliers know you have the ability to produce sales, you will be hounded to death by them, wined and dined, treated as royalty.

As you begin your search for products, always remember that suppliers need you more than you need them. Never forget this when negotiating prices and terms of wholesale purchase.

Directories

Locating a product to fill a need is as easy as letting your fingers walk through the Yellow Pages of your telephone directory. First, look up the name of the product, then find the subsection under wholesalers or manufacturers for that product. Do the same with phone directories from large cities; they're available at public libraries. Don't overlook the section under importers. If directory entries list only retail outlets of the product, don't hesitate to contact several of these and request names of their wholesale suppliers.

The next step is just as easy. Simply ask your librarian to let you see all of the directories of domestic and import goods for sale that the library has in its collection.

Of these directories, one most frequently used is the 11-volume *Thomas' Register of American Manufacturers,* produced by Thomas Publishing Company, New York City. This workhorse of product-finding sources will provide enough leads to keep you busy for days writing and calling to get product supply information.

A companion directory is *Sources of State Information and State Industrial Directories,* published by State Chamber of Commerce Department, Chamber of Commerce of the United States, Washington, DC. This directory reports addresses of manufacturing associations in each state and tells how to get additional information on products. For example, the *California Manufacturers Register,* published by Times Mirror Press, Los Angeles, lists thousands of manufacturing firms according to product, services, city, and county—categories that will help you locate products to use in starting your business.

Should you desire a product manufactured in another nation, directories are also available for this purpose. The master guide to all import directories is *Trade Directories of the World*, published by Croner Publications, Inc., Queens Village, New York. It contains a classified alphabetical list of directories and products by type. It covers thousands of foreign manufacturers, arranged by geographic location, and is complete with names, addresses, and telephone and telex numbers. It also lists major exporters and importers.

Newspapers and Magazines

Newspapers and magazines often advertise new products. Here are six of the best ways to use these publications to your advantage.

1. Study the Business Opportunities and Auction Offerings columns in your local newspaper.
2. Read big-city newspapers, such as the *New York Times, Los Angeles Times,* and *Chicago Tribune* for three months. Study their business columns and advertisements every day.
3. Read the *Wall Street Journal* and *Journal of Commerce* regularly, paying particular attention to the advertisements.

4. Study the classified and display advertisements in such magazines as *Income Opportunities, Money, Salesman's Opportunity, Selling Direct, Spare Time, Popular Mechanics, Popular Science, Science and Mechanics, Modern Franchising, Money Making Opportunities*, and *Moneysworth.*
5. Read the new product columns of every magazine serving your field of interest. Many of these products may be available on a discount, distributor, or franchise basis.
6. Check all leads out immediately.

Using your business letterhead, write to manufacturers of your choice and inquire if they have a manufacturer's representative or wholesaler in your area. If not, ask for the manufacturer's terms of sale, descriptions, and photographs of particular products you intend to offer.

Trade Shows

If you would rather see merchandise firsthand and wholesalers in your area do not offer a particular product line of interest to you, trade shows are an outstanding source for locating both new and established products.

More than 7,800 trade shows are presented in the United States each year, which means you should have little trouble finding one carrying the kind of product you want to offer. You can find the trade show nearest you in these publications: *Exhibit Schedule,* published by *Successful Meeting Magazine,* and *Trade Shows and Professional Exhibits Directory*, published by Gale Research, Detroit, Michigan.

At the library, you will also find show listings in trade and business magazines covering your product line. Don't forget to check with your local convention and visitors bureau to find out which trade shows will be held in your community or large cities near you. If you are actively seeking a product line, attending trade shows is a must-do adventure.

WHAT IF NO ONE MAKES THE PRODUCT?

If you've been unable to find the ready-made product you are after, the very next step is to find out if the product has been patented but never reached the marketplace. This is done by conducting a patent search. Information on how to conduct a patent search yourself is found in Chapter 6.

Conducting a patent search is, in fact, the method most often used by firms seeking new products and is an excellent way to locate a product you can make or have manufactured to start your business. The reason is that, while inventors do an excellent job of creating products and may even know how and where the product can be manufactured, they commonly don't know how to market the product. Some inventors may even have sales material already printed and a supply of the item from initial production. If you find a product that suits you from your patent search, contact the inventor to see if you can join forces and get the product successfully marketed.

If your search fails to turn up the product you're looking for and you find that no manufacturing firm makes the kind of product that fills the need you have identified, you have three alternatives:

1. Manufacture the product yourself.
2. Contract the work of making the product to a manufacturer of similar products.
3. Sell or license your idea for a product to an established manufacturer.

Manufacturing the Product Yourself

Individuals who make product improvements and home inventors, as distinguished from major corporations, account for a great many products in use today. If you fall into this category, you are another of those individuals on whom progress has always depended. U.S. Patent Office reports show that the vast majority of new creations begin with a lone worker who makes the first advance; details may be worked out by a team, but the prime idea is due to the enterprise, thought, and perception of one individual.

Unless the product you have in mind requires a great deal of space to manufacture, your home, garage, or small shop is an ideal place to begin making your product or at least a prototype of it. The fact is that countless big businesses started this way, particularly those making high-technology products that are easily adaptable to such humble beginnings.

Home manufacturing provides income for thousands of individuals. Everything from cork pullers to stereo components are produced this way. While it would be impossible to list all the home-manufactured products made in America, a brief list includes weather instruments, marble products, bronze art, horse trailers, go-carts, food dehydrators, designer doors, textiles—quilts, draperies, uniforms, blouses, baby blankets, and denim apparel—furniture, hardware, kitchen gadgets, water fountains, electronics of all kinds, hand tools, jewelry, sporting goods, musical instruments, various craft products, and thousands more.

The key to manufacturing your own product is knowledge, and knowledge is established by your interest as well as the time you spend in an activity, such as a hobby or pastime, perfecting the product and producing it in quantity.

Contract Out the Manufacturing of Your Product

If you don't have the tools or facilities to manufacture your product, you can job-lot the item or a portion of the item so it can be made by local factories, machine shops, fabricators, welding shops, and other manufacturers and outlets. You can assemble or finish the final product yourself once you have gotten the manufactured pieces.

Frequently, manufacturers will agree to warehouse your product and ship it according to agreed-on instructions. The advantage of such an arrangement is that, if you have very little space of your own, you won't have whatever it is you've decided to sell bulging out of your bedroom windows. The disadvantage is that the more hands through which a shipping order must pass, the longer the delivery time and the greater the chance of an order being fouled up.

Use your phone directory or your community *Directory of Business Services,* commonly known as the "City Directory" published by R.L. Polk and Company, Dallas, to locate a small shop or manufacturers of similar products in your area. Most small firms will produce items in lots of 500 to 1,000 or more at a reasonable job price or unit price. Thus, you pay only "X" amount of dollars for "Y" number of items produced.

If at all possible, find a small producer in your city or nearby area rather than a distant manufacturer. This way, you can personally make arrangements, check progress, and be available in the event delays or problems are encountered. Once your item is in production and sales begin to grow, you may want to contact larger manufacturers in other areas who can facilitate production in quantity at a lower unit cost or offer speedier turnaround time.

Selling or Licensing Your Product

If you decide not to produce the product yourself, you can often sell or license it to an established manufacturing firm. Generally, it is easier to license or sell a product to smaller, growing companies looking for new products and fresh ideas. Giant corporations with their own research and development teams may not be as receptive to new products. However, even they generally have departments and procedures for evaluating new submissions.

If you contact a company that has standard procedures for evaluating new products, you should follow their rules if you want to deal with them. Most will require that you sign a standard release agreement absolving them from any obligation, thus avoiding a lawsuit in connection with their examining your product.

If it is not already in the release, you may want to add language to ensure that the company will not produce the product without your consent unless, of course, it can demonstrate at the time you meet that it is already developing or considering a similar product. (A sample "No Disclosure, No Profit without Consent" agreement form is in Appendix I.)

A primary consideration in most negotiations of this kind is how eager you are to offer the product and rely almost entirely on the judgment of someone else for its production. If you need assistance in these matters, an attorney should be consulted. While your greatest fear may be that an unscrupulous company will "steal" your product or idea, this is rarely the case. Standard practice is for the company either to buy all rights to your product, pay royalties, or reject the product rather than face larceny charges.

Selling or licensing your product has both distinct advantages and disadvantages. A primary advantage is the possibility of immediate income without your direct involvement in manufacturing, distributing, selling, and so on. This is possible because a company can spread these costs over the full range of its product line, possibly producing quicker and greater profits than you can starting from scratch. A primary disadvantage is the likelihood that your profits from royalties or sale may be limited compared with what you could earn offering the product in your own business.

Manufacturing companies will generally be more receptive to a product that is patented or has a patent pending. This saves them the effort and expense of initiating the patent process and also demonstrates that you have a tangible product of value, rather than merely an undeveloped idea. If you have a patented product or patent pending, always remember to disclose this fact to prospective buyers, but never reveal the patent application date until final stages of a license or sale agreement are at hand.

If you decide to sell your product with all attendant rights, be careful that your asking price is high enough that you won't regret making that decision but low enough to not discourage the purchaser. A handy rule of thumb is to ask an amount equivalent to 10 percent of the anticipated item's sale price projected on the estimated volume of sales for a minimum of five years and a maximum of 17 years.

If this formula produces an amount that seems unreasonably large, you can adjust some of the variables to produce a more compatible figure, but at least you have some basis for your estimate. You should also decide, in advance, whether you prefer payment in one lump sum or, perhaps because of tax and other financial circumstances, spread over a period of months, quarters, or years.

If your product is licensed on a royalty basis, give consideration to whether your agreement will be exclusive, i.e., you have no right to make the same agreement with others, or nonexclusive, giving you full or limited rights to produce the product under a different name or make a similar agreement with others.

Consider Payment Terms. Do you want a guaranteed minimum with payment made annually, regardless of whether the manufacturer make sales? Will this be necessary to prevent the manufacturer from restricting your making the product, then in turn refusing to make and market the product itself?

Consider Production Terms. When will production begin and what quantities will be produced in initial and subsequent factory runs?

Consider Royalty Details. Will you be paid a specified amount for each unit sold? What will the amount be? Will the amount be adjusted up or down based on sales volume? Will you want payment on a schedule other than quarterly or semiannually? Will there be a special provision for the first year of production while the manufacturer tools up or pays special initial overhead production costs? If so, precisely when will the first payment be made?

Consider Duration of the Royalty Agreement. What are the specific beginning and ending dates of the licensing agreement? Will the manufacturer have the option to renew the agreement? Will such options be based on the remaining patent life of the product or on other considerations? Can either party sever the royalty agreement at specified intervals and, if so, under what conditions? Will degree of effort or volume of sales be taken into consideration? How so?

Consider Methods to Resolve Disputes. What settlement procedures will you both agree on in advance? What happens if one party claims that a provision of the agreement has not been met? How will the truth of such a claim be determined? Will there be penalties for noncompliance?

Obviously, licensing a product is much more complicated than selling rights with no strings attached; but depending on the product, a royalty agreement can be more lucrative over a period of time. Such an agreement is best negotiated by a registered patent attorney who can advise you on the hundreds of implications involving the manufacture and sale of products.

Generally, a basic royalty agreement will take only a few pages of text if the parties are operating in good faith and each party is knowledgeable and satisfied with terms of the agreement. Examples of such agreements are available in practically every public law library and are contained in standard references known as "Forms."

Just as in selling a product, a royalty amounting to 10 percent of the manufacturer's sales price for each unit sold is a good place to begin making profit estimates. A minimum guaranteed annual payment is a good idea, but no substitute for selection of a qualified manufacturer who will meet all terms of the agreement, including speedy and vigorous market penetration.

6

If You Invent
Your Own Product

A patent is an exclusive property right to an invention bestowing the right to exclude others from making, using, or selling the innovation for a period of 17 years in the United States, its territories, and possessions. Except by a rare act of Congress, a patent cannot be renewed.

PRODUCTS CAN BE MARKETED WITHOUT A PATENT

Because of the expense and time required to obtain a patent, manufacturers frequently market their products when the need is greatest, even if it is before or while they apply for patents. If you decide to do this, you can ensure that you are not infringing on an existing patent by conducting an inexpensive patent search yourself. Such a search can be performed either in the Search Room of the U.S. Patent and Trademark Office at Crystal Plaza, 2021 Jefferson Davis Highway, Arlington, Virginia, or at selected libraries. Libraries listed in TABLE 6-1 are but some of those in which a patent search may be conducted.

Each of these libraries is a mecca for home-style inventors, an absolute necessity if you have an idea to improve a patented product. "How to" books and microfilm available at these libraries contain a vast wealth of technical information, suggestions, applications, and even information on selling the idea. Bound volumes or microfilm contain most all the information you need and are excellent sources for generating ideas in your field of interest, even if you don't have a specific product in mind.

TABLE 6-1. Patent-Search Libraries.

State	Library
Alabama	Auburn University Libraries, Birmingham Public Library
Arizona	Tempe: Science Library, Arizona State University
California	Los Angeles Public Library; Sacramento: California State Library; San Diego Public Library; Sunnyvale: Patent Information Clearinghouse
Colorado	Denver Public Library
Delaware	Newark: University of Delaware
Georgia	Atlanta: Price Gilbert Memorial Library, Georgia Institute of Technology
Idaho	Moscow: University of Idaho Library
Illinois	Chicago Public Library; Springfield: Illinois State Library
Indiana	Indianapolis: Marion County Public Library
Louisiana	Baton Rouge: Troy H. Middleton Library, Louisiana State University
Maryland	College Park: Engineering and Physical Sciences Library, University of Maryland
Massachusetts	Boston Public Library
Michigan	Ann Arbor: Engineering Transportation Library, University of Michigan; Detroit Public Library
Minnesota	Minneapolis Public Library and Information Center
Missouri	Kansas City: Linda Hall Library; St. Louis Public Library
Montana	Butte: Montana College of Mineral Science and Technology
Nebraska	Lincoln: University of Nebraska-Lincoln, Engineering Library
Nevada	Reno: University of Nevada Library
New Hampshire	Durham: University of New Hampshire Library
New Jersey	Newark Public Library
New Mexico	Albuquerque: University of New Mexico Library
New York	Albany: New York State Library; Buffalo and Erie County Library; New York Public Library (The Research Libraries)
North Carolina	Raleigh: D.H. Hill Library, N.C. State University
Ohio	Public Library of Cincinnati and Hamilton County; Cleveland Public Library; Columbus: Ohio State University Libraries; Toledo/Lucas County Public Library
Oklahoma	Stillwater: Oklahoma State University Library
Pennsylvania	Cambridge Springs: Alliance College Library; Philadelphia: Franklin Institute Library; Pittsburgh: Carnegie Library of Pittsburgh; University Park: Pattee Library, Pennsylvania State University
Rhode Island	Providence Public Library
South Carolina	Charleston: Medical University of South Carolina

Tennessee	Memphis and Shelby County Public Library and Information Center
Texas	Austin: McKinney Engineering Library, University of Texas; College Station: Sterling C. Evans Library, Texas A & M University; Dallas Public Library; Houston: The Fondren Library, Rice University
Utah	Salt Lake City: Marriott Library, University of Utah
Washington	Seattle: Engineering Library, University of Washington
Wisconsin	Madison: Kurt F. Wendt Engineering Library, University of Wisconsin; Milwaukee Public Library.

A Record of Invention

If you decide to market your product before or while a patent application is being prepared, you can establish an unquestioned record of the date and existence of your product by filing a simple Patent Office form known as "A Record of Invention." You can obtain this form and a free booklet explaining its use entitled *Disclosure Document Program* from the U.S. Department of Commerce, Patent Office, Washington, DC 20231. Filing this form confers no patent privileges, but it can be of great assistance in any dispute over who was the originator of a product.

Once prepared, have the form notarized and a witness sign it; send the original and one copy along with $10 to the U.S. Patent Office. The Patent Office will date both, return the copy to you and retain the original for two years. Remember that, even though this form is filed, until you are granted a patent, you have no right to exclude others from making or selling your product.

APPLYING FOR A PATENT

For maximum protection, you may decide to apply for a patent. If your search revealed an exciting product for which a patent was granted more than 17 years earlier, you are free to produce and market that product.

What's Patentable and Who Can Own a Patent

A patent can be granted to the inventor or discoverer of any new and useful process, machine, manufacture, or composition of matter, or any new and useful improvement of a patented item.

You will not be granted a patent on an undeveloped idea, a useless device, printed matter, a method of doing business, an improvement in a device obvious to a person skilled in the art, or a machine that will not operate, such as an alleged perpetual motion machine. A patent cannot be granted if the product or invention was in public use or on sale in the United States for more than one year prior to the filing of a patent application. Even if you were the exclusive producer, user, or seller of the invention for more than a year, your right to a patent will be barred just as effectively as though discovery, use, or sale had been by someone else.

Any inventor may obtain a patent, regardless of age or sex, by complying with provisions of law. A foreign citizen may obtain a patent under exactly the same conditions as a U.S. citizen.

How To Do It

A patent application consists of an application fee plus certain additional charges (depending on the number of claims), a petition, a specification and claim describing and defining the invention, an oath or declaration, and a drawing of the invention. Models of the invention are rarely required.

As the originator of an invention, you are considered the official applicant of a patent if you make proper application to the Commissioner of Patents and Trademarks, Washington, DC 20231. However, only those attorneys and agents who are registered with the U.S. Patent Office may prosecute (obtain by legal process) a patent application on behalf of an applicant.

Patent procedures are highly complex, and terms have very specialized meanings. Even a misunderstanding of what appears to be commonly used words could result in your application's being denied or, if granted, your patent's being rendered useless because you drafted claims that were to narrow or too broad for practical use. Thus, if your invention is worth pursuing, for your own protection, you should seek professional assistance from a registered patent attorney to draft your claims and prosecute the application. This is so, even if you have conducted your own patent search.

The total cost of obtaining a patent generally ranges from $1,000 to $10,000 or more, depending on complexity and how much of the search is conducted by you rather than your attorney or agent.

It is not necessary to go to the Patent Office to transact business on patent matters. All matters can be handled by mail. However, interviews regarding pending applications can be arranged with examiners and, at critical times, may be helpful.

The Patent Office is not allowed to offer advice as to whether an inventor should apply for a patent. However, the Patent Office will answer written inquiries concerning the status of the application and will provide immediate information if the application has been rejected or the patent granted. If you have a patent attorney or agent, the Patent Office will not correspond with both you and the attorney concerning the merits of your application. Therefore, all inquiries and comments concerning your invention should be forwarded through your patent attorney or agent.

Protecting Your Patent

If a patent is granted on your invention, a final issue fee plus certain printing charges will be required to finalize the patent. Until the patent is granted, pending applications are kept in strictest secrecy, and no access is given to them except on written authority by the applicant or a duly authorized representative.

After the patent is issued, the official file containing the application and all correspondence leading to issuance of the patent is made available in the Patent Search Room and authorized libraries for inspection by anyone. Copies of these files may be purchased from the Patent Office at cost of reproduction.

Once a patent has been granted and recorded, the Patent Office has no further jurisdiction concerning infringement. If your patent is infringed, you should contact your patent attorney. You may decide to sue the infringer in the appropriate court, but it will have to be at your own expense.

PATENTS ARE TRANSFERABLE

Once granted, a patent is personal property and can be sold or even mortgaged. You can sell or transfer a patent or patent application that has been submitted and is active with the U.S. Patent Office. Such a transfer of interest is known as an assignment; and the assignee then has all the rights to the patent that the original inventor had.

A whole or part interest can be assigned; but remember that joint ownership holds many pitfalls unless restricted by a contract. A joint owner who has even the smallest assignment, but who is not restricted in use by a written agreement, can use the patent just as freely as the original owner.

For example, an inventor offers to sell a patent for $100,000 but finally settles with the prospective buyer on $10,000 for 10-percent interest in the patent. Now, the new part-owner—unless specifically prevented from doing so by separate written contract—could market the product as if owning 100 percent of the patent and need not disclose this to the part-owner who held the original patent. A new part-owner may make use of or sell the item for profit without regard to any other owner, or may also sell partial or full interest to someone else.

If you should become part-owner of a patent, it is your responsibility to make sure that any such transfer is recorded at the Patent Office within three months. All such assignments should be notarized and identified by patent number, date, inventor's name, and title of invention or they could be void, thus depriving you of future benefits.

OBTAINING MORE INFORMATION ON PATENTS

Your best exposure to patent information is to see firsthand the wide variety of materials, suggestions, and patent copies at the authorized libraries previously listed. If you are serious about a product or invention, one sure way of inspiring greater interest is to immerse yourself in these materials; you will find that an endless stream of ideas will captivate you to the point of your almost being unable to wait until you get home to begin experimenting and producing your moneymaking product.

If you are serious about starting a business and learning more about the world of products and patents, but do not have a library with actual patent material in your community, do yourself a favor, take some vacation time and go to the nearest qualified patent library. It will probably be the most rewarding and satisfying vacation you have ever taken, and it may pay for itself a hundred times over by stimulating that idea that makes you rich. To whet your appetite until you're able to visit an authorized patent information library, basic information can be purchased from the U.S. Department of Commerce, Patent and Trademark Office, Washington, DC 20231.

A pamphlet listing attorneys and agents registered to practice before the U.S. Patent and Trademark Office is available for $5; however, you can generally obtain the same information free in your geographic area by contacting the nearest District Office of the U.S. Department of Commerce or looking in the classified section of your telephone directory under the heading "Patents."

WHAT ABOUT INVENTION PROMOTION FIRMS?

Likely to be listed in the "Patents" section of your telephone directory are firms that offer—for a fee—to take the whole job of protecting and promoting your idea. Some firms may be quite helpful; however, caution is necessary in dealing with these promoters.

Federal Trade Commission investigations found that one firm, which charged fees ranging from $1,000 to $2,000, had 10 clients who made money on their inventions—that was out of a total of 35,000. Another firm with 30,000 clients had only three with successful inventions. If you elect to use idea-promotion firms, make sure

■ They provide you with solid evidence of their track record, not just a few flashy success stories, but verifiable statistics on the number of clients they've had and the number who have actually made money
■ They don't collect the entire fee in advance

■ They provide you with samples of their promotional materials and lists of companies to whom they've sent them (then check with those companies yourself)
■ You check the promotion firm's reputation with the local Better Business Bureau, chamber of commerce, patent attorney, or local inventor or innovators' club

OTHER OUTFITS CAN HELP WITH YOUR PRODUCT

Help with funding, promotion, and marketing may be gotten from other sources as well.

Invention Brokers

Invention brokers, listed in telephone directories of large cities, generally provide sophisticated management advice. Once convinced that a new product or invention has real profit possibilities, these firms will often agree to perform production and marketing services for a portion of anticipated profits. They may even help inventors raise capital and form companies to produce and market a promising invention. However, you can generally expect these brokers to be interested in more complex, new technology that will result in large sales commonly produced by rather large corporations.

University Innovation-Invention-Entrepreneurial Centers

University innovation-invention-entrepreneurial centers (IIEs) are new sources for getting ideas converted to tangible products. Operating in conjunction with the Small Business Administration's (SBA) Institutes (SBIs) and more than 450 of the nation's universities and colleges, they are attempting to bring higher learning to the doorsteps of home workshops and small businesses. Since these centers are rather new, they don't have much of a track record with technical research and development aspects of new products; however, they can be of immense assistance to the individual captivated by a burning idea who needs help with market research, feasibility analysis, and business planning.

The best known IIE center is located at the University of Oregon. For a modest fee, it will evaluate the chances of your idea making money on the basis of the following criteria:

Legality	Need
Safety	Promotion
Environmental impact	Appearance
Societal impact	Price

Potential market
Product life cycle
Usage learning
Product visibility
Service
Durability
New competition
Functional feasibility
Product feasibility
Development status
Investment costs
Trend of demand
Product line potential

Protection
Payback period
Profitability
Product interdependence
Research and development
Stability of demand
Consumer/user
Compatibility
Marketing research
Distribution
Perceived function
Existing competition
Potential sales

If you have a big idea that requires more resources than are at your immediate command, write for information to Experimental Center of the Advancement of Invention and Innovation, College of Business Administration, 131 Gilbert Hall, University of Oregon, Eugene, OR 97403.

If the Center concludes your idea has merit and is commercially feasible, it will help you contact established companies most likely to be interested in your product or it may even refer you to known sources of funds.

For further information about this program and its availability in your community, contact the university, college, or SBA field office nearest you. It could very well make the difference between a loss of investment capital or a big money-making winner.

Help with Energy-related Ideas

National Bureau of Standards offices offer assistance and even financial support for energy-related ideas and inventions. You can obtain full information by writing to U.S. Department of Commerce, National Bureau of Standards, Office of Energy-Related Inventions, Washington, DC 20234.

Basically, the Office of Energy-Related Inventions in the U.S. Department of Commerce's National Bureau of Standards will evaluate nonnuclear energy-related inventions and ideas for devices, materials, and procedures without charge. If the office finds that the invention or idea has merit, it will recommend further study by the Department of Energy. If it shows promise, the Department of Energy might provide support for the invention. This process can take from nine months to a year.

Inventors' Clubs and Associations

Inventors' clubs and associations are composed of others like yourself who are interested in inventing and producing new products. Many club members have had direct experience obtaining patents. They often can show you how to find out if your idea is original, tell you what it takes to produce and distribute a new product, and share other experiences with you. Talking directly with someone who has successfully produced and marketed a new product is an exciting way to keep your thoughts and imagination moving in the right direction.

To find out if you have an inventors' club in your community, send an inquiry to these organizations: American Society of Inventors, 134 Narberth Avenue, Room 101, Narberth, PA 19072; Association for the Advancement of Invention and Innovations, Suite 605, 1735 Jefferson Davis Highway, Arlington, VA 22202.

INITIATE! MAKE THINGS HAPPEN!

If the mother of invention is necessity, the father of invention is inspiration and effort. Ideas are created, things are invented, and money from this is made because of passionate motivation. When your interest in something is highly charged, that passionate interest produces vast quantities of energy. Use this high-powered energy to make things happen; do something!

Don't delay or you will find yourself mired in procrastination. Even if you don't have all the pieces to the puzzle, nevertheless begin. Step by step, all the solutions you seek will begin to unfold. When you have taken a project or invention as far as it can reasonably go, make your move; implement!

Often as much energy is required to take a project or invention the last 10 percent of its potential as was required to initiate the first 90 percent. Trying to reach perfection too early in a project can be paralyzing. Instead of trying to make one invention or project 100 percent better, perhaps you can be more productive making 100 projects or inventions 1 percent better. Worthwhile projects and inventions do not always have to result in immortal breakthroughs. Most successful inventions and projects are merely small improvements to accepted products or processes.

When you identify the idea central to fulfillment of your major purpose, go after it with enthusiasm and persistence. Pursue your passion. Astonishing achievement will be your reward.

7
Products
of the Imagination

Producing and marketing the written word or art work may appear different from producing and marketing traditional consumer products, but their business features are the same. The key is to find a need and fill it using the full array of proven business principles.

NEWSLETTER PUBLISHING CAN BE LUCRATIVE

People from all walks of life, many with little writing ability, are making substantial profits providing specialized knowledge and information through the medium of newsletters. Most newsletters consist of from two to six printed pages. People in need of timely, accurate information subscribe to such newsletters and often pay $50, $100, even as much as $1,000 and sometimes more for a one-year subscription. Imagine, if you have a readership of only 700 subscribers paying $100 per year; that will gross $70,000 for a four-page newsletter that may require only half a day of writing time.

Newsletters are so popular that opportunities exist in just about every field imaginable. One survey showed there were approximately 1,300 newsletters published in 1974. Today, there are almost 10,000 newsletters, and their popularity continues to grow at the rate of about 200 a year.

People who search out interests and activities of a specialized nature and then establish a readership have gone on to become leading experts in their fields. Many newsletter writers branch out into consulting, often commanding $1,000 a day in consulting and speaking fees.

Newsletters can be started with an initial investment ranging between $500 and $1,000, using borrowed money if necessary, and all business activities can be performed on a part- or spare-time basis.

Rapid advances in print technology through use of the personal computer have drastically changed the way newsletters are prepared. Desktop publishing, those buzzwords that mean the ability to design newsletters, reports, or practically anything else requiring printing at your desk, is revolutionizing the printing industry. Relatively inexpensive computer software is available to prepare, print, and paste up in just hours material that used to take days or weeks. Now you can produce typeset-quality publications, meeting traditional professional design standards, at a fraction of the cost right in your own office.

If you want to study a wide variety of newsletters in your own home, simply answer ads for them appearing in newspapers and magazines of interest to you. Your letter should ask for a free sample copy; you will be amazed at the steady flow of newsletters you will receive.

WRITING BOOKS AND ARTICLES

Each year in America, more than 40,000 books are published and tens of thousands of freelance articles are printed in well-known magazines and inhouse publications of large and small companies. This creates a huge demand for written material on a wide range of subjects. Many writing enthusiasts, who are not professional writers, have turned this pastime into a fortune.

What Should You Write?

You may have a strong desire to write but are uncertain about subject matter, whether to write articles or books, or whether fiction or nonfiction suits you best. The easiest way to clear up this uncertainty is to take an inventory of your dominant interests by following the steps described in the first chapter of this book.

Your best writing will always be generated from ideas and subjects that excite you. If you have a specialized knowledge in a fascinating subject area, ideas and words reflecting thought given to the subject should come easily. Excellent nonfiction of immense appeal to readers is produced precisely this way. Also, an analysis of best-selling fiction reveals more often than not that themes are bolstered by factual references or by the author's ability to combine specialized knowledge with fictional narrative. For example, James Michener's famous novel *Hawaii* is fortified by the author's specialized knowledge of the history, growth, and development of that island paradise.

Obviously, articles and books that sell well are those with wide audience appeal. Such appeal is most regularly found in the fulfillment of people's well-known universal desires. If you can write an article or book that satisfies these desires, you will most certainly improve your chances of acquiring financial rewards and quite possibly of producing a best seller.

Closely examine the following list of dominant desires and select one or more on which to focus your writing:

1. Enhance ability to make money or acquire riches
2. Increase acceptance by others
3. Reduce pain and improve health
4. Become more attractive to the opposite sex
5. Build greater self-confidence
6. Exercise greater influence over others
7. Gain stature, importance, and prestige
8. Satisfy appetite for food or beverage
9. Help others become more successful in their activities
10. Make leisure time more enjoyable
11. Improve skills and talents
12. Increase comfort
13. Make life more secure
14. Enhance self-expression and creativity
15. Save time or effort
16. Show others how to obtain more leisure
17. Enhance the likelihood of acquiring desired possessions
18. Satisfy the need for excitement, thrills, mystery, or romance
19. Appeal to the craving to be in style
20. Help others save money, provide for their futures, or enjoy retirement
21. Assist others in avoiding discomfort, unpleasant conditions, or accidents
22. Provide avenues for the protection of one's reputation and avoidance of criticism
23. Tell how to take advantage of opportunity or achieve social, business, or career advancement
24. Satisfy curiosity

How to Sell What You've Written

If your inclination leads in the direction of writing, your enthusiasm for a hobby, sport, or pastime can be converted to cash by submitting your material for consideration to any of the hundreds of publishing firms and thousands of editors.

Most community libraries have books and directories that can help you locate publishers and editors who are in the business of relaying your message to specialized audiences or the general public.

One of the most all-encompassing national resource documents used by aspiring authors to locate book publishers is *Literary Market Place* published by R.R. Bowker Co., New York City.

If you are inclined to write articles as well as books, you should get familiar with *Writer's Market* published by Writer's Digest, Cincinnati, Ohio. Published yearly, this is a comprehensive, convenient directory listing over 5,000 magazine, book, greeting card, and play publishers actively seeking contributors. It also shows where the paying markets are for magazine fillers, articles, gags, verse, stories, novels, and even photographs.

An outstanding set of five directories, which is an indispensable guide for locating thousands of publishers and editors, is *Working Press of the Nation*, published by National Research Bureau, Inc.. Burlington, Iowa. It's made up of volume I, the *Newspaper Directory*; volume II, the *Magazine Directory;* volume III, the *TV and Radio Directory;* volume IV, the *Feature Writers, Photographers and Syndicates Directory;* and volume V, the *Internal Publications Directory.*

Each directory lists publications and editorial personnel, along with their addresses and telephone numbers, in its own particular specialty. Volume IV also lists the names of freelancers, by specialty, and the magazines in which their work has appeared. It can be useful for locating a freelancer in your community willing to give you firsthand pointers on how to get articles published.

Using the sources just mentioned, select five to 10 publishers who would appear to have the most interest in the subject matter you've written about. It's a good idea to then write to the publications on your list asking for their style sheets. Style sheets tell would-be authors the particular requirements of a publication, for example, that the manuscript be typed double spaced or the number of words an article should contain.

Next, prepare a well-organized query letter. The query letter should ask whether the publisher is interested in the subject matter of your article or manuscript and specify your qualifications for writing what you have. Include a sample of your work and a self-addressed stamped envelope to facilitate the editor's reply.

In recent years, it has become customary for authors to submit their work to several likely publishers simultaneously in order to avoid publishing delays.

If you choose to do this, mention in your query letter that you are exploring publishing possibilities with several publishers, but only for the purpose of presenting your work on a timely basis.

If you would like further information on the intricate aspects of marketing your written book, entering into contracts, using an agent, and the like, you will find a raft of books on the subject in your local library.

Becoming Your Own Publisher

If you have trouble locating a willing publisher but have supreme faith in your book, you may decide to self-publish it. Joe Karbo, author of *The Lazy Man's Way to Riches,* self-published and sold his book through mail order. In one year, he sold 175,000 copies at $10 each, which amounts to $1.75 million.

You can start your own publishing company just as you would any other business and manufacture and sell your book or you can pay a "vanity press" to do the manufacturing and promotion for you. If you want to find out more about self-publishing, a must book for you is *The Self-Publishing Manual* by Dan Poynter, published by Para Publishing, Santa Barbara, California. It and many others on the subject are available at your local library.

THE MUSIC BUSINESS

Entertainers need a steady stream of new songs if they are to remain popular, and many songwriters have become wealthy overnight. If your great desire has always been to write a song, a key directory is *Songwriter's Market* published by Writer's Digest, Cincinnati, Ohio. It lists more than 2,000 places where you can sell songs and features the name and address of the person to contact, special requirements, payment arrangements, and other valuable information so you can direct the right material to the right market. All information in this book has been provided by the persons who actually decide which songs are and which songs are not accepted. Each listing is complete and up-to-date, so you can spend more time writing songs and less time searching for buyers.

You'll also get tips on contracts and copyrights, how to get your foot in the door; how to get your song heard by the right person, how to avoid the hazardous waters of song sharks, plus interviews with successful songwriters and music industry executives.

ART MAY BE YOUR WAY TO WEALTH

If you have an artistic bent, your talents could form the basis of a graphic arts business or perhaps you can create cartoons. Practical, business-related art is in high demand, particularly by very small businesses who cannot afford to hire expensive advertising agencies yet desperately need art work. A reasonable fee schedule, some concentrated leafleting to small, neighborhood-type businesses, and a portfolio of imaginative ideas on ways your art could increase your customer's business will help pave your way to wealth.

The Cartoon Business

Perhaps you have a knack for performing that unique American craft, which is not exactly art and not exactly writing but which Americans call cartoons. All types of business publications buy original cartoons of quality pertaining to their particular industry. Offering cartoons on a freelance basis is a good way to develop your skill; then by applying the success principles in this book, you can achieve whatever plateau of success you desire.

The best way to market your cartoons is to prepare a query letter and send it along with samples of your work to the people listed in the directories discussed above under the section "How To Sell What You've Written." Start by searching out those entries suggesting receptiveness to cartoons listed in *Writer's Market* and in volume V of the *Working Press of the Nation, Internal Publications Directory*. Follow up by doing the same with the editors in volume II, *Magazine Directory*, and finally volume I, *Newspaper Directory*. Just as in submitting manuscripts, send along a self-addressed stamped envelope to facilitate the editor's reply.

For inspiration, look at the phenomenal success story of cartoonist Jim Davis, creator of that feisty feline cartoon character, Garfield. Growing up on a farm near Fairmont, Indiana, the idea of drawing a comic strip became one of his goals.

Working for successful cartoonist Tom Ryan, Davis gradually evolved his own character—Garfield. He was confident about the new idea, but he worked on it for a year or so before trying to have the strip syndicated. When he did try, he was not warmly received. In fact, he was turned down by several of the top companies in the field. Finally Davis was signed by United Features, and Garfield made a public debut in 41 newspapers. He now appears in 1,000 newspapers not only in America, but also in Europe, Asia, Africa, and Australia.

Logos and Trademarks

You can also design your way to wealth. In the scheme of things not generally known, *logos*, or symbols, are extremely important matters in the business world. Big dollars are the common reward for designing these appealing, eye-catching symbols. A good logo must be recognized quickly and readily; it must be remembered and easily recalled by the audience seeing it.

Not that doing so is any easy matter, but applying the success principles described in this book can make difficult-to-design symbols appear effortlessly. Starting with an idea; applying imagination; establishing your goal; being persistent; and fortifying your effort with desire, faith, and belief can bring success if artistic endeavors are what you enjoy doing most.

The CBS television logo is a classic example of memorable abstract design of tremendous importance to business. Designed in 1951 by William Golden, it has become one of the best-known trademarks in the United States.

If you want inspiration so you can design your way to wealth, a solid reference is as close as your library. The "bible" covering every conceivable corporate, government, and notable symbol having worldwide significance is a big book entitled *Symbol Sourcebook: An Authoritative Guide to International Graphic Symbols,* published by McGraw-Hill Book Company, New York City.

If art is "your thing," why not try your hand at designing a new corporate logo and submitting it to the corporation? If it's accepted, you will immediately get that extra money, which itself is a symbol of success.

COPYRIGHTING YOUR MATERIAL IS EASIER THAN YOU THINK

A copyright provides a form of protection to authors similar to rights established for inventors by patents. A copyright is granted to authors of original works, including literary, dramatic, musical, artistic, and certain other intellectual endeavors. This protection, available for both published and unpublished works, makes it illegal for anyone to violate copyright statutory provisions—that is, steal your material.

The function of a copyright is to guarantee the author immediate, exclusive property rights of original material. Only the author can distribute, reproduce, and prepare derivatives of the copyrighted work or publicly display the work unless, of course, the author has licensed or assigned those rights to others.

Copyright protection automatically exists when original works are "created," and this condition is met when authorship becomes fixed in a tangible form of expression for the first time. Under a law that took effect on January 1, 1978, no publication or registration or other action in the Copyright Office is required. Protection is automatically conferred when a copyright notice is placed on all publicly distributed copies of the material.

The copyright notice consists of a symbol or abbreviation of the word "copyright," the year of first publication of the work, and the name of the owner of the copyright; for example, © 1990 John Doe. Applying the copyright notice on published material is the responsibility of the copyright owner.

It is no longer necessary to publish an original work to obtain statutory copyright protection. However, publication remains important to copyright owners because of established interpretations of the law.

While copyright registration is nothing more than a legal formality, it establishes a public record attesting to the basic facts of a particular copyright. Also, a copyright ensures maximum protection since it is generally a requirement before an infringement suit can be pursued in the courts.

You are legally entitled to submit an Application for Copyright Registration if you are the author of the original work, the copyright claimant, or the duly authorized agent of the author. You need not have an attorney file it for you.

If you choose to register your work, send the following items in the same envelope: (1) a properly completed application form, (2) $10 for each application, and (3) two complete copies of the original work for use by the Library of Congress. Send to United States Copyright Office, Register of Copyrights, Library of Congress, Washington, DC 20559.

There are two basic durations on copyrights. A copyright established on or after January 1, 1978, ordinarily has a term enduring for the author's life, plus an additional 50 years after the author's death. Copyrights established before 1978 lasted for the first term of 28 years and, if extended during the 28th year, for a second term of 47 years.

If you are unsure of the proper application requirements for your work, write to the Copyright Office for information and describe the work you wish registered. To obtain full information on copyrights, write for a copy of *Publications of the Copyright Office,* Information and Publications Section LM-455, Copyright Office, Library of Congress, Washington, DC 20559.

8
Providing a Service

Years ago the primary mission of small-business America was to manufacture and distribute products. Most independent business pioneers made money making things—automobiles, clothing, equipment, appliances and other tangibles. Along came technology, and rapidly, manufacturing became America's past, the service sector of business its future.

Services delivered by small businesses now account for 71 percent of the nation's output. Today, small-business America spends most of its time processing information, monkeying with computers, peddling financial and other intangibles, maintaining and doing service things for people.

For business success, your inclination and time may be best directed toward providing a service rather than offering a product. If so, you are certainly on the right track. Some services provided today were not even contemplated 10 years ago, and some services that will be needed 10 years from now are not known today. Some service businesses that seemed to just get by for years are suddenly booming because of changes in our society, economy, and life styles.

Through the vehicle of a service business, your expert skill or knowledge can be transmuted to riches of priceless value. Demonstrating a mastered talent has the potential to lift the most humble of us to positions of fortune, fame, and power.

If you take full and complete possession of your developed abilities, if you allow your mind full reign to concentrate on realistic income-producing services that you already know how to deliver, you can unlock doors to the solution of money problems. Prosperity, success, peace of mind leading to other values of life such as happiness and unchallengeable conviction of self-worth are only a few of the exciting rewards waiting to be collected.

HOW TO RECOGNIZE A SERVICE BUSINESS

What is the essence of a service business? How do you know one when you see one?

A service business is any income-generating enterprise that has as its primary purpose the exercise of knowledge or skill to accomplish a business goal. Unlike other types of business, it does not deliver a tangible product.

Sometimes the distinction between a service business and product business is blurred. Restaurants, for example, are often considered service businesses, but they deliver a special kind of product and thus are commonly known as food-service businesses.

Employment agencies are classified as service businesses as are laundromats, gardening and cleaning firms, detective agencies, collection bureaus, secretarial and computer service companies, and specialized schools, to name but a few. Generally, service businesses are time and energy intensive, as opposed to product businesses that are generally capital intensive.

A service business can be directed toward any one of thousands of activities. Most center around providing specialized knowledge, saving a customer time, or performing work that customers are unable or unwilling to do for themselves.

Take the case of Janet Christensen who started a detective agency from scratch in Seattle, Washington. Her specialty is finding missing persons. She earns income on the basis of her time, upwards of $30 an hour or $200 a day plus expenses. Tackling a case as she would a puzzle, she solves practically every one that comes her way. In her business, she uses time and ingenuity to apply every possibility she can think of to solve a case because, in her words, ''Success depends on being creative.''

The key ingredient is to develop an idea based on your interest, talent, knowledge, or skill. People successful in service businesses get interested in what they enjoy and want to do; they limit their involvement in activities not meeting these requirements and they convert their energy to accomplishment.

Remember that the hours you work must be geared to times of greatest customer need, which means you may have to provide coverage for weekends and nights as well as normal business hours.

LOOK FOR OPPORTUNITIES LOCALLY

You can often establish a service business based solely on local needs. Keep alert to local customs, patterns, population growth, and popular local activities. For example, when the computer broke down while the manuscript of this book was being prepared, the authors discovered that there were only two reputable repair shops within 20 miles, and each shop had a one-month backup on repairs. The need became painfully obvious, and the person skilled in computer repair discovering it will convert a collective desperation by others for similar service to a sizeable income.

One of the authors of this book used these same techniques to spot a need for a canoe-and-raft rental service on the historic American River in Sacramento, California. The river had always been a popular recreation waterway for those owning their own pleasure boats, but a rapid growth in population pointed to a need to make canoes and rafts available to those wanting to rent such crafts for a summer day of fun. This canoe-and-raft rental service was the first established in the Sacramento area; and subsequently, 14 other small businesses began offering a similar service, the genus of which was a basic need for recreation.

The most concrete suggestion that can be made for determining a need and converting it to a service business is to keep your eyes and ears open to events happening around you. Chapter 2 of this book precisely describes the kinds of conditions that generate service businesses.

You can get wind of service business opportunities practically anywhere. Avram Ruditzky got his idea for a service business from cocktail-party chatter with some physician friends. They were complaining about inadequate hospital record keeping. After some follow-up, he created Medical Registry Services Inc., a company that computerizes hospital records of cancer patients. In five years, he signed up 41 hospitals for annual revenue of about $1 million. In the next two years, he was up to 90 hospitals and projected annual revenue of $5 million.

Often, service businesses are created merely from impetus stemming from your own wants or needs. Sharlyne Powell, once overweight to the tune of 200 pounds herself, saw a need among the truly overweight to get together for physical workouts. She founded Women-At-Large, a firm that offers exercise classes for clients whose weight typically exceeds 200 pounds. Now closer to 150, the 5-foot, 5-inch Mrs. Powell sees her service business expanding rapidly in the next decade, it is already generating $400,000 a year in revenue.

Pastime interests are converted to cash in a wide variety of service businesses, including furniture stripping and staining, small appliance repair, dating services, sporting equipment repair, landscaping, and many others. Appendix B lists a large number of small businesses that are generating cash, many of which are service-type endeavors.

YOU CAN START A SERVICE BUSINESS ON A SHOESTRING

Based on your interest and an initial determination of need, a successful service business requires that you locate near and make your service known to potential customers.

A great many service businesses begin on a very small scale, with costs kept to a minimum because business can usually be conducted from the home. Since most of the work in a service business is performed at a location convenient to the customer, your home may be all that is required to receive calls from customers, to maintain records and prepare advertising material. Of course, as the business grows, renting a shop may become preferable.

A great many service businesses are begun to provide a second income; others are started to generate income during a period of unemployment. Generally, a person's time and know-how are the primary ingredients in operating a service business; an initial, but often minimum investment in equipment and advertising converts the business owner's time and knowledge to cash.

Nick Giacobone, owner of a limousine rental service in Torrance, California, applied this method and started a school to teach etiquette to limousine drivers. The course covers such subleties as how to address customers and riders, the proper attire, and how to uncork a bottle of champagne. At the end of the course, students must pass a road test by negotiating city streets and narrow canyon roads without spilling the instructor's glass of champagne. Giacobone, who loves cars and social events, had revenues of $750,000 in one year from his school and limousine rental service.

If you're looking for a service-oriented business, as you go about your daily affairs always keep attuned to events unfolding around you. When you hear someone complaining about some lack of service that is of interest to you, follow up and apply proven business success principles that will convert that service need to money.

Henry and Richard Block used just such an approach to build a multimillion-dollar business centered around seasonal tax return preparation. The H and R Block income tax preparation service is just one of many services that have made people wealthy.

BUSINESS-BUILDING TACTICS

Your service business has the best chance to prosper when you close the gap between basic customer needs and efficient delivery of talent or technology.

Service businesses, not being highly capital intensive, generally do not require large inventory expenditures or control. On the other hand, investment in advertising, equipment, and employee training is vital to optimize customer volume and service efficiency.

Service businesses are built by using a logical progression of sound business practices. You start where the customers are, convey your availability and qualifications, determine their need, clearly state your fee, deliver your service, and follow up to ensure satisfaction and get referrals.

When starting a new service business, you can acquire customers by typing a one-page flyer, taking this master paste-up to a quick-copy printer, and distributing copies in the neighborhood, thus notifying people of your business. This flyer should be a clear statement describing your service, specifying your qualifications and licenses, confirming that you have insurance, giving a typical schedule of fees, testimonials from satisfied customers, a work guarantee, and a phone number.

Don't hesitate to give copies of this flyer to the people you know from clubs and social groups with which you are associated: bowling leagues, sporting groups, religious groups, your child's school. All of these can become excellent sources of customers.

To Ensure Customer Satisfaction

A reputation of high character, prompt reliable service, and guaranteed work will bring more customers than you ever thought possible. Satisfied customers recommend you to others, which increases your volume and boosts profits. Always be sure that calls from prospects are answered promptly and courteously and that the person responding can provide reliable information.

Arrange a timely appointment and keep to a disciplined appointment schedule. Remember to call well in advance if rescheduling is absolutely necessary or if you unalterably find you're running late. Nothing aggravates customers more than scheduling themselves to see you and then cooling their heels uncertain of your whereabouts.

When you arrive at your appointment, be neatly and cleanly dressed. Be friendly, take time to listen to your customer, be certain of all aspects of the work to be performed, convey confidence that you can do the job, prepare an accurate written estimate, and give a specific time when the work will begin and be completed.

On getting the OK, confirm payment arrangements, keep your promises, supervise and/or inspect the work for precision and quality, and leave the premises clean and tidy. Before leaving, ask the customer's permission to place some leave-behinds, such as an advertising sticker fixed to the back of an appliance or a tag on an outside fixture or a piece of equipment you've repaired. You might want to leave a giveaway advertising specialty item, such as a potholder, telephone/date book, or key chain.

After the work is done, follow up by recontacting the customer to be sure you have delivered satisfaction. Ask to be referred to your new patron's friends and relatives and seek approval for a brief testimonial.

Advertising Tips for Your Growing Business

When additional advertising is required, look first at reasonable newspaper choices. For a minimum cash outlay, you can advertise your service in neighborhood "trader" newspapers that specialize in classified ads only and are read by tens of thousands. These trader newspapers are themselves small businesses that depend on classified ads for their business. Readers generally pick them up free at local grocery stores. Advertising rates are very reasonable compared with rates charged by traditional hometown newspapers.

Newspaper advertising can be especially appealing when it announces discounts to senior citizens or some other special group of patrons and notifies prospects of limited-time specials.

Other forms of inexpensive advertising include attractive displays on vans, trucks, and cars. Signs posted where you do the work are often appropriate, such as on construction or repair projects. In all cases, be sure to get permission and not offend the customer.

Radio spot announcements and local cable television are also available according to limits on your advertising budget. They help provide continuous recall, fitting a customer's unexpected need for the kind of services you render.

Be careful that your advertising doesn't produce too many customers before you are equipped to handle them. Service businesses have a unique way of depending on the time and talent of trained personnel. These resources must be available in ample supply when demanded by customers if your business is to grow. That's why owners of successful service businesses are generally top-notch managers. Expansion can only be achieved by making more hours available for service delivery, which means adding and training staff or working harder yourself.

Treated as a business, your service constitutes a practical means by which you and people you train can achieve a higher income. A skillful combination of proven service business-building practices and imagination can be the grandest form of your own self-expression; it can produce all the material things in life you desire.

Withholding anything short of the best service can be costly to your business. In the course of human events, and as an American, you have the absolute right to exercise personal initiative. You alone have a power that no one can seize from you—the power to reap the benefits from going the extra mile. Exercising this power is the source of all great achievement.

YOUR SERVICE IS A KEY TO RICHES

Prosperity from a service business is founded on a well-known law of mutual exchange. By applying this law, you can predict your fortune. The law is simply this: your financial reward will always be in direct proportion to the quality and quantity of the service you render. If you want a greater return, you must render more service.

Opportunities for rendering a worthy service today are enormous. You can go down any street in America and determine rather easily whether good and sufficient service is being rendered by and for the people living on that street. Using ideas in this book and your own thoughts, you can determine how best to provide a needed service.

Allow your miraculous mind to think about a goal of providing a service from all possible angles. Let your imagination speculate freely on the many different kinds of service that can be rendered. Use all your courage to force yourself to think positively about how your goal can be achieved. Establish a definite date and a clearly defined plan of action for accomplishing your goal. Refuse to believe that there are any circumstances sufficiently strong to defeat you. Begin now to act promptly and decisively to carry out your goal.

As you go about the task of fulfilling your goal, look at the abundance all around you. Be convinced that you have as much right to this abundance as any other living creature. To be successful on your way to the good life, understand emotionally as well as intellectually that any limitations you may have are largely self-imposed, that to control your life you must first control your thoughts.

If you hold your goal before you, everything else will take care of itself. Carry out at least one task in your plan of action each day and remember that ideas are worthless unless you act on them.

If you fully understand and apply this law, you will be among those who are truly successful because they have learned it. Don't overly concern yourself with the money that a service business will generate. Rather, be of service, build, work, dream, create—do these things and you will find there is no limit to the prosperity and abundance that will come to you.

Your success in a service business will always be measured by the quality and quantity of service you render; money is the mere yardstick for measuring this service. Getting rich requires only that you enrich others with your service.

Running you own service business affords the opportunity to make life an exciting adventure, never a bore. Doing a job for others in exchange for your financial reward provides incentive to live fully, to be alive, to look forward to getting up in the morning because you will be doing what you like to do. You will be rewarded, for as you believe, so shall it be done unto you.

9
Buying a
Business or Franchise

Perhaps you relish the stimulating features of business ownership such as high-income potential, realizing rewards in relation to your effort, freedom to be your own boss, and the privilege to have your full share of life's bountiful riches.

Perhaps you believe you are qualified to operate a business of your own because of unwavering faith in your skills, knowledge, education, or experience and abilities. You have supervised workers, administered budgets, exceeded goals, directed sales, or performed hundreds of other tasks culminating in business success.

While completely ready for the challenge to prove you can succeed on your own in the business world, perhaps you cannot quite muster the supreme venturesome spirit required to start a business from scratch. Maybe you are more inclined to be a manager than an entrepreneur. What can you do?

The answer may be to buy an already established, independent business or to invest money, time, and effort in a franchise.

THE STRATEGY OF GETTING STARTED

The U.S. Department of Commerce projects that 75 percent of small businesses and franchises operating today will change hands within five years. A third of the new owners will decide within the first year of operation that they don't cotton to a business owner's life style.

Another study by the Commerce Department concludes that successful business and franchise owners commonly display certain characteristics: an expert knowledge of the field or type of business they are in; initiative combined with willingness to work long hours; a positive attitude toward the business and its customers; organizing ability; an outgoing, like-people personality; a high level of physical energy; leadership ability displayed sincerely to inspire trust; self-discipline; willingness to pay attention to detail; and perseverance in the face of discouragement. A starting point to forming your own business ownership strategy is to honestly determine if you possess a very large measure of these characteristics.

While it is true that we live in a most free society and millions of businesses return a prosperous life to their owners, the fate of a new business owner is most often determined before actual ownership occurs. It is determined by the quality of the match between inherent merits of the business or franchise to be purchased and fundamental personality characteristics of the new business owner.

Buying the right independent business or franchise can be a timesaver relative to the process of creating and building a business from scratch. Be careful though, not to short cut the substantial investment of time and effort necessary to find the right business, to sift out a solid moneymaker from all the losers. In truth, a systematic search to find the business that fully meets preestablished criteria is the most crucial and difficult aspect of the purchase of any business or franchise.

ASSESS YOUR LIKES AND DISLIKES

Successful choice of a business or franchise to purchase will first depend on your likes, dislikes, experience, knowledge, and skill and the relation these have to operating elements of a specific business. There are thousands of fields of business. Within them are specific business operations of all shapes and sizes. Some are capital intensive, others are time and energy intensive. Some operate 24 hours a day, 365 days a year, others keep traditional nine to five business hours. Some rely heavily on one-to-one interaction with customers, others are suitable only for those comfortable working with things rather than people.

Go about the assignment of finding a suitable business with singleness of purpose. You have at your command two powerful mechanisms to ensure that your important business purchase decision meets all requirements. Use them wisely to make a sound purchase judgment.

First, reinforce identification of your aptitudes by rereading Chapter 1 and by diligently applying each step of the 10-point success formula so that you know and understand yourself thoroughly. Write out a clear, definite statement of the preconditions your business must meet. Decide in advance those attributes the searched-for business must have, matching them carefully with strong character strengths that you intend to devote to the business.

By this process you will be issuing detailed instructions to your inner-self. As you prepare criteria, you will be raising your mind's business-conscious level. You will be preparing yourself to unlock the doors to the solution you richly deserve. If you want success, there is no substitute for a perceptive match of your likes and skills with the strengths and weaknesses of the business you intend to buy.

The second powerful mechanism reveals itself in the process of determining the degree of need for the business relative to the rest of the world, your community, specific location, and customers. Reinforce identification of real and sustained need for goods or services by asking questions contained in the format for a business plan in Chapter 11. When you've done this, you will thoroughly understand the prospective business.

Equipped with knowledge garnered from these two powerful mechanisms, you can be assured that your business purchase selection meets all requirements for a sound business decision.

UNDERSTAND WHAT YOU BUY

Every established business or franchise for sale is in some phase of its overall business life cycle. These phases are described as start-up, growth, stability, decline, and rejuvenation. The only way to know the phase of a business or franchise is to carefully analyze its records. Think of the records of a business or franchise as its scorecard; only by careful review of business records can you know the score.

Don't be misled by the appearance of some degree of customer base and income. Buying a business is an investment; its expected return must equal or exceed anticipated return from competing investment alternatives. Aside from the priceless satisfaction of owning your own business, do records prove adequate profits now and in the future that justify investment of your hard-earned money and valuable time?

If you intend to run the business, it must be capable of returning to you reasonable annual compensation and reasonable yield on the up-front money you have invested. A very good way to evaluate initial asking price is to also know the compensation you can realistically expect from the business. Use this ballpark formula to screen business offerings:

$$\frac{\text{Business or franchise purchase price}}{\text{Annual compensation}} = \text{Factor} \div 100$$
$$= \text{Yield on investment}$$

For example, if the purchase price of an independent business or franchise is $200,000 and it returns an annual net profit after compensation of $20,000, you will be getting a 10-percent yield on your investment.

$$\frac{\$200,000}{\$20,000} = 10 \div 100 = 10\% \text{ yield on investment}$$

You must ask yourself how this yield compares with other investment alternatives, particularly those not requiring 50 to 70 hours weekly of your time?

COMPARING INDEPENDENT BUSINESSES AND FRANCHISES

A wise purchase of either an independent business or franchise can lead you to attainment of money, material possessions, and the degree of economic security you desire. Such conditions are not limited to a very lucky few. They are well within your reach, but only if you are adequately prepared to receive them. If you don't apply detailed principles of evaluation, that one slipshod business habit can lead to a curse of failure.

When you buy an established business, you are paying for the amount of worth developed by the seller. This is best measured by records of gross income, market share, size of customer base, and amount of profit. When buying an established business, it is unwise to pay for anything that has not already been made tangible by the previous owner. Certain intangibles, such as reputation, location, and goodwill, are not exceptions because they too are measured by income and profit records.

When buying a franchise, payment is made for all the same items of worth enveloped in an independent business, but realize you are also paying for expert on-going support, training, financing, assistance with record keeping, advertising, marketing, and the powerful reputation of a franchiser to produce customers for you virtually overnight.

If you cannot come away from your purchase evaluation convinced you are getting all the business elements you are paying for, then you have not yet completed your search. As you gather reams of information, brochures, advertisements, written descriptions, and a host of other materials on independent businesses and franchises for sale and as you compare and evaluate each one, know that you tackle this serious business assignment with the firm admonition to be patient.

All businesses for sale have strengths and weaknesses. Some of the weaknesses can be overcome by application of new ideas, energy, ability, and greater focus on the inherent strengths of the business. On the other hand, some weaknesses may be beyond anybody's control, they simply never will be overcome.

USEFUL TACTICS WHEN BUYING AN INDEPENDENT BUSINESS

Purchase of an independent business with an established reputation, location, and visible legacy from the previous owner, particularly when bought at a sensible price, can bring generous rewards. Businesses that change hands every day include everything from long-established major corporations transferred to new owners at billion-dollar prices to mom-and-pop operations at very low prices. In some cases, these transfers have created enormous wealth for new owners; in other cases, new owners have lost everything.

You begin using successful business-buying tactics by gathering and scrutinizing available information. There are three primary sources of information on businesses available for purchase: word of mouth, newspapers, and business brokers.

You can discover some very fine business-purchase opportunities by talking with business owners, accountants, bankers, and attorneys or by contacting business associations, chambers of commerce, and wholesale suppliers. Every day these entities deal with business owners and often are in key positions to learn first that a client or associate has been thinking about leaving the business. A little homework and follow-up in this area can produce a real treasure chest filled with prospects that could be right for you.

Newspapers are a valuable source of information about businesses for sale. Such information is dispatched in three ways: in business section articles that disclose that something is about to or has already happened to a business, its owner, or industry; in classified advertisements placed by business owners or their brokers; and in legal announcements, most often found in specialty legal-journal newspapers, telling of business auctions, probate sales, and estate sales. Regular review of these newspaper sources will keep you abreast of trends—what kinds of businesses always seem to be for sale or are rarely for sale, which locations are growing or declining, what are ballpark categories of going prices.

Brokers, either general commercial real estate or specialized business brokers, regularly handle business sales for clients. Look for their advertisements or seek them out in your telephone directory under "Business Brokers."

Every community is full of inspirational examples of folks who have made wise business-purchase choices and have thus gained independence, satisfaction, and wealth beyond the realm of any other occupation they ever tried. They have freed themselves from corporate rigidities, office politics, arbitrary bosses, dead-end futures, capped earnings, and thankless drudgery. They have gone on to realize the priceless satisfaction of personal and financial success in one of the most rewarding occupations in the world—being an independent business owner.

How to Investigate Before You Buy

Just as a physician evaluates vital signs of the human body to determine its health; to make a wise business-purchase choice, you must evaluate the vital signs of that business. These vital signs are:

1. Reputation
2. Customer base
3. Condition of fixtures, equipment, and inventory
4. Location
5. Total sales revenue
6. Profit
7. Projected growth

Analyzing conditions behind each of these vital signs will bring you the answer to the all-important question: Why is this business for sale?

Two of the most prevalent reasons businesses are for sale are they are losing money or they are at least not making sufficient money to justify continued investment of time, energy, or capital or their growth opportunities are limited. On occasion, a quality business may be for sale because the owner has built the business to peak capacity and will decide to sell the business at a prime price rather than risk diminishing sales due to future unknown events.

One SBA study concluded that, on average, the optimum lifetime of a small business from inception to maturity is seven years. Thereafter, sales revenue and profit stabilize or decline unless an infusion of something new or different occurs.

Rarely are businesses for sale for such oft-stated reasons as the owner's poor health, retirement, death, and so on. Generally, if these events occur in the instance of a thriving business, a family member or someone known to the owner will have first crack at buying the business.

As the potential buyer of a business, you have important work to do to glean from your search a handful of the most promising businesses. Those meeting your predetermined requirements of nature, type, size, location, and price are given the highest priority. Scrutinize each business in this category by analyzing every operational element and fathoming all vital signs.

Ask to see records of past sales and profits, applying the operating ratios discussed in Chapter 11 on preparing and evaluating a business plan. Analyze previous income-tax returns for the business and then forecast sales and profits over the next one to five years. A caution flag is raised if a seller will not provide this information; since without it, you cannot logically evaluate the business.

If an analysis of this information reveals weak or declining profits, you must decide whether the chief reason is poor management by the owner, unfavorable economic conditions, or inherent weaknesses in the business itself. If you determine the chief reason is poor management, then before buying the business, you should prepare a revised business plan and objectively evaluate the realistic prospects of a new and improved plan to offer turnaround capabilities.

When you conclude from this analysis that all systems are a go, negotiations for purchase can commence.

Negotiating the Purchase

Getting help from a qualified business appraiser to determine a fair value purchase price is a wise investment. The objective is first to establish a realistic value of tangible assets such as inventory, furniture, fixtures, equipment, supplies, accounts receivable, and real estate. Evaluation of intangible assets, such as goodwill, customer base, lease value, and supplier relationships, is generally more difficult to ascertain and often represents the fulcrum for purchase-price negotiations.

Negotiation strategies often employ the use of various business-price valuation formulas; however, one of the easiest to use combines the resale worth of the tangible assets with the estimated value of intangible assets multiplied by a factor to arrive at a purchase price. Here is the procedure:

1. Obtain adjusted tangible net worth. Do this by estimating resale worth of all tangible assets, both current and long-term, then subtract current and long-term liabilities. $ _____
2. Get the net earnings (profit) for the most recent one-year period before any salary of the seller and before taxes. $ _____
3. If the business is well established, multiply the amount in step 2 by a factor of 5 to 8; if the business has only a moderately favorable name, product, or location, multiply the amount in step 2 by a factor of 3; and if the business is profitable but new, multiply the amount in step 2 by a factor of 1. $ _____
4. Add amounts produced by step 1 and step 3 to establish a price. $ _____

Additional factors to consider for effective negotiations are whether any lawsuits are pending, the lengths of any leases and whether they are renewable or transferable to a new owner, and whether revised zoning or licensing requirements will affect a new owner.

Final Steps to Proud Ownership

You become the proud owner of your business when sale and transfer of business assets and operations are completed. For smooth passage through escrow and recording, always get help from an attorney to prepare a written sales agreement. Be sure that conditions of sale include clear title to all physical property; a statement of agreement on finance terms; assurances that the seller will not deplete assets or sell inventory in a clearance sale; and covenants that all information, financial reports and statements, and liabilities are true, factual, and have been disclosed to the full extent possible.

FRANCHISING MAY BE RIGHT FOR YOU

On the busiest street corner in Houston, Bob Landauer works in the hottest segment of one of the fastest-growing sectors of the U.S. economy. He sells pizza. Mr. Landauer holds an MBA from New York University, but turned in 24 years with Peat, Marwick, Main & Co. for a Pizzeria Uno pizza franchise. Now he belongs to a segment of business growing 10 percent a year.

Projections are that by the year 2005, franchising will be a $1-trillion-a-year industry and will account for half of all retail sales. There are almost three million franchise outlets. Beyond those owned by individuals or married couples, an additional 20 percent are owned by male-female partnerships. About 11 percent of all franchise outlets are owned exclusively by women.

Franchise outlets have often proven to be marvelous devices to unlock the doors of business ownership. A correct selection can produce income and satisfaction rewards sufficient in both quantity and quality to satisfy all reasonable business ownership desires. Assistance by a reputable, experienced franchise parent can provide the same plane of opportunity enjoyed by more traditional business pioneers. Tried and proven franchise procedures invariably bestow a sense of control that can guide you to greatly improved circumstances of life. Constant contact between franchiser and franchisee can be a powerful two-way communication link of notable importance to your business success.

Franchising Is Not for the "Free Spirit"

As in any business, harmony of human relationships among all concerned parties, including family members or partners, is vital to producing fruits of work in a spirit of friendly cooperation. A positive mental attitude takes first place in the list of techniques to combat the common cause of friction sometimes appearing in franchise arrangements.

The strength of a franchise is the standardized methods and procedures relied on to govern and operate the outlet down to the last detail. Your mind must be conditioned to accepting these rigid procedures because they are the foundation on which the franchise structure produces money and all other forms of business satisfaction you seek. You will receive the first test of your capacity to condition your mind for this acceptance the minute you disagree with standardized methods of operation.

You are best advised to determine in advance if this condition can create a problem. It depends on your own personality characteristics since, standing alone, no difference of opinion need become a serious liability. You have the power through thought to obtain the fullest expression of the attainment of your objectives. A formidable truth is that thought is the only power over which you have complete control. Use this power to convert potential franchise differences of opinion into assets of priceless value.

What Are the Fastest-growing Franchises?

Almost everything imaginable is being franchised today—photocopy services, temporary-help agencies, accounting firms, collection agencies, oodles of food service and auto service operations, physical fitness operations, medical clinics, the list goes on and on. The fastest-growing franchises are listed in TABLE 9-1.

TABLE 9-1. Fastest Growing Franchises.

Franchise Name	Total Number of Franchises
1. Domino's Pizza	1,970
2. McDonald's Hamburger	6,150
3. Burger King Hamburger	3,555
4. Jazzercise (physical fitness)	3,073
5. Fantastic Sam's (hair care)	860
6. Wendy's Hamburger	2,106
7. Ice Cream Churn	700
8. Rainbow International Carpet Dyeing and Cleaning	950
9. Thrifty Rent-A-Car	600

Purchase fees and start-up costs range from the low thousands of dollars to $325,000 for a McDonald's. This requirement of often large cash or financing terms and conditions demands that you think big when buying a franchise.

Pros and Cons of a Franchise

The key attraction of a franchise purchase is the power of your capital to deliver a turnkey business opportunity. This doesn't mean you won't have to work hard and put in long hours once you open the business; however, the stimulation, satisfaction, and financial rewards are most often worth it.

In many respects, the advantages and disadvantages of owning a franchise are the same as owning an independent business. A person comfortable as a manager who understands the value of an inflexible, time-tested procedural format will often do best with a franchise; after all, this is the economical and efficient strength of franchise operations. On the other hand, entrepreneurs can be notoriously poor franchise owners because they tend to like risk, are unable to contain their ideas for change, and always believe they can do something better.

In addition to operating restrictions placed on them by the franchisers, franchisees are chiefly concerned with employee problems, low profit margins, competition, and inadequate franchiser support. Franchisers try to overcome potential problems by providing management training, employee training, recruitment aids, and operating manuals, in addition to assistance with site selection, facility design, lease negotiation, and franchise-fee financing.

A franchise contract spells out responsibilities of franchiser (grantor) and franchisee (grantee). If it fails to do so completely or is vague in important aspects, the result can be conflict.

Franchisers are most exacting about product quality, territorial responsibility, and sources of operating supplies. You should be most exacting about training and other support matters.

Get assistance from your attorney to make sure the franchiser contract is beneficial and solid on important operational elements, including definition of an established and protected territory, honored commitments to provide advertising, facilities, equipment, training, supplies, and any other business operations support.

How to Find the Right Franchise

Your library will give you immediate access to three quality sources of information on franchises. The *Guide to Franchises*, published by Dow-Jones-Irwin, Homewood, Illinois, covers and compares essential benefits of 570 different franchises operating in the United States. It includes information about capital requirements, financing assistance, training, managerial support, and other financial provisions.

The Directory of Franchising Organizations, published by Pilot Books of New York City, lists hundreds of franchise opportunities and gives concise descriptions and required investment. It even contains a franchise evaluation checklist to assist in making comparisons among the wide assortment of franchises.

The *Franchise Opportunities Handbook*, republished each year by the U.S. Commerce Department, lists offerings of 1,265 franchisers and summarizes how they operate, their sizes, years in business, equity capital requirements and aid they provide for financing, training, and management. Copies cost $13.50. Write to the Superintendent of Documents, U.S. Government Printing Office, Washington, DC 20402.

Look Carefully Before You Leap

If you're serious about buying a franchise, be sure to use all the same techniques described above in the section on buying an independent business. Remember that purchase price and fees must be in line with actual performance of other owners of the same franchise network and with financial-return projections of the exact franchise you intend to buy.

If you are comfortable with administering established procedures, supervising employees, and perhaps making big financial commitments, the process of thinking big could propel you to a vast fortune as a franchise owner.

QUESTIONS YOU NEED TO ASK

Buying an independent business, franchise, or distributorship can be a shortcut to success on your wealth safari; but like any other journey, it is not without potential detours and pitfalls. Before purchase, questions you must settle in your own mind include:

■ Do you have knowledge and experience in the type of business?
■ Are you sure it is the kind of business you want to devote a sizeable portion of your life to carry on?
■ In the case of an independent business or established franchise, what is the real reason the business is for sale?
■ Is it the type of business or franchise that has limited growth prospects and therefore tantamount to buying a job?
■ Does the business or franchise have growth prospects likely to make you rich, thus making it worth the purchase price?

10
Financing
Your Business Dream

Traditionally, two-thirds of the funds needed to start a new business come from the owner's savings or loans from friends. The remainder comes from banks and other financial institutions, credit from suppliers, and credit from providers of fixtures and equipment, inventory, and tangibles.

Certain types of businesses are not likely to appeal to banks or financial institutions, at least until they have become well established and are sure of a profit. Retail stores and many service businesses, such as restaurants, are examples of the kinds of enterprises that banks shy away from until they prove they can make money. On the other hand, a business offering products or services of a new technologic nature tends to have more appeal to banks and other lending institutions as well as to venture capitalists.

What, then, are you to do if you need business capital? For starters, go back and read the earlier chapters of this book. If you have faith that your idea will work, you must employ imagination to get your business started, using every means available to you. Your primary supplier of funds must, of necessity, be your own personal funding sources.

QUESTIONS TO ASK YOURSELF

In what kind of shape is your personal credit? Are you fully using your imagination, time, and energy to turn your hobby, favorite sport, or pastime to cash? Are you prepared to back up your faith with personal savings? Are you willing to pursue your business with conviction and, if necessary, increase your personal debt? Who do you know that has such personal faith in your convictions, knowledge and abilities, and the promise of your business that they will advance money to you on faith alone, at least until you are able to establish a business record? Have you told friends, relatives, and associates about your business program? Have you substantiated its potential for generating income to the point that they can be persuaded to kick in a few hundred dollars?

Remember that borrowing money, whether it be for personal or business purposes, rests on established credit-worthiness principles. Whether you are able to borrow money today depends on what you did with money in the past. How solid is your money-payback reputation? Do you have a solid credit rating? Have you been prudent with your financial resources? Are you overlooking untapped sources of money? Do you have to improve your personal credit rating before you can realistically expect to be advanced any further credit?

If raising your credit rating is not possible without additional income, perhaps you should reconsider the hobby, sport, pastime, or idea you momentarily regard as most intriguing, but expensive to finance, in favor of a more practical variation for which know-how and materials readily available will produce additional income.

Of course, you may have had financial misfortune and your past credit rating may have slipped. But once you engage your great mind to generate a workable idea, apply your imagination to implement it, and put forth your effort to make it produce income, you can generate credit again. At that point, the best way to expand your credit base is to take out a new loan from an altogether different funding source and pay it back before final payment is due. If you are asked to establish a reason for the loan, simply state it is for an investment purpose; this is a generally recognized reason. But remember, from the bank's point of view, the nature of the loan is personal, it's not a business loan.

If you live in quiet desperation, you have only to decide to change this condition by applying a different attitude of mind, and a new bountiful life will be yours. As a process, getting enough money to implement your idea is just a means to this end. Think of it as merely one of several steps to achieve your fulfillment. However, do not be so preoccupied with the need for large amounts of start-up money that you lose perspective about the various ways your idea can be implemented immediately. Instead, use your imagination to seek alternatives. Nothing succeeds like offering the right product or service, in any form whatsoever, so long as it has the most promise of generating immediate income. Taking the smallest step will most assuredly start you on the road to riches.

How much money does it take to start a business? In some cases, very little; in a great many cases, less than the cost of buying a new car. TABLE 10-1 gives you some idea of what others found to be their start-up costs.

TABLE 10-1. Initial Investment for Business Start-Ups.

Start-up amount	Percentage of businesses	Number of businesses
Under $5,000	17	43,026
$5,000-$9,999	14	35,433
$10,000-$19,999	16	40,495
$20,000-49,999	25	63,273
$50,000-99,999	15	37,963
100,000-249,999	8	20,248
250,000 or more	5	12,654

Source: U.S. Small Business Administration, *Small Business and the Economy of the 1980s* (January 1988).

TAPPING YOUR OWN RESOURCES

Desiring enough money to begin your business must transcend idle daydreaming and go beyond mere wishful thinking. Instead, the ability to locate sources of money requires determination, imaginative thinking, enthusiasm, vitality, and the conviction that you will honor all commitments on the road to greatness, regardless of the level to which you aspire.

Home Equity

If you own your home and if you have not already tapped the equity in it as a money source, you may be surprised to find that your residential real estate has appreciated substantially in a recent inflationary period. If this is the case, it may constitute the largest single source of immediate cash available to you, often producing $10,000 to $50,000 overnight.

This asset can be converted to ready cash by two widely used methods. The first is refinancing your existing mortgage. This method lowers your payments and extends them over a longer period of time, thereby freeing money for other uses. It may also produce a lump-sum cash amount. The second method involves taking a second or third mortgage. This often produces a large lump sum but increases your payments.

Using either approach requires extreme caution, however, because interest rates may be much higher now than they were when you originally financed your home. It's important to carefully evaluate your present income to keep from overextending your ability to make the new higher payments.

Using this source of funds, therefore, requires absolute and total conviction that your idea is sound and your efforts will produce added income. Tapping this source of funds takes faith in yourself and assumed risk, but no more than you would be asking of a banker when applying for a business loan. Funds obtained from home equity have generated business start-up money for thousands of people, but tapping this source must be done with prudence and the application of sound business practices.

Personal Credit Sources

Credit unions and other savings associations often have a signature loan procedure, allowing you to borrow an amount of money dependent on the size of your salary. If you have used this source of funds in the past, you may find that increases in your salary have since qualified you for a higher maximum signature loan.

If your credit is good and your bills are current, your bank may be willing to advance you a personal line of credit available on demand. Various banks offer this service to their preferred, credit-worthy customers, along with a full range of other personal banking services. Check with your bank to see if you qualify for these programs.

Relatives and friends are often willing to lend money because of personal regard and faith in you and your ideas. If you borrow from them, however, do it in a business-like way. Write up a note (forms for which are available at most stationery stores) showing the amount and method of repayment, dates that principal and interest are payable, and then honor this commitment without fail. Also keep these lenders informed with periodic progress reports on how your business is doing.

Credit Cards

Bank cards, such as MasterCard and Visa, and even such credit programs as Diners Club and American Express have become so versatile, they can frequently be used to buy a good share of the items, materials, equipment, and printing you will need for business purposes. Also, they can be used to stretch your cash by covering a wide array of personal expenses. Cash freed up in this way can be used for business-related expenditures, particularly those not able to be charged, while you are establishing credit with your suppliers.

Also, some of the major items you will use for business purposes, such as travel, an automobile, and business equipment, can be purchased on a personal installment-loan basis. Credit cards and services offered by such major department stores as Montgomery Ward, Sears, and J.C. Penney are also perfect for purchasing materials and major pieces of equipment that you need for your business.

Life Insurance

If you have a whole life insurance policy covering yourself or members of your immediate family, your insurance agent can arrange to have a personal loan advanced to you by the insurance carrier. The amount of the loan will, of course, be based on the cash value of these policies. Generally, such loans are made at interest rates far below other loan and credit-card finance charges. If you decide this source of funds is suitable for you, remember once again to use caution not to overextend your ability to repay the loan or keep up insurance-policy premiums.

Investments

Stocks and bonds registered in your name can be used as collateral to obtain a loan amounting to as much as 60 percent of their current value. However, be sure to investigate all the details thoroughly with the lender, your banker, and your stock broker, so you understand the precise terms of these loans, the variability of interest rates, and the specific conditions regulating when these loans can be called in.

U.S. Savings Bonds may also be a ready source of cash; but if they have not matured, you may suffer a loss of interest.

IRA and Keogh plans can also be a source of funds, but cashing them in may have some downside implications. Before using them, you should have your tax advisor fully evaluate early withdrawal penalties. You should also determine if you are permitted to borrow against any unique pension plan that you may have or that has been established for you.

Credit Extended by Your Suppliers

The purchase and payment of business goods and services revolves around billing periods of 30-day intervals, which are frequently extended to 45- and 60-day periods. Material and equipment suppliers, advertising media, print shops, jobbers, wholesalers, and practically every other business supplier will agree to bill you for services, if you are known to them and your credit is trusted. It is well recognized in the world of business that credit extended by suppliers is a much more significant means of financing business operations than bank loans.

Credit extended by suppliers is termed "trade credit" and is usually made available by suppliers in order to encourage credit-worthy and reliable customers to continue to buy from them. However, it is also well known that the mechanics of billing, once established, are an efficient and orderly way to maintain business records and regulate business transactions. Therefore, it is customary to take delivery of goods and services, but not pay until billed.

Producing income through your business takes on added special significance when you realize that suppliers are actually financing your operations while you generate new orders. Most certainly, you will be unable to maintain this pattern unless your product or service is generating a satisfactory degree of income. But if your product or service is of quality and value, at least you have the opportunity to make money first and pay for a healthy share of the costs later.

Using trade credit may be a big advantage to a small business, but it comes not without the clear obligation to pay your bills. Learning early in your business career that the art of conducting business requires integrity, mutual trust, and scrupulous honesty will establish a solid foundation for growth and boundless prosperity in the future.

Always remember that your creditors are entitled to payment according to terms you have negotiated, and you are entitled to the good-faith consideration that you are responsible and creditable. Remember, too, that as your business expands, you will unavoidably be in a position to decide whether to extend credit to your customers. By establishing a consistent business philosophy in your formative years, as your business matures you will be guided by proven policies that will simplify decision making on credit and other important business matters.

No doubt, seeking trade credit calls on you to muster supreme self-confidence and to make good on your promises. But it is the ability to exercise this kind of strength and courage that equips you to expand your horizons as far as your vision and energies can carry you.

LEASING RATHER THAN BUYING

Since many small businesses have difficulty raising capital, you may want to look at leasing as an alternative financing arrangement to buying when acquiring business equipment. All types of business equipment, from motor vehicles to personal computers, from manufacturing machinery to office furniture, have been acquired for small business use through leasing.

A lease is a long-term agreement to rent equipment, land, buildings, or any other asset. In return for most—but not all—of the benefits of ownership, the user (lessee) makes periodic payments to the owner (lessor) of the asset. The lease payment covers the original cost of the equipment or other asset and provides the lessor a profit. There are three major kinds of leases: financial, operating, and sale and leaseback.

Financial leases are most common by far. A financial lease is usually written for a term not to exceed the economic life of equipment. It usually provides that periodic payments be made, the equipment reverts to the owner at the end of the lease term, the lease is noncancelable, the user has a legal obligation to continue payments to the end of the term, and the user agrees to maintain the equipment.

Operating or "maintenance" leases usually require that maintenance of the equipment is the responsibility of the owner. Such leases can usually be cancelled under conditions spelled out in the lease agreement. Computer equipment is often leased under this kind of arrangement.

The *sale and leaseback* is similar to the financial lease. However, the owner of the equipment sells it to someone else then simultaneously leases it back. This arrangement lets you free up money, otherwise locked in an asset, for use elsewhere; buildings are often leased this way. If you already have some equipment but are tight for cash, you may find this arrangement suitable for relieving temporary cash-flow problems.

You may also hear leases described as "net leases" or "gross leases." Under a *net lease*, the user is responsible for expenses such as those for maintenance, taxes, and insurance. Under a *gross lease*, the owner pays these expenses. Financial leases are usually net leases.

Finally, you might run across the term *full payout lease*. With this arrangement, the owner of equipment recovers the original cost of the equipment during the term of the lease.

In recent years, the use of leasing has increased as a method for small business to acquire use of equipment and other assets. The number of companies offering such leases has increased dramatically, and leasing is now a billion-dollar industry.

Commercial banks, insurance companies, and finance companies do most of the leasing and are usually capable of making lease arrangements for almost anything used in business. Others in the leasing business include equipment manufacturers and firms that deal in specialized equipment.

The obvious advantage of leasing is acquiring use of equipment without making a large initial cash outlay. Compared with a loan arrangement to purchase the same equipment, a lease usually requires no down payment, while a loan often requires a 25-percent down payment. In addition, a lease requires no restriction on a firm's financial operations; with it you can spread payments over a longer period and so lower your payment amounts; and leases provide protection against the risk of equipment obsolescence.

There also may be tax benefits in leasing. Lease payments are deductible as operating expenses if the arrangement is a true lease (and IRS agrees that it is).

CUSTOMERS ARE A SOURCE OF FUNDING

When customers pay up-front money for expected goods and services, they are financing your business. The degree to which you can convince them to do so largely depends on your methods; and make no mistake, there are plenty of methods available.

Mail order is a perfect example of customers willing to pay up-front cash before receiving merchandise. Magazine subscription is another example where customers are often willing to pay for up to three years of merchandise before ever receiving it.

Many service businesses have gotten started by offering up to five years of service free for paying an established amount in advance. Even when you provide a service for someone or customers buy a product and pay cash immediately, they are financing your operation; the more customers, the greater the amount of cash. Requiring the payment of a deposit before services are rendered or goods are delivered is a widespread form of customer financing.

The key to customer financing is to be ready, willing, and able to provide the promised goods or services. Persuading potential customers, in other words advertising that you meet this condition, increases the number of customers doing business with you and, therefore, increases financing available to you. Exchanging your goods or services for advertising also enhances cash accumulation as new customers are reached with a renewed burst of effort.

Evaluate your business. Use imagination. Create your own success. The rewards may be nothing short of spectacular.

GETTING MONEY FROM OUTSIDE SOURCES

You should use caution when borrowing money, and you should apply these principles:

- Never borrow more money than you immediately and actually need.
- Always shop for the lowest interest rates and most advantageous repayment schedules.
- Generally, short-term loans are cheaper than long-term loans, particularly if you borrow only as real need occurs.
- Long-term loans usually have a lower interest rate than short-term loans, but are more expensive cumulatively.
- In an inflationary period, borrowers can repay loans with cheaper money. However, lenders usually build an inflationary premium into their loans to protect their principal.

Going to the Bank

Banks generally limit long-term loans for business start-ups to 50 percent of the money needed. The reason for this is that banks do not want to be more of an owner of your business than you are.

Bank lending officers look for borrowers with good credit ratings, experience in the proposed business, businesses that are showing a profit, and business plans that demonstrate ability to repay the loan. Interest rates and repayment schedules vary from bank to bank. Thus, it is worth your time to shop for the money you need.

Most lenders will require you as a small business owner to guarantee the loan, name a comaker or endorser of the loan, that is, a third party to repay the loan if you find you cannot. Often SBA will act as such a guarantor.

If your signature alone is insufficient, lenders will require collateral, securities, mortgages, real estate, accounts receivable, life insurance, leases, or any tangible property that will guarantee the loan should the business not succeed.

Going to the Government

In addition to banks and similar private institutions, governments—federal, state, and city—have an assortment of programs to assist with the financing of new businesses.

SBA. At the federal level, SBA may make direct loans to a new small business. It is, however, more common for the agency to guarantee up to 90 percent of a bank loan. By law, SBA will not make a direct loan if a business can obtain funds from a bank or other private source.

SBA will not consider a direct loan unless the application has been declined by at least one bank—two in a city with a population greater than 200,000—and even then cannot always be counted on to provide a direct loan. It will, however, often guarantee a loan from another source.

For any loan that SBA guarantees, it insists that you match the amount of the loan with an equal amount of your own money. This is done to ensure that you will take a big interest in what happens to the business.

SBA direct loans may be used for construction; expansion; conversion; and purchasing machinery, equipment, supplies, and working capital. SBA also has a series of loans to provide help in specific areas. These include revolving lines of credit, guarantees, displaced business loans, and handicapped assistance loans, among others.

Both banks and SBA require thorough documentation to back up the loan request, including:

■ A complete business plan, projected monthly profit and loss statements, cash flow projections, and a projected balance sheet for the first year of business, plus an explanation of how the loan will be used
■ A resume of the applicant's work experience with emphasis on any experience gained in the particular industry the business is in

■ A personal financial statement showing your personal net worth (see Appendix C for format)
■ Income tax returns for the previous three years
■ Credit references
■ A copy of any lease agreement, insurance policy, distributorship, or franchise agreement, if applicable

SBA can give assistance in procuring government contracts. It provides advice and assistance to new business owners just starting out through the Service Corps of Retired Executives (SCORE) and the Active Corps of Executives (ACE) and attempts to provide business opportunities to socially and economically disadvantaged individuals.

Other Agencies. To encourage exporting, the International Trade Administration offers advice from foreign trade specialists and an information clearinghouse. The Minority Business Development Administration, the Maritime Administration, the National Telecommunications and Information Administration, and the Office of Science and Technology have specialized programs to assist minority and female entrepreneurs. The Farmers Home Administration (FmHA) of the Department of Agriculture has a business and industry program to develop commercial enterprises in rural areas through loan guarantees and direct loans. In the program specifically for farmers, FmHA has loans and loan guarantees for ranchers, farmers, agricultural enterprises, and even aquaculture producers.

While SBA and Departments of Commerce and Agriculture provide the bulk of government assistance to small business, Departments of Health and Human Services, Interior, Energy, Transportation, Housing and Urban Development, and State; Veterans Administration; Overseas Private Investment Corporation; and Export-Import Bank offer some combination of guaranteed loans, direct loans, or grants.

Clearly, the government has a significant number of programs worth exploring, but it must be stressed that the processing of applications for government loans or loan guarantees is a lengthy procedure taking many months. It is perhaps better to consider government assistance as an additional or secondary source of financing once the business is under way, rather than as a source for start-up funding.

STILL OTHER SOURCES OF FUNDING

When you find you need money for your business, you must be persistent in exploring every possible source of funding and use all the organized knowledge and enthusiasm you can muster to approach every potential investor, banker, lender, or creditor. Getting money for a business is a continuous job. It is every bit as important as the operating aspects of the business, and you should adjust your mental attitude so that you accept the task of raising funds simply as a part of doing business. If you run into obstacles, reinforce your faith and belief with the burning desire for the things you want. You will be surprised to find that the intensity of your desire will cause beneficial things to happen.

Private Placement Stock Offerings/SBICs/Finders

If you have exhausted all other sources of funds, a commonly used method to raise additional money is to circulate a private placement stock offering to a number of those you find willing to invest in the business. This kind of stock offering is exempt from the rigorous regulations imposed by the U.S. Securities and Exchange Commission on public stock underwritings.

A limited stock offering of this kind must be described in a Private Placement Memorandum, which fully discloses all information that might be required by a prudent investor. Such an offering is limited to 35 investors of sufficient means to afford the risk. SBA can provide information on how and where to go to get assistance in preparing a Private Placement Memorandum. Legal assistance is essential. SBA can also give you names of firms known as Small Business Investment Companies (SBICs), which receive funds from the federal government for the purpose of investing in small businesses.

Another source you can use to locate funds is called *finders*. These are individuals who have extensive contacts with private wealth. They charge a percentage of the funds they raise, somewhere between 1 and 8 percent. Ask your banker, chamber of commerce officials, or SBA if they can direct you to finders in your community.

VENTURE CAPITAL MAY PROVIDE THE BOOST YOU NEED

A number of venture-capital organizations invest money by specializing in funding new, innovative and exciting businesses. While banks seek guaranteed returns largely through interest and evaluate whether you can deliver based on past performance, venture capitalists look to the longer run—future growth, dividend returns, or large profits through sale or future stock appreciation of the business.

Banks are *creditors*. They look for safety in the product market of the business. Venture capital firms are *owners*. They hold stock in the business, adding their invested capital to the business's equity base. They invest only in firms they believe can rapidly increase sales and generate substantial profits. These are generally firms with sales in the $250,000 to $1.5-million range that can return three to five times their investment in five to seven years. Consequently, venture capital firms tend to invest in sophisticated, high-technology ventures; but they do often express an interest in smaller proposals, novel solutions to everyday problems, new marketing ideas, and unique inventions.

How Venture Capital Firms Work

Venture capital is a risky business because it is difficult to judge the worthiness of an untested business. The typical venture capital firm receives over 1,000 proposals a year. Probably 90 percent of these are rejected quickly. Often, they don't fit the goals of the venture capital firm or the established geographic, technical, or market areas where the firm does business. By far, the preponderant reason proposals are rejected is that they are poorly prepared and are not supported by a thorough and complete business plan. (Everything you need to know to write a business plan is covered in Chapter 11.)

The remaining 10 percent are investigated with care, and venture capital firms will often hire consultants to evaluate the product, particularly when it is a new invention or technologically complex. References, potential customers, suppliers, bankers, and others shown in your business plan are consulted, interviewed, and tested. The financial condition of the firm is audited. Production costs are analyzed. The legal form and registration of the business are investigated. Most important, the character and competence of owners and key managers are evaluated.

These preliminary investigations may cost a venture capital firm $5,000 to $10,000 per company investigated, and such screening will typically produce only 10 to 15 proposals of interest. Then more thorough and expensive investigations reduce the number of proposals under active consideration to only three or four. Eventually, the venture firm invests in only one or two of the businesses.

When a decision is finally made, the venture firm prepares an equity financing proposal that details the amount of money to be provided, the percentage of common stock to be surrendered in exchange for these funds, the interim financing method to be used, and the protective covenants to be included. Finally, the financial arrangement is completed.

Clearly, the owner of a small business seeking equity financing with a venture firm must consider the future impact on ownership and control, since taking in a venture capitalist as a partner may virtually guarantee that the owner will be obligated to sell out, go public, or buy back the business.

If you are ready to seek venture capital, an outstanding reference on the subject is *Guide to Venture Capital Sources* published by Capital Publishing Corporation, Chicago. It will provide the guidance you want and need in seeking venture capital.

11

A Business Plan—
Your Master
Key to Success

If you are inspired by this book's proven hobby-to-business conversion formula; if you have applied the step-by-step approach described in its pages; if you have established your business and generated income through the vehicle of offering a product or service; you may not know it, but you have 90 percent of what you need to get big-money financing. The remaining 10 percent consists of nothing more than writing a business plan that covers operations for the next year or so, then attaching it to applications for loans or equity financing.

If you have actually established your business—if your business is truly generating income—then you have a business record on which all loans and equity financing are based. This is the point where formal lenders, banks, venture capitalists, and investors will back you with ready cash if you present them with an impressive business plan.

Whatever format you use, a dynamic business plan must be an expression of what you intend to accomplish through organized action using financial resources the lender agrees to provide.

TYPICAL BUSINESS PLAN FORMAT

Whether you want money for a business start-up or for your established business, you must convince lenders and investors of your worthiness by placing before them, for close scrutiny, your business plan. The plan must be in writing, and it must describe certain key elements of your business. It must not be prepared hastily, haphazardly, or under pressure. It must be carefully prepared or it may give an impression of instability and lack of planning.

Cover Page

Identify name of the business, address, telephone number, and name of owner.

Table of Contents

List of subjects covered in the business plan and their page references.

Introduction

Write a brief introductory paragraph identifying the business name, type of business—whether it is a sole proprietorship, partnership, or corporation—address, name of owner, and telephone number where owner can be reached.

Capital Requirements and How Financing Will Be Used

Describe the principal need for financing, why you are requesting or seeking the money, and how you intend to pay it back. Carefully answer the following questions.

How Much Money Is Needed? Provide specific figures. Prepare a budget forecast, a projection of borrowing requirements, and a cash flow schedule.

Describe Specifically What You Will Do With the Money. If it is to buy inventory, how much inventory and what kind? Will you use the borrowed funds to launch an advertising program? Of what will such a program consist? Will the funds be used for research and development or product improvement? Describe all other uses of the money.

Identify the Length of Time the Money Is Needed—The Term. Is need for the money of a temporary nature? Is it needed for long-term requirements?

Describe How You Will Repay the Money. Fundamental questions of every lender are: Do you have ability and capacity to repay the loan? and Are your sales adequate? Disclose your specific plan for repayment, including a specific repayment schedule.

Describe What You Intend to Use for Collateral. Will it be fixed assets such as your home, real property, or equipment?

Specify the Nature and Amount of Return on Investment. If the return will be in the form of interest, how much? Are your estimates competitive? If you are raising capital through equity financing (sale of stock rather than a loan or bonds), when do you anticipate dividends? Describe your stock offering and prepare a prospectus. Prepare a specific return on investment forecast.

Disclose Your Financial Projections. Indicate your profit goals—are they reasonable? How do your profit goals compare with actual past profit facts? How do these figures compare with those of other similar businesses? Indicate profit trends (past performance) as well as projections (future performance). Show the relative contribution of each product line or service to total sales. Show the relative burden of expenses according to each product or service. Show which items or services are most profitable, which are less so, and be forthright about which, if any, are losing money. Also show which products or services are faster or slower movers relative to all others.

Describe Your Present Financing. Currently, what are your primary sources of capital, your debts and liabilities? Are they short term or long term? Provide a description of working capital management, cash budgeting practices, profit planning, and analysis of existing or previous financing efforts.

Nature of the Business

Describe what kind of business you are in or intend to be in. The amount of detail you include depends on a wide variety of factors that are highly personal to each situation, the type of financing you are seeking, and how much money you need.

Specify when the business started or is intended to be started, the market you are serving, and what goods and services you are offering. Explain, generally, how the product or service is sold, made, performed, and advertised and how shipping and delivery occur.

Indicate the legal structure, i.e., whether the business is a sole proprietorship, partnership, or corporation, the names of officers, directors, key managers, owners, or partners, and the basic compensation practices for each.

Provide a description of basic business operations, machines or equipment used, and amount and kind of labor required to carry out the business. Describe all pertinent manufacturing services or selling activities. Identify all known strengths or weaknesses of the business. Is your product or service superior, different, or less expensive than those of similar businesses? Do you have a superior cost control system? Provide a brief sales and profit history; indicate previous rate of growth, sales revenues, costs, expenses, and projections for each category.

Indicate whether the business is capital intensive (requires a large degree of capital to start the business or continue operations) or labor intensive (labor costs constitute the major expense and a large work force is required).

Specify the type of problems the business has encountered, such as with suppliers, shortages of materials, labor disputes, marketing, advertising, restrictive government regulations or practices, and so on.

Describe generally how sales occur, how payment is made, and what has been the income history of the business so far.

Identify your major expenses. Are they fixed costs, such as rents, equipment purchases, office expenses, wages, utilities, insurance, and so on? Or are they variable costs, such as materials purchases, sales commissions, advertising, or spoilage? Are they business start-up costs, such as licenses and permits, professional services (lawyer, accountant, consultants), telephone and utility installation, decorating or remodeling, down payment on purchase or deposit on lease of place of business, furniture, equipment or vehicles, advance advertising, initial inventory, and insurance premiums?

Describe the buildings or facilities used in your business, whether they are owned or rented, and what impact their location has on the trade of your business and operations.

Explain your management system. Do you maintain orderly books of account and other business records? Do you exercise modern, efficient, and economical management practices? Do you make cost-effective purchases, perhaps expending funds only when necessary, or do you make volume purchases to obtain lower prices? Identify any other advantages brought about by your purchasing methods. Are your purchases in line with expenditures? Do you exercise sound inventory control; wise financial planning; strict budget practices; and effective, consistent, cost-cutting methods? Are your budget estimates generally in line with expenditures?

Nature of the Industry

Generally describe the industry your business is part of and overall conditions prevailing in the industry. Describe trends, both good and bad; whether the industry is growing or declining; and key factors affecting the industry as a whole. Is your type of business, its products or services, in short supply or in a state of over-extended abundance? Explain how outside factors, such as shortages of materials, economic conditions, labor problems, or restrictive or fostering government practices are affecting the industry. Report any other relevant information you have acquired, witnessed, or found in your business, and conduct a library search of state-of-the-art materials concerning the industry so you become an expert in your field.

Your Business History

Since a beginning small business will usually depend primarily on personal financial resources (equity), trade credit, lease financing, and only secondarily on bank financing and issuance of stock for capital needs, you must disclose your personal and business track record to your lenders. What have you previously financed and repaid? What has been the history of your business growth? Have you operated the business successfully from your home and do you now desire to move to a fixed location? What were your initial and subsequent capital investments? What have you found that your business does best?

Accomplishments and Milestones

Describe what your business has accomplished to date; identify any measured milestones and progressive accomplishments, such as completing product development, manufacturing design, production feasibility projects; and, of course, report that universally accepted standard of business accomplishment—sales. What have been your purchases of materials, equipment, furnishings, or vehicles? If the business is not yet in operation, when will there be a tangible working model of your product? When will you be able to provide the first business service to a paying customer? How will you get your first order? Have promises of orders been secured? How soon will payment be made?

Customer Base–Market Share Projections

Describe in specific terms who your customers are, where they are located, and how you intend to reach more of them. Using specific figures, indicate how many potential customers you can realistically reach. Are your customers primarily individuals; other small businesses; small, medium, or large corporations; or government? Describe your current and your potential customer base. What is your current percentage share of your market and how do you plan to increase your share? Define your measurements.

Product or Service Characteristics

Describe the product or service that you offer, current uses and functions, size, weight, quality, and any anticipated new uses, branch-offs, or offshoots. Report on whether your product or service is superior to others in durability, appearance, uniqueness, convenience, price, reliability, prestige, attractiveness, delivery, serviceability, warranty, or any other important factor.

How have you determined there is an unmet need for the product or service? How do you know you will be able to enter or penetrate the market? What are the anticipated obstacles? How will they be overcome? Can your product or service be easily substituted? How will this affect your business? Is the product or service a fad or will there be continuing need?

Describe how the product or service was designed, the market tested, and why customers want it. Describe production methods or service delivery methods and techniques; how production or service occurs, is inspected, and completed. Report your practices in conducting design or service-delivery reviews and cost-reduction methods.

Indicate if you hold any patents, trade secrets, copyrights, or trademarks.

If you offer more than one product or service, describe how the product lines or services complement each other and whether they will continue to do so in the future.

Indicate whether you intend to offer new products or services. Where will the new ideas come from; have you or will you be conducting patent searches and attending trade shows to expand your product line or service with similar products or services?

Identify your current and anticipated production resources. Do you have excess production capacity or insufficient equipment? Do you use superior manufacturing techniques, the most modern technology, specialized equipment, innovative assembly practices, or economies of scale?

Provide a cost breakdown of product or service components, tooling, and equipment costs. Have you identified critical parts of your product or elements of your service that can be modified or improved to increase profits? Do you inspect your product or service regularly to improve methods and increase profits?

Indicate whether you buy material according to predetermined standards and specifications to control material acquisition costs. Do you have inventory management problems involving raw materials, goods in process, or finished goods? If so, indicate your plan to correct them. Remember, inventory represents money since it refers to the purchase of stocks of anything necessary to do business. Such stocks are generally costly to purchase and keep on hand. Since inventory can represent a large portion of business investment, your bank or lender will want to know if you are managing inventory properly to maximize profits. Do you do a good job of balancing costs with amounts of inventory on hand? Do you keep track of inventory turnover rates? Your banker or lender will want answers to all these questions since excess inventory ties up money in materials, storage, taxes, insurance, and so on.

If you hire employees, do you have an effective employee training program to improve efficiency and reduce labor costs? Have you improved efficiency with a procedure checklist that you and your employees systematically go by?

Pricing Strategy

Describe how your price is determined for products or services—what it is based on and how far you can raise or lower it before sales will be affected. Is your price in line with expenses? If you have conducted any pricing surveys, indicate what the results show. Does price depend on your volume? What important factors will affect each? Can you get price advantages by superior technology, equipment, or techniques? Show an expense analysis as expenses affect price, leading to either cutting expenses or obtaining greater benefit from them. What reducible expenses can you locate? Indicate prices you anticipate charging in the future.

Marketing Strategy

Describe your existing sales program. Indicate any improvements you intend to make. If you have conducted any marketing studies, report the results. Indicate the channels of distribution currently in use—your own sales force, manufacturers' representatives or agents, wholesalers, retailers, distributors, jobbers, factory outlets, direct mail, magazine mail order, rack sales, consignment, or vending machines. Report on sales and show whether you are meeting sales goals. If you aren't meeting sales goals, indicate the likely reasons. Is it because of the general business climate, competition, pricing, advertising, lack of sales promotion, credit policies, and so on? When you identify problems, specify any steps you plan to take to correct them to increase sales.

Advertising Methods

Describe the overall advertising plan you are currently using. Indicate whether you retest your means of advertising to find out what type of advertising works and what doesn't. Do you have plans to improve advertising? Do you plan to drop advertising that doesn't pull in customers and launch advertising programs that do increase sales? If you have conducted any advertising surveys or studies, indicate results and identify the directions that seem most promising.

Profit Projections

Describe your current profit picture. Indicate whether you are currently making a profit and what the trend has been. Show your operation's profit and/or loss cumulatively for past years, for the current business year, and projected over the next year. Take account of sales in relation to expenses. Indicate whether your profit margin is adequate; if not, will it be improved and how? What is your break-even point (the point at which gross profit equals expenses)? Tell what efforts you are making to implement cost improvements and the anticipated effect they will have on profits.

Indicate efforts you are making to reduce accounts receivable, inventory, and other expenses. Can you improve sales with giveaways or other promotional means? Do you follow sound business practices in purchasing and receiving materials and minimizing waste? Are your profits affected by returned goods, and can you increase profits by reducing returns? If you have analyzed customer complaints, show results and indicate revised methods to produce a better product or service to improve customer satisfaction and sales.

Indicate all methods you can use to increase profits. Can you add to your product life or service, increase the average sale per customer, use display space or advertising more effectively, or in other ways enhance market penetration?

Show whether productivity is on the increase or decrease. Include various ratio analyses and findings, as follows:

1. Current ratio (current assets divided by current debts) as a measure of cash or near-cash position (liquidity) of the business
2. Quick ratio (current assets minus inventory) to test the ability of the business to meet current obligations
3. Total debt to net worth ratio (the result of total debt divided by net worth then multiplied by 100) as a measure of how your business can meet its obligations from equity
4. Net sales to total assets ratio (net sales divided by total assets) as a measure of the efficiency with which you are using assets
5. Operating profit to net sales ratio (divide operating profit by net sales and multiply by 100) to determine your profit position relative to sales
6. Net profit to total sales ratio (divide net profit by total sales and multiply by 100) to determine your return on investment
7. Net profit to net worth ratio (divide net profit by net worth and multiply by 100) to provide information on productivity of resources you have committed to business operations

Also indicate the amount of gross revenue from sales of goods and services and the amount of income from other sources, such as interest or portions of your business that have been sold.

Growth Rate Projections

Describe results of your forecasting efforts. Include sales and profit projections. Identify any expansion plans. Report results of your financial statement analysis and, using established trends, project growth patterns for a five-year period.

Suppliers

Identify, by name and address, your current suppliers and the amount of business you do with each of them. Tell what trade credit terms and amounts your present suppliers provide. Indicate whether there are other suppliers in your community or in other parts of the country that will advance additional credit or supply merchandise or material and to what extent they will do so. Describe the extent of cooperation you have with suppliers.

Competition

Specify how many competitors are in your market. Identify your major competitors and explain what makes your product or service superior to their products or services. Also explain any similarities. Describe the extent of competition, what steps you plan to take to successfully compete, and what obstacles your competition presents. Identify any other matters involving competition, such as whether price cutting occurs frequently, and any known tendencies of your competition to substitute its own products or services for yours.

Insurance and Product Liability

Describe the types of insurance you carry and identify their costs. Indicate whether the liability limits of your policies are keeping pace with the times. Identify all your insurance needs. Do you have adequate coverage for product or service liability problems? For example, do you have a solid product or service safety program? What program are you implementing to minimize product safety liability? Explain any product or service safety goals. Do you anticipate that cash reserves can be decreased or insurance costs can be lowered with an improved safety program or by dropping a particular product? Explain any product safety or service liability considerations.

Impact of Government Policies and Regulations

Explain and describe any government policies or regulations that impact favorably or place limitations on your ability to conduct your business.

Future Milestones

List and describe goals, timetables, and programs designed to increase sales, profits, and growth. Specify measurements you use to determine achievement.

Appendix

The appendix of your business plan should contain all relevant financial reports, tables, and statistics not included previously:

1. Pro forma projections
2. Owner's resume
3. Owner's compensation plan
4. Balance sheet showing:
   a. Current assets
   b. Fixed assets
   c. Other assets
   d. Current liabilities
   e. Long-term liabilities
   f. Net worth
5. Profit and loss statement
6. Detailed diagrams, photographs, and drawings if necessary to convey a vivid image of important items
7. Projected budget
8. Previous year's tax returns

SOME THINGS TO KEEP IN MIND

The quality of your skills in running your business (management ability) is a primary, perhaps the most crucial, factor in determining whether a lender will agree to provide a loan. This is because more businesses fail because of poor management practices than for any other reason. Sound management must be practiced if loans are to be obtained and used profitably. Your ability to know and control your business' financial condition, cash flow, cash projections, and borrowing will, in large measure, determine your ability to repay the loan.

All too often a beginner in business insists that large sums of money are needed for business or to solve business problems when, in fact, the real solution depends on ideas, imagination, organized knowledge, and persistence, fortified by unrelenting desire, belief, and faith. If money is indeed the remaining necessary ingredient after all the other success principles have been exhaustively applied, then you must reach out and you will find the particular connections that will produce needed capital. However, lenders will accept no substitute for your ability to keep good records and manage your business finances.

Borrowed money may ease financial pressures temporarily; but without consistent application of the disclosed success principles and sound management, further indebtedness only intensifies basic problems. Money alone can neither provide nor replace relentless use of the success formula and quality management practices.

12
Marketing Your Product or Service

The term "marketing" may sound confusing, but it is really nothing more than knowing who your customers are; knowing where they are; knowing what they want; conveying the message to them that you have what they want; recognizing when their needs and wants are about to change; and, in all cases, getting what they want to them when they want it.

Here are two important questions to constantly keep before you. First, are the means and methods presently used to reach your existing customers conveying your message effectively? Second, what improvements in means and methods can you make to convey your message more effectively, to serve existing customers better, and to attract new customers?

KNOW YOUR CUSTOMERS' NEEDS

A few years ago, the Brookings Institution completed a comprehensive study of successful and unsuccessful marketing practices. The difference between success and failure hinged on a really simple thing—sensitivity and awareness of customers' needs.

It makes no difference whether this conveyer of sensitivity and awareness is an individual or a giant corporation. The world market has plenty of room for both to make more money than ever dreamed possible, if they will only remain aware and sensitive to their customers' needs.

Ed Allyn presents a perfect example of someone who once again proves that customer needs and your own inclinations can be the mother of invention as well as the vehicle to extra cash. A former teacher who motorcycled to Canada while on vacation, Allyn found that a foam rubber seat cushion was not enough to prevent severe saddle soreness. In desperation, he used an air mattress to seek pain relief for his tush. Allyn found both some much-needed relief and the idea for an air-filled cycle seat.

He scraped some money together and formed the Allyn Air Seat Company in Lenox, Massachusetts. After some experimenting, he produced an air seat so tough that a truck could run over it and it wouldn't collapse. He contracts out manufacturing and packaging of his seats and, working from his home, markets them to cycle, sports, and hardware stores. He also advertises in trade and consumer magazines, catalogs, and sells through mail order.

In one year, Allyn sold 2,000 air-filled seats. Two years later, he was selling 10,000 seats and grossing just under $100,000, with a projected growth rate of 40 percent a year. When last heard from, Ed Allyn was developing a unique line of soft luggage for cycles and was well on the road to achieving his goals.

After a new product or service has been introduced and is a resounding success, marketing experts are often quick to point out that no special genius was required to see the need for the product and to capitalize on it. This may be true, but where were these same experts *before* the innovator proved success for the new product or service?

Witness the American automobile industry in the early 1970s. The industry could afford the best marketing experts money could buy, yet those experts didn't have command of the essential ingredient of success: awareness and sensitivity of their customers' needs. It was the foreign-car manufacturers who capitalized on the demand for a quality, small economical car. Ignoring customers' needs almost drove some of the world's largest automobile manufacturing companies to bankruptcy.

A similar mad rush of giant mass merchandisers to look alike, to sell the same products at the same prices, to offer only the same services in the same old way opens the door of opportunity to individuals with a better idea.

For example, North Carolinian W. Daniel Renn was in his middle 20s, down to his last $400, and out of a job when he came across an idea that was to change his life. Merely by chance, Renn's father-in-law showed him a home fire alarm with a unique battery-powered feature. Unlike traditional electric-powered alarms, this new alarm would not fail at crucial times since fire could not cut off its power source.

Captured by the idea and with nothing better to do, Renn wrote a letter to the manufacturer, Falcon Safety Products, and asked if he could begin offering the product.

Meanwhile, executives at Falcon were not having much success marketing the alarm with traditional methods. In fact, the original inventor had grown so disgusted with "same old way" sales promotion programs, he'd sold all rights to the alarm for a few thousand dollars.

Renn began his new business with nothing more than 20 home fire alarms and the right to offer them to customers. He spent his spare time developing, refining, and sharpening his ideas about why anyone would want a home fire alarm. Figuring what he had to offer was not just a product made of wire and metal, but personal safety and human peace of mind, he decided to approach homeowners directly.

When the first 20 homeowners he approached bought his initial inventory, he become inspired by the taste of success. Using his apartment as an office, Renn began recruiting a sales force. However, he would let no one offer an alarm to a homeowner until that person was thoroughly trained in all the product's lifesaving features, had rehearsed the sales presentation, and had committed it to memory.

One year after starting his business, Dan Renn and the cadre of professionals he schooled produced $300,000 in sales. One year later, sales bounced to $1.5 million. Four years later, sales exploded to $4 million, but they didn't stop there. Six years after starting a business centered mainly around teaching others to sell, Renn and his students produced a whopping $6 million in sales, and Dan Renn became fabulously wealthy.

Demand for the right goods and services properly rendered will always exceed supply; that's a law—a law as durable as any law of nature. But just as with any other law of nature, you must thoroughly understand it and diligently apply it before you can benefit from it.

Understanding this law and applying it to marketing means knowing your customer, then focusing on your customer as the center of all business activity. Methods or variations for doing this run in the millions, but the highly personal aspect of knowing the customer remains the same essential ingredient whichever method or variation is used.

LEARNING TO PRICE PRODUCTS AND SERVICES

Being in business means more than generating income; it also means making a profit. You won't be in business long, regardless of how much revenue your effort produces, if your product or service isn't priced to make a profit. Measurements of profit are expressed both in gross profit and net profit terms and vary with the type of business—retail, wholesale, service, manufacturing, construction, mail order, and so on.

You need to know what the gross profit and net profit figures are for your business before establishing prices. If you are already selling products or services, you obtain these two figures from your business profit-and-loss statement (sometimes also called operating statement or income statement). (See Appendix F for a sample profit-and-loss statement.) If you are not yet in business, you can produce these two figures by preparing an estimated profit-and-loss statement based on estimated prices and estimated costs of doing business.

PRICING PRODUCTS

Assuming that you are not already in business, you must estimate a total sales (or revenue) figure from the number of products you expect your customers to buy at an estimated price. Next, you subtract from this total sales figure the direct cost of goods sold. This is either the cost of buying your inventory or the cost of materials and labor to produce your inventory. This will give you your gross profit figure. Dividing the direct cost of goods sold by the number of products estimated to be sold gives you the average cost of merchandise.

Next, take your gross profit figure and subtract from it the estimated expenses of doing business not related to directly producing your product or buying inventory. These are selling and administrative expenses, utilities, rent, supplies, equipment depreciation, payroll taxes, and any other indirect expenses. This gives you your net profit figure before taxes.

How This Pricing Formula Works

Assume your business, Outdoors Unlimited, intends to market a product having a sales price of $40 each. When projecting sales, you estimate customers will buy 9,250 products. Therefore your total projected revenue is $370,000 (9,250 products @ $40 each). Your projected, year-end profit-and-loss statement may appear as in Table 12-1.

In this illustration, your business, Outdoor Unlimited, made a net profit of $32,337. If this profit figure had been precisely zero, your business would be operating at the break-even point. Since your objective is to make a profit, you would need to cut estimated costs of doing business, raise prices from your price estimate, or do a bit of both.

Raising Prices for Profit

Assuming you choose to increase profit by raising estimated prices, go back and get the figure representing the average selling price of merchandise. Your intention will be to markup this figure. For example, say the average selling price of merchandise is $40, and you want a 10-percent markup from the current price. What will be your new selling price? Markup is figured as a percentage of the

TABLE 12-1. Outdoors Unlimited
Profit-and-Loss Statement for the Year Ended December 31, 1999.

REVENUE:

9,250 products sold at $40 each:	$370,000	
COST OF GOODS SOLD:	185,000	

Cost of goods sold ÷ number of products = average cost/product

$185,000 ÷ 9,250 products = $20 average cost/product

GROSS PROFIT (MARGIN):		$185,000

($370,000 − $185,000 = $185,000)

EXPENSES:

Depreciation	$1,156
Salaries and sales expenses (including your own)	91,343
Supplies	16,187
Insurance	424
Rent	18,500
Payroll taxes	9,134
Interest	964
Utilities	5,473
Maintenance	8,000
Other (miscellaneous)	1,482
TOTAL EXPENSES	$152,663
NET PROFIT BEFORE TAXES	$32,337

new selling price. Thus, if you want a 10-percent markup, the base price of merchandise will be 90 percent of the average selling price. This formula will help:

$$\text{New selling price} = \frac{\text{Current price}}{\text{Current price as a percentage of selling price}}$$

$$\text{New Selling price} = \frac{\$40}{.90}$$

$$\text{New selling price} = \$44.44$$

So, your new selling price becomes $44.44 (current price $40, plus markup $4.44 or 10 percent of selling price). If your business sells only one product, you will raise the price of that product accordingly. If your business sells many products, price markups can vary to produce an average 10-percent markup.

Lowering Prices

If you decide to have a sale and thus mark down (discount) selling price, say by 10 percent, use this formula:

$$\text{Discount} = \frac{\text{Regular price} \times \text{Discount amount}}{100}$$

$$\text{Discount} = \frac{\$44.44 \times 10}{100}$$

$$\text{Discount} = \$4.44$$

$$\text{Discount Price} = \$40 \ (\$44.44 - \$4.44)$$

PRICING SERVICES

The process of establishing selling prices for your service business is much the same as product pricing. The key difference is that you establish a price based on a unit of service, say an hourly or daily rate or the completion of a project task, rather than on each product. Another difference is the way you arrive at your estimated gross profit figure. Since a service business does not rely on product inventory, the cost of goods sold is the sum of direct labor costs and the cost of materials used directly to produce the service.

Just as with a product business, your total sales (or revenue) is the result of customers buying so many units at an estimated price. Subtracting from this figure the cost of direct labor and materials produces your estimated gross profit figure. Dividing this figure by the number of units of service estimated to be delivered produces the average unit cost of service.

Now take your gross profit and subtract from it the estimated expenses of doing business not related to direct labor and material costs. This gives you your net profit figure before taxes. All the remaining aspects of pricing a service are the same as pricing a product.

RAISING PRICES CAN BACKFIRE

In setting prices, the goal must be to maximize profit without driving away customers, yet maintain sufficiently competitive prices to attract new customers.

Before raising prices, remember to scrutinize costs to see if expenses can be reduced using technologic efficiencies, different work methods, or other economies.

The volume of products sold and services delivered can also impact prices and profit. When you are able to contain cost increases yet deliver a higher volume of products or services, you will increase per-unit profit.

The rate of inventory turnover also impacts prices and profit. Inventory is cash tied up in merchandise, and too much cash in this form is nonproductive. On the other hand, too little inventory may cause costly delays in filling orders. The number of times your average inventory is sold and replaced each year can be a signal of strength or weakness in your business. A low inventory turnover rate may be a sign of excessive or indiscriminate buying or accumulation of unappealing merchandise. High turnover is normally an indication of business strength because merchandise is selling well and contributing rapidly to profits.

PLANNING PROFITS BY BUDGETING

Another useful tool to control costs and inventory-related expenses is a process known as budgeting. It helps you deal with both the present and the future and increase the likelihood of turning expectations into reality.

Working up a business budget allows you to stretch capital and determine whether or not your profit goal is within reach. When budget figures are put together, you have answers to such questions as: How many sales are needed to achieve desired profit? What fixed expenses will be necessary to support sales? What variable expenses must be curbed or increased? The process of budgeting forces you to consider your basic objectives, policies, plans, and resources so you are better prepared to direct the future and prevent crises.

A budget is nothing more than a tally of income and expense elements. By breaking out your sources of revenue and categories of expense, you are equipped to plan necessary changes to increase profits. If sales of one product or group of products are exceeding projections, this is a tip-off to focus more attention on that area. If some expenses are higher than projected, you can start looking for ways to cut them. In short, a budget can head you in the right financial direction just as a map helps you travel roads and highways.

Use Your Profit-and-Loss Statement

The simplest way to budget is to start with what you already know. You get this information from your most recent profit-and-loss statement or business income tax return. Look carefully at each of the categories of income and expense. Ask yourself which sources of revenue can be increased and which items of expense can be reduced. Identify fixed expenses, such as rent and utilities (items not easily changed), as contrasted with variable expenses, such as salaries, advertising, supplies, and travel costs, that allow greater use of discretion.

Next, decide where you want to go. Develop a new set of figures as your target for the next 12 months. Break down these amounts into quarters or even monthly targets. During the year, these periodic divisions give you a handle on expenses and other activities. They help you anticipate peak periods so you can schedule inventory purchases, special promotions, and advertising campaigns in line with anticipated sales.

Use your budget to seize control of what you are doing and where you are going. Carefully evaluate your previous quarterly or monthly operating period. Are you producing sales and holding down costs in line with targeted projections? If not, what should be changed? Always compare anticipated goals with actual results. Share this information with your employees so they are encouraged to put forth a good effort. Ask your employees for suggestions and search to uncover reasons any targets are not met.

Next, prepare any necessary revisions to your budget so you will have an improved, workable plan for the next operating period. Remember that far too many business owners try to conduct business without a planned budget. They don't have any goals; rather they seek only to survive from week to week and month to month. Don't be one of them. Use your profit-and-loss statement to develop a workable budget so your business will be conducted according to plan.

Finally, use your budget to fix the optimum price for your product or service in relation to your overall income and expenses. Know that prices fixed according to your own real operating experience will keep you in business and help you remain attractive to your customers.

Be aware that no one pricing formula or budget tool will produce the greatest profit under all conditions. The *best* budget is one prepared regularly, evaluated systematically, and modified to meet changing conditions.

The *best* price for your product or service is not necessarily the price that will sell the most units. Nor is it always the price that will bring in the greatest number of sales dollars. Rather, the *best* price is one that will match your market, maintain existing customers, help to attract new customers, and ultimately maximize your business profits.

13
Getting a
Ready-made Sales Force

Whether you are offering a product or service, the extent of your business will depend on generating sales. Depending on your inclinations and knowledge, you may want to sell your product or service directly, but it's not an absolute requirement; and if you are not good at selling or don't like to sell, you can easily hurt your business by doing it.

You must remember, however, that if you do not sell your product or service yourself, then someone else must be paid to do the selling for you. Whether you offer your product or service through sales agents, mail order, radio, television, or newspaper advertising, at flea markets, by telephone sales or rack consignment, all of these methods require that you pay for the selling service. The method of payment for these services need not always be up-front cash; nevertheless, payment will sooner or later be required.

INSTANT PROFITS USING A SALES AGENCY

If selling your product or service requires someone to generate business by calling on your potential customers, using a sales agent or obtaining a commissioned sales representative through a personnel agency will be less costly than hiring your own sales force.

Selling for others is the business of independent sales agents who work alone or who are employed by sales agencies. They make their money by representing several clients on a commission basis. They solicit orders for clients in agreed-on territories. Your function will be merely to set prices, terms, and other conditions of sale, ship the merchandise or provide the service, and bill the customer directly.

Sales agents go by various names. A few examples are manufacturer's agent, manufacturing representative, and "rep." The labels vary according to industry.

Using an independent sales agency or sales agent to promote your product or service has several important advantages. Since they are paid a percent of sales as a commission, you accrue selling expenses only when actual sales occur, and such costs thus become a predetermined selling expense based on sales. Also, sales agents give you immediate entry into a defined territory, they make regular calls on customers, and they can provide quality selling ability. Most sales agents are experienced professionals, have an in-depth knowledge of their territory and industry, and are highly motivated because they get paid only on results.

In selecting a sales agent, you should determine what the agent's record of success is in products, services, and territories similar to yours, how long the agent has been in business, what is the agent's reputation, and whether the other lines carried by the agent are compatible with yours. Once you know the kind of agent you are looking for, it is relatively easy to select the right one. Listings of sales agents are available from the Manufacturers' Agents National Association, PO Box 16878, Irvine, CA 92713, and are also given in your telephone directory. They also can be found in classified advertisements in trade magazines whose readership is geared toward the type of manufacturer's representative you seek.

Commissions charged by sales representatives are generally 10 percent of the sales price on items selling for less than $100 and 5 percent on the sales price exceeding $100. These are reasonable fees considering you are free of all employer overhead costs, such as social security, income taxes, unemployment and worker's compensation taxes, and travel expenses, to name just a few.

A good sales representative should be expected to produce a reasonable number of sales within 90 days from the first day of canvassing an established territory.

An essential characteristic of a successful business person is the ability to attract others who can assist the business. Selecting and using independent sales representatives takes a little initial work, but the rewards can be sizeable. If you think great thoughts and dream of success, you must begin to use the talents of others; in this way, your own effectiveness can be maximized.

Remember that success in business is not the private property of a fortunate few. Success can be and rightfully should be yours if you have the courage to begin. If you will exercise the courage available to you to begin doing today that which you have only dreamed of, you will discover you have at your command all the talents to start that business of your own and be successful.

EXPAND YOUR WEALTH BASE
THROUGH CONSIGNMENT AND RACK SALES

In the last 20 years, our rapidly changing world has come to rely on self-service and convenience store channels of distribution to cut costs and speed customer purchases. This creates a new opportunity for small business to get products to market using three alternative approaches: consignment, rack sales, and rack selling on consignment.

SELLING PRODUCTS ON CONSIGNMENT

Consignment selling is not a new or untested method for presenting merchandise to consumers. Some products always have been and still are sold on a consignment basis even in the most modern, big-business-owned chain stores. Such products include eggs, bread, dairy products, light bulbs, batteries, garden seeds, potted plants, produce, magazines, newspapers, and seasonal items, such as greeting cards and Christmas decorations, among many others.

Consignment means placing merchandise in outlets with an established dealer who pays you only for merchandise that sells. The dealer also retains the right to return to you, without obligation, merchandise that does not sell. Thus, selling on consignment provides the dealer with an attractive incentive to stock your merchandise and you with a ready-made showroom for your merchandise.

Consignment selling affords you, the beginning manufacturer or wholesaler, some important advantages:

■ You have the choice of a wide variety of retail outlets and locations and thus can optimize exposure of your products to the buying public.
■ The retail dealer has an incentive to stock your products because no capital is tied up in inventory.
■ Since risk of investment loss is minimized, dealers are encouraged to stock newly introduced merchandise for which there is no established sales record.
■ Dealers are encouraged to stock seasonal and perishable items that they might otherwise avoid because of unpredictable conditions.
■ You have your merchandise exposed to the buying public instead of having it stored and isolated in a warehouse waiting for a buyer's order.

The principal disadvantage of consignment selling is that you tie up funds waiting for merchandise to be sold, but this may be offset by having your merchandise on public display ready for purchase. Other disadvantages are that the dealer may be a poor credit risk or might promote merchandise already owned over your consigned products. It is therefore important to try to place items on consignment that are not competing with the dealer's own products.

Consignment Agreements

When placing merchandise on consignment, you enter into an agency relationship with the dealer. That is, the dealer takes no ownership of merchandise but merely acts as your agent. Without a written agreement to the contrary, liability for loss or damage of the merchandise remains with you. Thus, you may want to prepare a standard written agreement in advance that says the dealer will assume a share of the loss in case of shoplifting or damage to merchandise, and that the dealer will exercise normal care in display and handling of merchandise. Also, you should agree on the exact commission to be awarded to the dealer upon sale of merchandise. Depending on the product and price, dealers prefer commissions of 50 to 60 percent of the sale price; but again, depending on the product and price, they frequently accept 30 percent.

Length of time (weeks or months) the dealer agrees to display merchandise and the intervals at which the dealer will pay for sold merchandise can also be made clear by agreement. Other considerations for which agreement can be arranged include the specific location within the store or shop where merchandise will be placed, delivery and pick-up intervals, and conditions of storage of any merchandise that is not on display, particularly in the case of perishables. Unless the dealer objects, make every attempt to specify that inventory delivered less inventory collected equals inventory sold. In the event that merchandise is damaged and in the absence of any agreement that the dealer will share in the loss, ask that the damaged goods be retained for your records to ensure fair play.

Hometown Advantage

An important feature of consignment selling, whether performed by you or a sales agency, is the ability to make a splash in your own local area, then branch out into your region.

While there's always been a bit of local and regional pride in home-owned businesses, in recent years that pride has swelled to huge proportions. This kind of marketing knowledge creates opportunities for small entrepreneurs who go head-to-head with billion-dollar corporations. Adroitness at consignment selling can be the precise marketing tool you need to capture strong local sentiment and bring hometown products and services to market.

Look at the success of Sophia Collier and Connie Best, the New York duo who started their American Natural Beverage Corporation from scratch by capturing the mystique of New York's thriving Soho scene. The two pooled their savings and began producing a truly natural beverage called Soho Soda. In the beginning, nobody wanted to distribute their soft drink, so the young women loaded their Jeep with the new creation and went around to small stores in Soho, Greenwich Village, and Chelsea offering it on any terms acceptable to small retailers. By the end of one year, they had sold 72,000 bottles of soda and made $1. Three years later, after achieving local success, distributors flocked to their door to get distribution rights. Now the company has over 100 distributors, 52 employees, and is generating $20 million in sales across the country.

The combination of a locality name on a label and consignment selling of a product can often be a real winner. For example, the word "Vermont" on a specialty food product has tremendous marketing power. And Sally Von Werlhof found she could move a lot of western-wear clothing by playing up the fact she makes her goods in Kansas City, America. She attributes this marketing technique with helping her company's sales grow by 33 percent each year.

These are but two examples of how small, but smart entrepreneurs, fully aware of local-market trends and nimble enough to use any distribution tool available, can outmaneuver America's giant corporations.

RACK SELLING

In the last 20 years, rack sales have grown to giant proportions. It is estimated that more than 70 percent of all retail items can be displayed attractively on racks. Arranging to have your line of merchandise displayed on a pegboard rack or in a point-of-purchase container is a quick and easy way to generate profits. Such racks or containers are generally made of wire and masonite or cardboard, and you can either purchase them from container manufacturers or design them yourself and have them made to your specifications. They can provide an ideal vehicle to feature advertising messages you choose and prominently display your company's product, name, and logo.

The primary advantage of using racks for display-point purchases is the wide selection of locations that can accommodate them. Wherever merchandise is sold, you're likely to see a rack or container offering blister-packed items. Chain stores and small retailers most certainly use them; but they are just the tip of the iceberg. Gift shops in hotels, airports, and hundreds of other places, including hospitals and restaurants, present merchandise to walk-through customers by the convenient use of attractively packaged goods on display racks.

You may want to personally make arrangements with dealers to display your merchandise on racks that you or the manufacturer provide. However, doing so may entail sales ability and, once again, you may prefer to obtain the services of an independent sales agent to establish your rack locations. The more locations you have, the greater your sales and profit potential. Remember, however, that you must devote time or enlist the help of others to service this robot sales force on a regular basis.

COMBINING RACK SELLING WITH CONSIGNMENT

Retail dealers and operators of other commercial, high people-traffic locations are always on the lookout for ways to increase profits. Increased revenue from easy-access impulse or necessity sales is an attractive income booster. More income can be especially appealing when use of merchandise racks is combined with the no-risk-to-dealer features of consignment selling.

One very good reason to use the rack selling–consignment approach when you're just starting out is to do market testing. You may not know if the target market will be as receptive as hoped. This can be a fairly inexpensive way to learn which market segment produces the most sales or if a new product will sell at all.

Another good reason to combine rack selling with consignment is to encourage wholesalers and retailers to stock your items in a convenient and risk-free fashion. When wholesalers or retailers know you have made it easy to stock your item and they see the prospect of a commission for exerting very little effort, both you and they can be quite pleased with the income-producing results.

Several substantial manufacturing firms in America began operations in the owner's home or small shop, marketed products through rack sales and consignment selling, advanced to direct sales, and eventually captured a fair share of the market. If this is your desire, it doesn't have to remain just a dream, it can become the incarnation of your own living reality.

SELLING YOUR SPECIAL HANDICRAFTS

If your hobby-converted-to-a-business product happens to be a handicraft, new opportunities for consignment are rapidly springing up in the form of craft co-ops. Craft co-ops are generally store-front locations run by members of a group pooling resources to display and sell goods made by group members. You can find them in your phone directory under "Craft Galleries—Cooperatives." The resurgence of interest in carefully made, original handcrafted items occurring throughout America and the innovation of craft co-ops are producing high-volume sales for many gifted and productive home artisans.

If you have an entire line of handcrafted goods, including various craft arrangements, sculptured candles, pottery, dry-flower arrangements, sculptured metals, and others, you can make generous profits by combining a schedule of consignment outlets, flea markets, swap meets, art shows, and department store appearances for high-traffic volume sales. At an average retail price of $15 for each product, monthly sales of just 300 items will produce gross sales of $4,500 per month or $54,000 per year. Closely controlling material costs and operating expenses should net a healthy spare-time income.

If you want to know more about selling handcraft items, check your library for a copy of *Craft Worker's Market*, published by Writer's Digest Books, Cincinnati, Ohio. This handbook is a must for all who wish to sell fiber art, glasswork, woodcrafts, miniatures, pottery, leatherwork, scrimshaw, metalsmithing, dolls, decoupage, needlework, and basketry.

It lists more than 3,000 places to sell and exhibit your work. Information in every listing is supplied directly by buyers and exhibitors, so you know exactly whom to contact and how to do it. Also included are payment rates, special requirements, and other information you need to sell your crafts. There is even information about the business records you'll need to keep, how to keep them, and much more.

BARTERING CAN MAKE A REAL CASH DIFFERENCE

Bartering as a means of exchanging goods and services has existed throughout human history, yet it continues to be a thriving form of business-building. In fact, business-to-business and business-to-customer bartering has grown to such significant proportions that the Tax Reform Act of 1986 requires formalized barter transactions to be reported the same as any other income received through broker arrangements, clubs, or societies.

You often hear television commercials announce that game show contestants have been given transportation on a major airline in exchange for promotional advertisement considerations. This is a form of bartering. A reported 65 percent of all corporations listed on the New York Stock Exchange conduct at least part of their business through barter. And so do an estimated 7.5 million small businesses, 350,000 of which carry on formal barter arrangements through membership clubs.

When establishing a new business, the attraction of maximizing bartering is the ability to acquire operating goods and services without borrowing or spending much money, thus preserving cash flow. You can enhance profits by using your own goods or services, normally more readily available in a new business start-up. Bartering can reduce production costs if you are a manufacturer by using spare capacity without adding overhead.

Essentially, there are three kinds of barter systems: swap meets, private barter arrangements, and commercial barter. You may find using any one or all of them will prove a springboard to growth.

Swap Meets

The swap-meet form of barter is the most basic and perhaps the easiest way to learn that paying in kind with goods and services is every bit as respectable as paying with cash. Bartering is common at flea markets and swap meets; and at times, items are displayed by participating wheelers and dealers as much for trading as for selling.

Seasonal-type goods are often traded this way. Frank Sahlman, Jr., owns a ski shop in Squaw Valley and turns over thousands of dollars of inventory by taking in seasonal ski items and trading them when they are most in demand. Sahlman claims not only that this is good for business, but that he also gathers 75 percent of his family's personal needs through barter.

While barter can assist you to weed out inventory of overstocked or slow-moving goods, products, and merchandise, the entire system is adaptable to trading your services as well. Service-oriented businesses often have unused capacity that can be traded for their business-building wants and needs.

Private Barter Arrangements

This is the I'll-fix-your-kid's-teeth-if-you'll-draft-my-will kind of bartering arrangement. It is performed on the basis of what two consenting parties find to be fair value. A carpenter agrees to do needed work in exchange for accounting assistance, or a computer whiz agrees to trade some time and skill for carpet cleaning, or whatever. The University of Detroit claims to do a fair amount of business this way, swapping university sports tickets, seminar fees, part-time admissions, and even the cost of entire tuitions for such operating needs as air conditioning units and vehicles.

Some of the old standbys that continue to be traded include advertising, radio and television spots, hotel rooms, airline passage, lawyers' fees, secretarial services, sign painting, copywriter skills, and a variety of other services that businesses often find difficult to do without. To a large extent, swap-savvy businesses can form a self-enclosed gathering of professionals, service providers, retailers, and manufacturers who, by supplying one another with operating needs, also contribute to one another's profits.

Commercial Barter

When groups of businesses actively barter, the concept of even exchange can get complex, and that has led to creation of formal barter associations. They make an exchange of goods or services easier and less time consuming, facilitate an extremely wide range of exchangeable services, and add to the benefits enjoyed by highly diverse parties. These services are performed by formal barter membership clubs, otherwise known as trade exchanges.

One huge bartering association in America traded more than $100 million worth of goods and services in one year. Bartering volume for all trade exchanges is approaching $600 million and promises to continue to grow at a rate of 15 percent a year through good times and bad.

The medium of exchange for bartering transactions is *trade credits* that can be spent on-site or over the phone to acquire any product or service within the domain of the association. It is this system of trade credits that allows association members to exchange items or services of equal value.

Computerization makes credit and debit accounting of trade credits possible and results in triangular trade and multilateral commerce. This ability is greatly enhanced as more and more exchange clubs link up with one another or merge to form a truly nationwide exchange capability.

For example, a manufacturer in San Francisco was stuck with $17,000 worth of cowboy hats by a slow local market. When he offered them for barter through a nationwide exchange, a retailer in Knoxville, Tennessee, jumped at the opportunity and took the entire lot for an exchange of trade credits. In another case, Wilson Sporting Goods had a surplus of $100,000 worth of specialty golf balls that were exchanged for barter trade credits. In the largest single barter deal known, Xerox Corporation used the services of Barter Systems International to exchange approximately $2 million worth of copiers for a basket of goods and services that included real estate, cash registers, telephone recorders, and moving services. Some small business owners, unable to pay employees top wages, use trade credits to give workers bonuses in the form of health club memberships, condominium rentals, and free vacation trips.

There are an estimated 300 bartering clubs in the United States. A typical club charges members a one-time set-up fee of about $350, an annual continuing service fee of about $100, and may require a broker fee of up to 10 percent of trade credits transacted through the club. In turn, the club provides a directory of members and services available for exchanging goods and services, keeps accounting records of all transactions, sends each member monthly statements of credits and transactions, and conducts seminars on how to make the most of club membership. Most clubs advise that business barter dealings be limited to 10 percent of gross sales.

TO FIND OUT MORE ABOUT BARTERING

While bartering may never fully replace benefits derived by the accumulation of money, it may be used profitably by avoiding the expenditure of cash, thus enhancing your wealth base and freeing funds for other forms of investment.

The recent explosive growth of bartering clubs in America is itself becoming a new business opportunity suitable for full- or spare-time operations. One barter-club founder started a barter service with $2,000, and now she brokers more than $10 million in a trading year. Lois Holtzman Dale started New York-based Barter Advantage Inc. from scratch and has built the firm to the point where it grosses three-quarters of a million dollars.

If you would like to learn more about how to barter your products or services or even how to start a barter dealership in your own community, you can contact either ITEX International, One Lincoln Center, PO Box 2309, Portland, OR 97208, or the trade association for barter exchanges: International Association of Trade Exchanges, 5001 Seminary Road, Suite 310, Alexandria, VA 22311.

FREE THINGS ARE TAKEN FOR GRANTED

It can be argued that bartering is a method for obtaining goods and services essentially free of charge. Some say bartering will never amount to much for this very reason. Things that we pay money for, we value; and things we obtain for practically nothing, we place little value on—generally, we take them for granted. The paradox is that exactly the reverse is true. Most everything that is really worthwhile in life has come to us absolutely free.

Consider, for a moment, the example of the human mind. It comes to us at birth free of charge as standard equipment. It contains riches beyond our wildest dreams, yet most of us take it for granted. Most of us torture and drug it and generally use it for little jobs instead of big important ones. The human mind can do any kind of job we assign it. Yet studies have proven that most of us operate at about 10 percent or less of our mental capacity.

In one sense, our mind can be compared with extremely fertile land. It will return in kind whatever seed that is planted. If we plant in fertile soil seeds of poisonous nightshade rather than nutritious corn, the soil will return the toxic weed in great abundance, just as it would have returned healthful breeds of corn. The mind works the same way, though it is much more fertile than the land.

Like the soil, the mind does not care what seed we plant. It will return what we plant—a concrete worthwhile goal or confusion; hopes, dreams, ambition or fear, misunderstanding and anxiety; success or failure—but it does not care what we plant. Regardless, you are the master gardener; you control and direct your mind and thereby the character, circumstances, and destiny of the life you possess.

Decide now what seed you want to plant in your own mind. You want to be in business; you want to be rich. All you have to do is plant those seeds in your mind, care for them, nurture them, work steadily toward those goals—they will become a reality, they will be yours.

14
Get Rich through Mail Order

Even if you have no experience selling products, you can generate big profits with your own mail-order business.

Each year, over 47 million people subscribe to more than 10,000 magazines, and an additional 63 million households regularly receive newspapers suitable for mail-order advertising. Upon reading advertisements in their favorite publications, subscribers buy more than $26 billion worth of products each year through mail order. This is in addition to the $86 billion in sales generated by direct mail and mail-order catalogs.

If you have ever wanted the freedom and flexibility of your own business, mail-order merchandising may be just what you are seeking. Think about this: have you ever seen a mail-order business for sale? Pick up any newspaper and you will find businesses for sale by the hundreds—some doing well, others going broke; but rarely do you come across anyone selling a mail-order business.

You can buy products wholesale and sell them through mail order; or better yet, if the product is something that you manufacture, you have the choice of offering it retail through mail order or you may even sell large volumes of the product to established mail-order houses.

A most appealing feature of a mail-order business is the ease by which it can be operated from any geographic or residence location. It makes little difference whether you choose to live in a major metropolitan area or a pleasant town in the country, a successful mail-order business can be conducted wherever you reside.

To begin, you need only advertise an appropriate, inexpensive product in one of the hundreds of specialty magazines available for mail-order sales. As orders come in and you begin to establish a nationwide customer base, additional items may be added to your product line. You can then expand the business by sending customers a circular, on a regular basis, which presents a few additional items. Then when the number of products warrants it, advance to a catalog.

Magazine advertising rates range from $50 to several thousand dollars per advertisement; mailing lists range from $30 to $100 or more per thousand names. However, their real worth depends on the need for your product and the ability of your advertising to show honesty and appeal.

Many successful mail-order businesses have been started by one person and then expanded to the proportion of a major corporation. Consider the case of Gerardo Joffe who, as an immigrant from Germany, had to learn to speak and write the English language, then borrow $5,000 to start his mail-order business known as Haverhill's. Five years later, Joffe sold the firm to Time Incorporated for $1 million. Not satisfied with this success, he started another huge mail-order business known as Hennicker's and was on his way to another million dollars.

More recently, Bill Nicolai of Seattle, Washington, established Early Winters Limited, a rather unique outdoor equipment mail-order business offering an elegant array of gadgets and goods for roughing it the soft way. A few years ago, he was the firm's only employee and the only product offered was a tent for mountaineers. Now the firm employs 205 workers, grosses almost $12 million annually, and offers a wide assortment of novel, sometimes posh, equipment and clothing through the vehicle of a 132-page catalog.

HOW TO FIND PRODUCTS FOR YOUR MAIL-ORDER BUSINESS

For products made in the United States, the most important sources for locating new merchandise in your field of specialty appropriate for mail order are trade shows and trade magazines that feature new products (these are described in *Standard Rate and Data*, available at your library).

The most important sources for locating new merchandise produced in foreign nations are the following publications: *Made in Europe*, PO Box 174027, D-6, Frankfurt/Main, 17, West Germany; *The Importer*, c/o East Asia Publishing Co., 2-11 Jingumae, 1-Chome, Shibuya-ku, Tokyo, 150, Japan; *Hong Kong Enterprise*, 3rd floor, Connaught Centre, Central Hong Kong; *Asian Sources*, c/o Trade Media Ltd., PO Box K-1786, Kowloon Center, Hong Kong; and *Direct Marketing*, c/o Hoke Publications, 224 7th St. Garden City, NY 11535.

Is Your Product a Mail-Order Winner?

Generally, products that can successfully be sold through mail order meet these requirements:

1. The product is not readily available in stores.

2. Rarely is the product offered by major mail-order houses, but, if offered, is available only at a substantially higher price.
3. Purchasing the product by mail affords the customer recognizable buying convenience.
4. The potential market for the product is sizeable and identifiable, and can be reached easily and inexpensively through publications of specific interest to customers in the same product field.
5. Size and weight of the product are proportionate to the price and value of the product, i.e., offering a 200-pound anvil through mail order may be interesting but extremely risky.
6. Material substances and product shape meet postal regulations.
7. The product's fragility and packaging requirements are proportionate to its price and value.
8. Perishability can be controlled and the cost of doing so is not prohibitive.
9. Instant recognition can be obtained with a brief description or illustration in the space of an economical advertisement.
10. The product should be a repair-free item.
11. Where possible, the product should be personalized, i.e., have the buyer's name or initials appear on the product.
12. The product should be of a nature to generate repeat sales and preferably be suitable to generate sales for related products.
13. Need for the product should endure, and it should not be subject to faddish obsolescence.
14. The products you offer should all appeal to the same market.
15. The product should be one that you have obtained exclusive rights to sell, or at least exclusive mail-order rights, for a specified period of time.
16. The price covers all expenses and includes margin for profit while appearing moderate in relation to value. Use this rule of thumb to determine the price of an item advertised singly, such as through a magazine.

Your Total Cost		Times Factor		Maximum Advertised Price
$3 or less	×	4	=	$12 (but not less than $4)
$3.01 to $6	×	3	=	$18 (but not less than $12)
$6.01 to $10	×	2.5	=	$25 (but not less than $18)
Over $10	×	2	=	Various (but not less than $25)

The recommended, maximum advertised price in terms of total cost of the product to the seller, as shown, applies only when overhead costs are at a minimum, such as when beginning a mail-order business from your home. As the business grows, the times factor will have to be increased to cover additional overhead expenses as they occur.

17. To avoid warehousing and inventory problems, you can arrange for your supplier to ship the product in individual units to customers rather than in large quantities to you. This practice is called drop shipping. It means you obtain orders, send them to the supplier who, in turn, ships the product to your customer.

SURE-FIRE MAIL-ORDER ADVERTISING STRATEGIES

As a general rule, products of a specialized nature or interest should be advertised only in specialized publications catering to that specific interest or advertised by direct mail to specialized mailing lists.

Print Advertisements

Generally, daily newspapers are not profitable media for specialized items, but may be suitable for some products of general interest. They can be used for one-time only testing to see if your advertisement pulls sufficient orders to warrant further advertising in other periodicals. Well-known magazines with a wide readership, such as *Sunset, Yankee,* or *Better Homes and Gardens,* are far better for general-merchandise advertising purposes. Specialized magazines are far better for merchandise of specific interest to groups such as golfers or skiers or you name it.

The most common, but proven method of advertising a product for beginners is to prepare an advertisement containing a headline, a few lines of concise information, including price, and an illustration of the product. This method of advertising in a magazine offering moderate rates allows the beginner to test public response with a limited capital investment.

The "bible" used for selecting a magazine or newspaper suitable for your product is *Standard Rate and Data,* available at most libraries. This directory consists of several volumes, but the three volumes that will be most important are *Consumer Magazine and Farm Publication Rates and Data, Business Publication Rates and Data,* and *Newspaper Rates and Data.*

Information displayed in these references will assist you in choosing which publication is most appropriate for the advertising you intend to do, including the dates of publication, the number of copies of each magazine distributed, character of readership, closing dates for receiving advertising, mechanical requirements to accommodate the advertisement, and other essential information.

An important feature in the reference is a summary listing of all magazines with mail-order and/or shopping advertising pages.

In determining which magazine is best for advertising your particular product, important factors bearing on rate of return are the number of potential customers in the magazine's readership who will be specifically interested in your product and the degree of appeal that the product has to those customers.

Each magazine establishes its advertising rate on the basis of circulation size, type of magazine, readership, cost, and many other factors. Consequently, advertising rates range widely. Advertising rates will also vary depending on the size of the advertisement, whether it's in color or black and white, and whether the advertisement is display, classified, or included in a mail-order shopping section. The profitability of your advertisement depends on the return for each dollar spent rather than on cost of the space. The number of people the advertisement will reach is not nearly so important as whether those people are interested in the particular type of product you offer.

Another important consideration is whether circulation size of the publication and advertising volume are increasing, remaining stable, or decreasing. By checking previous issues and circulation figures, you can gauge and compare patterns of competitive magazines and determine the most favorable growth patterns or geographic advantages.

A solid test of the appeal of your product and effectiveness of your advertisement may be obtained by running it three consecutive times in the magazine having most promise for your product. Four weeks from the date your first order was received, you will have obtained 50 percent of the total orders from the first advertisement placed in a monthly magazine. This allows you to estimate the productivity of your advertising in time to make changes if needed.

Preparing the Advertisement

To get started, take a careful look at mail-order advertisements appearing in magazines you enjoy. Notice the headline, text in the body of the advertisement, size, and placement of any illustration, price announcement, and ordering information.

A magazine-advertisement headline must stand out from other text in the magazine. Select a typeface that will be noticed and easy to read. Try to convey a magic message in a few short words. Text in the advertisement should emphasize what the reader will get, not what the product does or how it does it. Use a few short lines to link the product to key benefits wanted by the reader.

Move the reader to action by offering a unique benefit, such as a special discounted price, a free gift, a free no-risk trial and guarantee of satisfaction, a limited time offer, or an offer of two for the price of one.

An illustration should be large enough for the product to be easily recognizable; the design should be clear and crisp. Graphics should conjure action emotions, command attention, create immediate desire, and excite the reader to urgency.

Price of the product should be clearly stated and evoke action. Notice how Haverhills did this in a newspaper display advertisement for a halogen-power flashlight:

We are one of the largest national mail-order houses. In order to make our operation ever more efficient, we need to increase our customer files by at least 25,000 names per month. The best way to do this is to make an irresistible offer of quality merchandise. Our Halogen Powerlite is one of these. We offer this to you as a list builder and at the hard-to-believe price of $12.95. But we have an even more astonishing deal: *Buy two for $25.90 and we'll send you a third one, with our compliments—absolutely FREE.*

If size of the advertisement permits, include a brief order form. Better yet, give the reader a toll-free phone number as well as an address and accept credit-card payments. Studies prove these devices greatly increase response.

Use a coding system to monitor which magazines and which issues are producing orders. This is simply done by including a department number representing issue months as part of the address. For example, Dept. A1 means magazine A advertised in the January issue.

A magazine mail-order program must be planned well in advance since art work may be required, and the advertisement must be received by the magazine at least two months before it is to appear. If the product is a seasonal item, be sure the advertisement begins to run at least two months before the actual key date. Depending on the nature and type of season, it's best to run the advertisement at least three times.

Know in advance how many orders you need to break even and how many orders you need to make a reasonable profit. (More about preparing advertisements is found in Chapter 15.)

Television Advertising

Traditional broadcast television has rarely been the preferred medium for mail-order promotions except for a few items such as recorded nostalgia or holiday-season promotions. The reason is that traditional television advertising is very expensive because advertising rates are based on the presumption that almost the entire viewing audience is interested in the mass-marketing message.

Rarely, however, does the viewing audience sit by the television set, pencil in hand, waiting to note a telephone number or scribble an address for order placement. The exception to this is an advertisement run frequently at late-hour broadcasting times when rates are cheapest or on local or smaller stations that have last-minute commercial time because of cancellations. But, as a general rule, television advertising represents an expensive, shotgun advertising approach rather than the targeted, rifle sharpshoot that you need for economical, effective mail-order advertising.

As a small-business owner, you should be very sensitive to the occurrence of a dramatic marketing shift called segmentation. This means, more than ever, mass markets are splintering into subgroups, and each has to be approached differently. For television, this means that the three major networks are no longer able to serve the more personal appetites of more than 240 million Americans and their widely differing television viewing tastes.

Cable Television Advertising

"Cable America" is experiencing explosive growth as it attempts to satisfy segmented audience choices. Cable television reaches almost 42 million American homes, constitutes almost one-half of all television homes, and is increasing at the rate of about 400,000 every month. This expansion is opening new opportunities for you and all advertisers—particularly for mail-order businesses—as segmentation allows narrower target merchandising. The cost of advertising is still quite high relative to traditional forms of direct-response advertising, but averages about 30 percent less than traditional television broadcast advertising.

In addition to offering you greater segmented targeting, cable offers small, direct-response businesses another attractive feature known as "per-inquiry" advertising rates. As cable firms seek their share of available advertising dollars from you, they are more receptive to being paid a commission on each response generated by a commercial rather than on the basis of time used.

Traditional television commonly charges you a dollar amount per 60-second spot, and that amount is reduced in increments as more spots are purchased. The traditional television station presents convincing arguments that its signal beamed into hundreds of thousands of homes will produce sales for you; but once media time is purchased, the station has no direct stake in each actual response. On the other hand, cable stations are more willing to be your partner by being paid an amount on each actual response received. This allows you to control advertising costs, tie advertising rates directly to actual product sales, calculate advertising expense the same way you calculate other expenses on a per-item basis, and establish prices accordingly.

The Direct Marketing Association has produced guidelines for advertisers who market products through the medium of cable television. You can see they are much the same as guidelines used by direct-response firms, whichever medium is used.

1. The product should be unique, completely new, or present significant variations on similar items already available at retailers.
2. The product should be so compellingly wanted or needed that the customer is willing to wait for delivery.
3. The product should not be available from local retailers.
4. The product should be demonstrable.
5. Price savings should be perceived to be so great that the customer is motivated to not pass it up.

Radio Advertising

Occasionally you may hear mail-order promotions advertised on radio, but like traditional television, it is not the preferred medium to reach customers. Generally, most spots don't give the listener time to understand the worth of what is advertised or to jot down order information.

The exception is a product so closely related to programs of special interest, such as gardening, financial advice, or religion. In such cases, a half-hour or an hour program on one subject broadcast to intent listeners may be just the opportunity you need to reach a focused audience.

SECRETS OF SUPER DIRECT-MAIL CAMPAIGNS

If you have a keen interest in mail-order advertising approaches, using direct mail rather than magazine advertisements is another profitable method to obtain orders. Generally, the smaller your business, the more important direct mail is for reaching customers. However, even large corporations embrace direct-mail advertising, which in one year accounted for $15.5 billion in advertising dollars, almost as much as television, and produced $74 billion in consumer sales and another $26 billion in fund raising.

Direct mail as an advertising medium is vastly more precise than either television or newspapers. Using a wide assortment of available mailing lists, you can send descriptive sales literature to potential customers in a market known to purchase similar items by mail. Combining several products in the sales material reduces the selling cost of each item because the cost of mailing is shared by the number of products offered.

Elements of successful direct-mail advertising material include (1) an effective tease headline on the envelope that in the time of a split-second glance will stop the potential customer and start creating curiosity or desire; (2) an upbeat introductory sales letter that will overcome inertia and produce immediate action; and (3) a persuasive brochure that describes the uses and advantages of the product, answers questions, and pulls sales by using compelling, powerful graphics and stating a clear attractive price.

Creating a Mail-Order Package

What generally works best in a mail-order package is an outer envelope that doesn't pretend to be anything other than what it is—advertising mail—but it must create such strong interest that its contents will be read immediately rather than set aside or thrown away. A key distinctive word on the envelope such as "free" will often do the trick, but perhaps you can come up with something more novel and pungent.

The amount of copy contained in the letter doesn't make much difference so long as it is not long and dull. Use indented material and bullets to break up long paragraphs and catch the reader's eye. Like the envelope, the letter should immediately capture the interest of the reader.

An effective direct-mail letter used to advertise subscriptions to *Popular Mechanics* and appeal to hands-on repair buffs opened this way:

Good friend, this invitation isn't for deadbeats, rip-off artists or "gentlemen" who hate to get their hands dirty. It's for the rest of us. It's for the guys who aren't afraid to get down under the sink with a pipe wrench. Guys who don't mind sticking their hands in the toilet tank to adjust the ball cock because they know it's going to save a $16 plumber's bill.

Another successful direct-mail effort was a seven-page letter offering a 26-day, $10,000 trip around the world. Presented as a challenge to the reader was the price tag, length of the trip, and even danger. These were played up as main features that not everyone could handle, rather than disadvantages to hide. The advertiser had just $5,000 to spend on promotion; but the letter was so captivating, it sold $600,000 worth of tickets. The promotion also proved that even very expensive products can be sold effectively via direct mail.

Advertisers give many reasons why consumers should buy, but one reason is more compelling than all others. Try hard to identify that one reason, then concentrate all your energies behind it. Doing so, capturing the master motivation to buy is vital to producing sales and profits for your business.

Testing the Package

Perhaps direct mail's biggest appeal is the cost-effective scientific testing that can be done to ensure that you are reaching precisely who you want to reach. Test mailings can be evaluated using coded order cards. By mailing a series of advertising packages to carefully selected customer types, you can determine the effect of key variables, such as the outer envelope, the sales letter, brochure, graphic design, and price. A 2-percent response rate is considered good, and a sizeable mailing can, of course, produce millions of dollars.

Mailing Lists

Lists of potential customers may be obtained from mailing-list brokers or list compilers or they may be comprised of your own past customers. A wide assortment of customized mailing lists is available from firms that are in the business of offering such lists. *Direct Mail List Rates and Data*, published by Standard Rate & Data Service, Inc., of Wilmette, Illinois, is available at many local libraries. It describes available lists and gives their cost. You can identify the lists you think are best for you and then contact the owner.

Another way to get a good idea of the range of lists that are available is to send for a free catalog to the firm of your choice. Firms are generally identified in your telephone directory under the heading "Mailing Lists."

Two of the nation's largest mailing list firms are Hugo Dunhill Mailing Lists, Inc., 630 Third Ave., New York, NY 10017, and Edith Roman Associates, Inc., 875 Avenue of the Americas, New York, NY 10001. These firms supply addressed labels and provide other mail-order services for a fee. Once the labels are obtained, they can be applied directly to your material. The cost of postage to mail your material can be reduced by obtaining a bulk mail permit from the U.S. Postal Service.

HOW TO GET MORE INFORMATION ABOUT MAIL ORDER

If you decide that mail order is an ideal way to convert your favorite hobby, sport, pastime, or idea to cash, you may enhance your understanding of this fascinating business by consulting three important references. The first is *Direct Mail/Mail-Order Handbook*, published by The Dartnell Corporation, Chicago. The second is *How to Get Rich in Mail Order* by Melvin Powers, published by Wilshire Book Co., North Hollywood, California. The third is *Mail-Order Busi-*

ness Directory, published by B. Klein Publications, Inc., Coral Springs, Florida.

In addition, you can acquire personal knowledge of successful mail-order promotions by studying advertisements appearing in magazines; by answering advertisements offering to send free information; by studying the catalogs, sales letters, brochures, and direct-mail literature you receive, and by paying particular attention to all follow-up literature. These are ideal ways to learn from the promotions of successful mail-order firms and to see, firsthand, the methods used by the mail-order industry.

If you are serious about using direct mail to promote your products and services, do yourself a tremendous favor. When you contact Hugo Dunhill for a copy of the mailing-list catalog, also ask for a free copy of these must-have marketing and sales aids: *How to Prepare an Effective Direct-Mail Letter; How to Prepare a Direct-Mail Brochure That Sells;* and *How to Prepare a Seminar Brochure,* an easy-to-follow, step-by-step guide to selling seminars.

Where to Go for Help

If you already have a product or service suitable for direct-response advertising and have a personal computer, many programs have been written to ease your order-taking and order-processing activities. One of the best is the Quick Order Processor (Q/OP) system. This program features online order entry, customer inquiry, inventory control, complementary and substitute selling, all aspects of record keeping and reporting, sales and profit analysis, complete catalog and advertising analysis system, online customer service, back order, special-order and drop-ship processing, mailing-list management, online purchasing and receiving, United Parcel Service (UPS) shipping-manifest generation, detailed financial analysis, same-day shipping features, and much more. Write for information to Nashbar Associates, Inc., 4141 Simon Road, Youngstown, OH 44512.

If you need assistance with sales-letter preparation, printing, and mailing-list management, write for information to On-Line Business Systems, Inc., 2801 Northwestern Parkway, Santa Clara, CA 95051.

If you have mail-order products and want someone else to handle all customer-order, warehousing, shipping, and other order-fulfillment tasks, contact BSA Incorporated, 39 Cindy Lane, PO Box 38, Oakhurst, NJ 07755. This is one of the best full-service, order-fulfillment companies in the business.

PROFIT BY KEEPING ACCURATE MAILING LISTS

Mailing lists made up of your own customers and serious prospects are valuable whether or not you sell products and services by direct mail. You pay good money for past and present advertising and other customer-getting results. Each customer and serious prospect represent hard earned dollars; therefore, listings of them are good as gold. These listings constitute your customer base and should be maintained as accurately and kept as current as possible. Analysis of these lists tells you the characteristics of your customers so you know what to look for when searching out new customers.

A proven law of sales is that your current customers are most likely to give you repeat business for additional purchases of more and different items. Maintain these lists and make a point of using them often to advertise your products and services.

Mailing-list brokers are craving quality mailing lists to rent to other firms looking for prospects meeting characteristics of your customers. Thus, every time you make a sale or get the name and address of a serious prospect, you get a name that can be turned into money. Eventually, you can rent your list to mailing-list brokers, and this can be a very profitable side line.

One of the largest newsletter publishers in the business has a full-time staff working to handle sales of the lists of that company's own subscribers. More profit is generated from rental of these lists to other companies than from the sale of newsletters and books that company publishes.

IMPORTANT THINGS TO REMEMBER

The secret to success in mail order is the ability to match attractively priced products to customers through an advertisement in an appropriate magazine of interest or through a mailing list of customers known to have purchased similar products. Of course, it is always necessary to conduct business efficiently; seek and test new products; test a variety of prices, mailing lists, and publications; keep the loyalty of your customers by regularly offering quality merchandise at key intervals; and provide prompt friendly service.

As responses come in, you must keep detailed records on the number of inquiries received, the cost of the advertisements and lists, the average cost of each inquiry, the number of orders received, the dollar value of the orders, the amount of the average order, the percentage of orders received, the best magazines or lists for producing inquiries and orders, and the profit and loss from each endeavor.

15
Power-packed Promotion Methods

If your potential customers don't know you exist, they can't buy your product or service. There are many ways to reach out to those who can use what you have to offer. Some approaches, like advertising, telemarketing, and appearing at trade shows, will require payment for the selling service. Others, such as publicity, are provided by the communications media at no charge.

An incredible revolution is occurring in the way products and services are announced to the world. No longer do advertisers rely on only one method to reach customers. Rather, successful advertisers use multiple promotion methods available to everyone in business.

ADVERTISING YOUR WAY TO RICHES

Advertising is a form of selling, the essential difference being that communications media, such as newspapers, magazines, radio and television, rather than personal contacts, convey the sales message to the buyer. A convenient definition of advertising is any sponsor-paid form of nonpersonal presentation and promotion of ideas, goods, or services with the objective being to produce a predetermined response.

In business, you spend money on advertising to accomplish one or more of these objectives:

1. To tell customers about the benefits, features, and price of your product or service, which includes telling them that what you have is superior to what the competition is offering

2. To tell customers who and where you are, and why doing business with you benefits them more than doing business with your competition
3. To promote a feature of your product, service, or business that compels purchase or at least a look-see now
4. To establish a business image on the basis of what you want perceived when your kind of product or service is thought about. Another term for it is *building reputation*.

If you are not perfectly clear on which of these objectives you want your advertising to achieve, then most likely you will be wasting your money.

Once you *are* crystal clear on which of the above objectives you want to achieve with advertising, then you must take these steps:

1. Analyze your market; determine as precisely as you can who you want to reach.
2. Set your goals; predetermine what would constitute a successful advertising campaign, and do it in measurable terms, such as within 30 days increasing sales by X dollars.
3. Develop an advertising budget.
4. Use your imagination to create a consistent advertising strategy.
5. Decide on the advertising medium most likely to produce results in the most cost-effective way.
6. Analyze and evaluate results compared with your predetermined, measurable objectives.

As a general practice, small, service-type businesses rely more heavily on radio and television advertising, while product-oriented small businesses rely more heavily on written media, such as newspapers, magazines, and direct-mail advertising.

Unfortunately, advertising can be a rather expensive form of selling, and payment is generally required immediately with absolutely no guarantee that the advertising will produce buyers. While a low advertising budget might rule out television advertising, at least initially, other forms of advertising can be used effectively, and costs can be kept to a minimum if you thoroughly know your market.

DEFINING A MARKET

There is no such thing as one market. This great country, with the greatest purchasing power in the world, is divided into a number of *markets* for individual products or services, each with specific needs and requirements. When these needs are recognized, advertising a special product or service to that market will produce results.

An example of one market among many is the *youth* market. The size of this market is 73.1 million, and it ranges in age from 5 to 25. However, this market can itself be divided into four distinctly different submarkets—children, teens, collegians, and young adults. Each group must be reached by its own advertising media, influenced by its own motivators, and sold through its own appeals.

Such a spread in age and characteristics will normally point to the need for closer scrutiny, not only of the primary market, but also of the segmented or splintered submarkets. For example, within the youth market is the *young-adult* submarket, which, in turn, consists of married couples and singles. While a portion of this market will be found to be hard-pressed financially, most will have money to spend. They will, however, tend to be more limited in their spending than middle-aged, financially established adults.

The *college* submarket differs from the young-adult submarket because of its geographic concentration, separate and distinct campus culture having its own fads, fashions, and values.

The *teen* submarket comprises 30.3 million consumers who are not without impressive spending power. Almost three out of five of them hold either full- or part-time jobs, and weekly earnings of U.S. teenagers are estimated to be about $638 million. Add allowances, which four of every 10 teens receive, amounting to $85 million a week, and the teenage market's clout at the cash register totals about $37 billion a year. Nearly all of it is disposable income since most don't pay rent or utility bills. Rather, they are spending their money on new, in-style products, cosmetics, record albums and tapes, movies, electronic games, clothing, and fad items. Advertising in such magazines as *Seventeen*, *Co-Ed*, *Teen*, *Young Miss*, *Glamour*, and *Tiger Beat* can produce sales of everything that appeals to this market.

One exciting common characteristic of the entire youth market is its willingness to accept new ideas and try new products. Another characteristic, important from an advertising point of view, is that today's youth spends a proportionately large amount of time listening to selective radio and cable television stations and reading special-interest magazines—all specific media whose rates are comparatively reasonable.

If you truly know your market, you can find an affordable advertising medium to reach it, but it takes a little imagination and merchandising innovation. You don't have to be a Sears or J.C. Penney to make advertising work for you, but you do have to be an independent thinker and absolutely flexible in selecting the advertising method best for you.

When you set out to reach your market, be prepared to explore a wide variety of advertising approaches until you find the one that most noticeably conforms to the buying habits of your customers. Concentrate on your market and then use everything at your disposal to reach your customer, even if it is only a small, 1-inch advertisement in a specialized magazine or a month-long leaflet campaign in your neighborhood.

ADVERTISING BUDGETS

Very few small businesses have enough money to buy all the expensive forms of advertising they want. But successful small businesses use, instead, what is at their disposal; namely, time, effort, imagination, and product or service appeal.

Use your time first to set aside a total dollar amount for advertising. Then break the total into smaller amounts according to the specific objective you want to achieve.

The size of your advertising budget makes no difference; this approach will work even if you have less than $500 to spend. The idea is to match your advertising budget to the type of advertising that will do the most good, but not before you have considered every form of advertising available to you.

USING AN ADVERTISING AGENCY

If you are fortunate enough to have a sizeable advertising budget, you should seek the advice of a reputable advertising agency. An important resource for locating an advertising agency in your vicinity is the *Standard Directory of Advertising Agencies,* published by National Register Publishing Company, Inc., Skokie, Illinois. This directory is a resource to over 4,400 advertising agencies and advertising services. It's arranged by subject and contains a section listing agencies catering to specialized groups, products, and interests.

A good advertising agency will evaluate your product or service and determine advertising problems and objectives; then in accordance with a predetermined budget, plan a suitable advertising campaign. If you give the OK, the agency will handle all the technical aspects of creating the advertisements, place them according to plan, check to be sure they run correctly, review the billing from the media, and send you only one monthly bill. These services will generally cost between 15 and 30 percent of your advertising budget. If the agency wants to charge more, look for another agency.

BEING YOUR OWN ADVERTISING AGENCY

If your budget cannot afford an advertising agency, your time will be a valuable asset. Use it to explore the pros and cons of various media available to you, and to make continuous contact with your potential customers, even when using little more than an inexpensive handout. Effective advertising is continuous advertising; and continuous advertising generates sales that improve the level and form of advertising, thus attracting new customers.

Low-budget Advertising

Low-budget advertising begins with word-of-mouth advertising among friends, coworkers, social groups, neighborhood groups, and members of your place of worship and branches out to people who, in turn, are known to them. You can enhance word-of-mouth advertising by giving all who you know a handout or an inexpensive free gift. For example, if you have an appliance-repair business, you can ask to put a small advertisement sticker on the bottom or back of each item you've repaired. This approach can be highly successful for most equipment or appliance businesses where service is required only occasionally rather than on an everyday basis.

Products can be effectively advertised the same way; but given the nature of products, a logical low-budget extension of this idea is to use signs to advertise products at flea markets, garage sales, and swap meets. Giving away specialty items, such as free helium-filled balloons, at these neighborhood showrooms will also generate interest in your products.

Beyond handouts and specialty giveaway items, low-budget advertising is available in the form of print media, including telephone directories, neighborhood classified *advertiser*-type newspapers, limited direct mail, and specialty-magazine advertising.

Mabel Henderson built up her Los Angeles, simulated stained-glass window and mural-painting business by vigorously handing out circulars to everyone whom she contacted; and Margaret Tobler grosses $29,000 or more a year just working weekends at the huge San Jose, California, swap meet continuously advertising patio furniture that her husband makes at home. Both are advertising effectively because they are doing so continuously and vigorously.

If you need art work to create an imaginative sign, circular or display advertisement, many commercial artists offer their services at reasonable prices. Check the appropriate section of your telephone directory, usually under the heading "Advertising Art" or "Artists–Commercial" and call on them for an estimate of prices. Always ask them to show samples of their work.

An established business can often be advertised effectively and inexpensively in conjunction with a charitable fund-raising event. Generally, advertising costs are shared with the charitable group, and it is relatively easy to attract media attention, thereby obtaining free publicity as an added benefit.

For example, a brilliant but often overlooked advertising technique is to promote a contest, raffle, or drawing where you give away your products or services as prizes with proceeds going to a worthy charity. The combined advertising efforts of your business and the charitable group, along with the free radio or television publicity that can be marshalled in support of the charitable purpose, will almost always result in a successful advertising campaign.

Print Advertising Secrets

Print advertising, whether in a newspaper, a magazine, or a circular, simply consists of an eye-catching phrase, question, or slogan; information about the product or service, including price with emphasis on special features; and identification of the business name, address, phone number, and hours. If you are advertising in an established publication, most have media departments that are happy to assist small advertisers create an advertisement, select style and font layouts, and prepare art work. Desktop publishing programs developed for personal computers allow you to accomplish the very same thing in your own home or office.

The exercise of preparing an advertisement begins with a concerted effort to learn more about what other advertisers are doing that makes their advertisements effective. From newspapers, magazines, and circulars, gather a sampling of advertisements that really appeal to you. Also gather some that you dislike. Consider as objectively as possible what it is about them that is appealing or detracting. Check the different type styles, borders, illustrations, and other features.

Do the advertisements that you prefer tell who, what, when, where, and possibly how or why? Does the headline stop the reader by capturing attention and drawing the reader into the advertisement? Are descriptions concise, interesting, and persuasive? Are the advertisements kept simple with sufficient white space so they are easy to read? Do the photographs or illustrations have a key purpose in relationship to other portions of the advertisement?

After you have completed this initial research and roughed out a few advertisements of your own, take them to the media department of the publication or, in the case of a circular, to the printer and take advantage of the assistance they willingly offer.

Remember that, where space permits, descriptions should always stress the advantages of the product or service rather than the product or service itself. If the product or service does something quicker, easier, and more conveniently; saves money; lasts a lifetime or whatever, these features should be emphasized.

After you have experimented with different type sizes, borders, and arrangements and looked at several preliminary layouts, you should be ready to give the OK for a *camera-ready* original and various-sized prints you may need in your advertising campaign.

A helpful book that covers all the advertising do's and dont's for the business beginner or veteran is *The Dartnell Advertising Manager's Handbook*, published by Dartnell Corporation, Chicago. This resource can be of great assistance when facing major advertising decisions.

TRADEMARKS, LOGOS, SERVICE MARKS, AND TRADE NAMES

Businesses commonly center advertising on trademarks to create recognition and maintain demand for products and services.

The formal definition of a *trademark* is any word, name, symbol, or combination of them adopted by a business entity to distinguish it from others. Logos and brand names meet this formal definition and they, too, may be registered and protected under federal law.

Forms of Trademarks

The forms trademarks take are:

Service marks—Used by service businesses, as distinguished from manufacturers or merchants, to provide recognition.

Collective marks—Used by cooperatives for the same purpose as service marks.

Certification marks—Used to certify regional origin, mode of manufacture, accuracy, quality, or other characteristics.

Trade names—Used to identify and distinguish one business from another.

Brand names—Used to identify and distinguish one product from another.

Logos—Symbols adopted by businesses to distinguish one from another.

Establishing Rights

Trademark rights are established by adoption and actual use, and no rights exist until actual use occurs. These rights are protected under common law.

The U.S. government permits the registration of trademarks in order to verify claim of ownership and validate exclusive right to use in commerce.

Forms for the registration of trademarks are available from: Commissioner, U.S. Patents and Trademarks Office, Washington, DC 20231. A complete application consists of (a) a written application properly notarized, (b) a drawing or presentation of the trademark, (c) five specimens or facsimiles of the trademark as actually in use in commerce, and (d) a filing fee.

Upon registration and date of issue, trademarks have a duration of 20 years. To prevent automatic cancellation, however, a trademark owner must file an affidavit showing continued use in commerce within the registration's sixth year. Thereafter, the registration may be renewed at the end of each 20-year term as long as the trademark continues to be used in commerce.

ACHIEVE SPECTACULAR SUCCESS WITH FREE PUBLICITY

You can promote your product or service inexpensively and generate hundreds or even thousands of dollars worth of business through ingenious free-publicity techniques.

Public Interest Stories

One approach is to contact every local newspaper editor, columnist, and public affairs director and every talk-show producer or talent coordinator in your community and explain what is unique or newsworthy about your business, product, or service. Using the same technique as those interviewed on the Johnny Carson Show or prominently featured in your local newspaper, you can reach thousands of potential customers through the media's eagerness for public-interest stories.

This is exactly the approach used by Gary Dahl, the guy who created the Pet Rock. He sold 1 million of them with an ingenious publicity campaign, and he didn't spend a penny on paid media advertising. Gary introduced his famous Pet Rock at the San Francisco and New York gift shows. He established a price of $4 from which he estimated making $1 on each sale. His first big order of 500 came from Neiman-Marcus, the giant Texas retailer; and he was soon distributing 10,000 Pet Rocks every day. But his big break came after he sent out press releases that described the rocks as close personal friends, yet easier to keep than pet animals. *Newsweek* picked up on the press release and gave him nearly a full-page write-up complete with photograph (which would have cost more than $29,000 as paid advertising). Reaching *Newsweek's* 18 million readers, Gary was deluged with invitations for radio and television appearances. In all, he gave some 300 interviews, and his story was printed free in 1,400 newspapers and magazines around the world.

You can use the same approach. Using your letterhead, prepare and send along to newspapers and magazine editors a press release, a 5-×-7-inch, black-and-white glossy photograph of your new or different product or service, and a descriptive information sheet. Essential information should cover what your business is, what it does, any unique characteristics or features on how it does it, how it provides new benefits to users, what distinguishes it from other products or services on the market, how much it costs, and where and how it can be obtained. A cover letter should courteously request a free editorial when space permits. The same material can be sent to local television and talk-show producers.

New Products

You can obtain names of the many popular magazines and business publications that regularly feature new products and services using as a reference *Bacon's Publicity Checker*, published by H.R. Bacon and Company, Chicago. Available at many libraries, this valuable resource lists magazines and periodicals according to subject category, thus allowing you to hone in on those publications with a readership having a specific interest in your particular product or service.

Since editors include special features on new products or services in order to maintain interest in advertised items and keep readers informed on the newest innovations in a particular field of interest, you will save money and time by submitting your request only to those publications whose readership interest is in the same field as your product or service.

Raffles, Contests, and Stunts

The third approach to free publicity is the selective use of extravagant raffles and contests or unusual publicity stunts. For example, if you want to advertise a fishing lure, equipment, or service business that you recently converted from a hobby, why not promote the grandest of all fish derbies? You might model it on the $1 million derby held in Seattle, Washington.

That event was publicized as the most grandiose derby in history, and 23,000 anglers paid an official $10 entry fee for the right to catch a specially marked salmon with a $1 million reward on its head. The derby promoter released the salmon marked with a special tag at an undisclosed spot in Puget Sound. Any angler catching that particular salmon between 6 A.M. and 6 P.M. on derby day would walk off with the prize of $50,000 a year for 20 years. Of course, your particular raffle or contest, no matter how extravagant, should ensure that there will always be a winner.

A proven method for getting free publicity is to announce a contest centered around a raging fad. In the past, hula hoops, boomerang throwing, far-out costumes, or dance marathon contests served as effective attention-getters. One year the fashion rage seemed to be the Deely Bobber—those Styrofoam things on two springs attached to a headband that bob on top of your head much like antennae. Announcing a ''most unique Deely Bobber'' contest or giving a free prize to any customer wearing a Deely Bobber at a time when they were popular was a clever way to get all the publicity you wanted.

As a matter of interest, creation of the Deely Bobber is itself a start-from-nothing business-success story. Stephen Askin of Los Angeles got the idea from the "killer-bee" outfit made famous on television by the late comedian John Belushi. Askin premiered the Deely Bobber at the California Gift and Trade Show, and the product hit the stores three months later.

Askin's insect-inspired creation soon spread as fast as an insect infestation. Teenagers bobbed to the beat, executives bobbed through board meetings, and a host of otherwise sane-looking people rapidly forked over $3 for the real thing at Macy's or Bloomingdale's, and $1 or $2 for facsimiles sold on the sidewalk. In less than two years, about 2 million DBs were sold, bringing Askin $500,000 just for starters.

Americans seem to have a growing fascination with amusements and crazy costumes, reflecting an innocent need to keep the spirit of Halloween alive all year long. Bizarre, out-of-the-ordinary promotion schemes reflecting Halloween tendencies are just the ticket if you are looking for attention-getting gimmicks to advertise a business. Fashion shows; product displays of an extravagant variety; someone promoting the business dressed up like a bear, lion, or hippopotamus—all are effective publicity angles. When these activities are combined with deeply discounted prices or free food and refreshments, they work even better.

Unusual stunts are also ingenious devices to lock in free publicity. Larry Walters, an adventurous fellow from North Hollywood, received nationwide publicity when he attached 45 helium-filled weather balloons to a lawn chair and, wearing a parachute, took a ride up to 16,000 feet. After the event, Walters said he would be happy to endorse Sears' lawn chairs.

Publicity stunts do not have to be quite so extreme to receive attention by the media or your customers, but the principle is the same. The amount of free publicity you can obtain to promote your product or service is limited only by your ingenuity, imagination, and courage to begin.

BUILDING A CUSTOMER BASE WITH THE TELEPHONE

Businesses differ from one another, and rarely do you find two that are exactly the same. This is because people own and run businesses and people themselves are not the same. Even giant franchises, such as McDonald's, which turn out products by the billions using a specific, disciplined procedure in all locations, find they must cope with differences—mainly people differences.

Regardless of these differences, in the overall context of operating a successful business, all businesses share the common goals of needing to attract customers, produce sales, and make a profit. Whether you are the only person/employee involved in your business or you hire a large staff, people in your business must have a conscious awareness of these goals and strive continually to attain them.

One of the most overlooked devices for meeting these goals is the telephone. Perhaps like everything else we're so familiar with, we tend to take our telephones for granted. After all, practically every home and business in America has one or more. But therein lies the very secret of why the telephone is a terrific customer-base-building tool.

You can make good and profitable use of your time using the telephone to meet your business goals. One undeniable advantage of the telephone is its ability to allow you to interact with your potential customers—answer questions and overcome objections, uncover new opportunities, and locate customers using people-to-people direct communication. Studies have proven time and again that use of the telephone for business-building purposes produces fast results. Nevertheless, a great many businesses ignore the potential of telephone calling to build a customer base. Some view the method as a serious insensitive intrusion—an objectionable violation of privacy.

Telephone marketing, or *telemarketing* as the system is called, has an impressive track record. It has been used successfully to achieve business objectives whether it be to obtain magazine subscriptions, to locate customers for a carpet cleaning or repair business, or you name it. It is estimated that over $200 million worth of goods and services are sold over the telephone each day; and the cost of conducting business over the telephone is still small in comparison with other business expenses.

Telephone calling can be budgeted very accurately. Results can be measured weekly and even daily. Approaches can be modified or completely changed as your campaign progresses. Alternative messages can be tested against one another. And your telephone marketing program can be expanded or cut back any time the results warrant it.

Supplementing your direct-mail or leafleting activity with a telephone campaign may prove to be the most efficient media mix you've ever discovered because a telephone provides instant two-way communication and encourages people to make decisions. Direct mail and leaflets may be used to spark an idea and notify your potential customers of the availability of your products or services, but by following up with a telephone call, you can clinch the sale.

Planning Your Telemarketing Campaign

A telephone sales campaign can only be as successful as the planning that goes into its development. The essential parts of your plan consist of carefully spelling out objectives in advance of the campaign, establishing clear operating procedures, making clear-cut assignments of time and responsibility to carry out the program, evaluating results, and engaging in the telephone campaign with dedicated commitment.

Two essential keys are preparing the message in advance and having the message delivered by a highly trained person with voice appeal. If you must hire someone to do your calling, compensation can be a combination of a base-salary plus commission determined by results. In advance of the first call, a complete script must be carefully worked out, questions to be asked must be developed, benefits of the product or service must be spelled out, objections must be anticipated and replies worked out, and alternative closing statements must be developed.

Once your script has been polished to what seems to be perfection, it is time to do some testing. One way to proceed is to place four sets of 15 test calls—60 calls total. After each set of 15 calls, you should evaluate each part of the call for its effectiveness, and you should examine the objections that have come to light. This evaluation will almost certainly indicate modifications that should be made. After 60 calls, you should finalize the script.

You or your people should practice with the final script until delivery becomes natural and spontaneous. Listen to your own voice on tape; and if more than one person is doing the calling, listen to each other's presentations and don't hesitate to make constructive criticism.

This done, it's time to begin your campaign following these do's and don'ts:

1. Prepare mentally for your calls by turning off your own unrelated concerns and concentrate on your prospects' needs. You should be enthusiastic and positive or you shouldn't be calling.
2. Prepare physically for your calls by having all needed materials, information, and literature at your fingertips so you are never lost for answers to questions.
3. Always put yourself in the other person's situation with the constant reminder that the purpose of the call is to provide helpful information that the potential customer will want to hear.
4. Always keep smiling. "Dial a smile" and the person at the other end will hear it.
5. The pitch of your voice should be low but not gruff, high enough to be heard but not shrill. Your voice should exude confidence and reassurance, yet be friendly, natural, and conversational.

6. The ideal rate of speech for telephone selling is between 120 and 150 words a minute. No one likes to be "attacked" by a fast-talking salesperson. Too slow a delivery invites impatience and interruption.
7. Be a good listener. When two people are talking, no one is listening. Let the other person ask questions and be alert to telltale signs that your newfound business friend is about to make a decision.
8. Don't be in a hurry to hang up unless you have closed the sale. Even then, restate what has been agreed to so there can be no misunderstanding. Thank your new customer by name before hanging up and then go on to the next call.

Where to Get More Information

You can turn telephone calling into a successful business and by so doing call up an immense monetary reward. Remote marketing, at times using computer-calling technology, is a highly sophisticated way to reach and motivate clients, locate prospects, and build your business.

You can learn more about how telemarketing can improve sales, increase orders, and enhance customer relations, plus upgrade telephone skills and learn new sales techniques and how to effectively collect overdue bills by contacting your local telephone company. Most local telephone companies conduct workshops and seminars on these and other telephone-related subjects. They even provide videotapes demonstrating a variety of skills on such subjects as improving listening, developing professional voice, recognizing verbal clues to personality, timing calls, and teaching ethical practice to avoid insensitive intrusion.

You can also obtain assistance from telemarketing-research and selling-service firms. They will be listed in your local phone directory under "Telemarketing."

EXHIBITING AT TRADE SHOWS

If you have developed a new product or have the ability to home-manufacture a useful product, attending trade shows can boost you to riches.

In prebiblical times, merchants, manufacturers, and artisans from all parts of the then-civilized world would gather at specified times of the year to exchange their goods. Ever since, in spite of new ways to market products and services, people have been getting together to display their wares at trade fairs or, as they are more commonly known in the United States, trade shows.

Trade shows feature these advantages:

1. They offer an opportunity for both the buyer and seller to meet face-to-face, as the products shown are demonstrated and handled.

2. They offer a preselected audience with specified interests, who attend them for the common purpose of learning about products.
3. They offer an opportunity to reach people who are ordinarily not accessible to sales representatives and to uncover unknown buying interests and new products.
4. They are places where buyers can do comparative shopping, discuss their problems with technical people, iron out arrangements for mutually beneficial business transactions, and shorten the product selection and buying processes.
5. They offer an opportunity to establish a market, introduce a new product, locate new merchandise, and establish relationships necessary for conducting future business.

By reviewing the "Exhibit Schedule"—the yearly special edition of *Successful Meeting Magazine*—or Trade Shows and Professional Exhibits Directory, by Gale Research, Detroit, you can find a show that seems right for you. You will need to get more information about the shows you're interested in, and you can do so by writing the show management and asking for literature prepared for prospective exhibitors. Try to attend shows that most nearly match your product lines and interests. This will help you conserve funds and deal with products and services most compatible with your own.

Setting Up Your Exhibit

Once you have decided which show to attend, if you have a product to sell, you will want to reserve exhibit space. The most common unit of space for beginners is a 10-×-10-foot booth. There is often a price differential that depends on location or proximity to the main arena.

Next, you should design an exhibit, which must be portable. Set this up as far in advance of the trade show as possible in order to maximize the effectiveness of your display. If you have sufficient funds, get professional assistance in designing your exhibit. Generally, the price of trade-show space includes little more than a right to enter the show, a draped area, and a sign with your name on it.

The kind of exhibit you end up with depends, to a large extent, on the kind of message you are trying to put across, its complexity, the nature of your audience, and your budget. You may do very well with little more than some attractive backdrops and photographs, along with a table or two on which to lay out goods or conduct a simple demonstration. Or you may need to design and construct an elaborate display that might include a video or slide show.

Between these two extremes, you can made or buy attractive but simple display units. Some consist of a portable kit of rods and panels, held together by joining members, that can hold shelves, graphics, or merchandise. If you are not handy at making such displays, they can be purchased directly from manufacturers or local exhibit designers and producers. Sometimes they can even be rented.

Generally, trade-show space is rented for three or more days of that particular show; and while the show runs, your booth becomes your place of business. An exhibit booth is neither a warehouse nor a store window, although it has characteristics of both. Like an advertisement, it needs something to catch the eye. This can be a large photograph or sign, or better yet, something active or three-dimensional.

Once the interest of the visitor has been obtained, the exhibit must lead into a selling story, a demonstration, or some sort of presentation. Finally, there should be an effort made to advance the sale or tie down a commitment.

Handouts, brochures, sales aids, and specialty advertising items, such as key chains and the like, should be made readily available for the customer to take for later review and use.

It is estimated that hundreds of thousands of products are offered, resulting in more than $89 million worth of sales each year at trade shows held in the United States. Follow the practical tips on how to get the most out of the trade-show medium described here, and your skillful display of goods or services at trade shows will produce impressive, big-money trading results.

TAKE COMMAND OF SUCCESS OPPORTUNITIES

The secret to marketing is best described by the term *target your market*. Unless you define your market, know what your customers want, and understand what moves them to buy, you are leaving the fate of your business to chance. Targeting your market provides the opportunity to determine the optimum advertising, promotion, publicity, and sales-approach mix to bring business success.

Equipped with this knowledge, you can establish realistic sales goals. This, in turn, allows you to manage your business by evaluating measurable results of your marketing efforts.

16

Accomplish More in Less Time with Help from Others

There comes a time in the life cycle of every successful growing business when you need assistance from others to achieve your major purpose.

RECOGNIZING WHEN YOU NEED HELP

Generally the need for help in your business is stimulated by a desire to improve the quality or quantity of performance or manage growth effectively. In each case, the measure of your success is determined by fulfilling the following essential responsibilities. You must:

1. Know and understand the business you are in; concentrate on your central mission
2. Develop a plan to accomplish the most necessary work and establish priorities
3. Organize the work by identifying and grouping tasks; establish a timetable for completion of these tasks
4. Take inventory of your own personal abilities; list your own strengths and weaknesses
5. Focus your attention on what you do best; make the most of your special talents and effective use of time
6. Identify work that is best done by others, being mindful of your own limitations
7. Anticipate help needed from others by reviewing your actual business operating experience; prepare a schedule showing when this help will be needed

Without realizing it, you may already be hiring others to do work for you. In the conduct of your business, paying a fee for professional services is a form of hiring. You engage these services when there is a need and when others can perform the work better or more cost effectively. Services of an accountant, tax expert, attorney, advertising agency, print shop, telephone answering service, or travel agent are examples of work you may already be hiring others to perform.

While this form of hiring, otherwise known as contracting-out services, can be an excellent alternative, steady business growth, short-term surges in volume, or need to equip someone to take care of business during your absence may require greater access to people performing tasks on a daily basis. Estimating the amount of work to be performed, identifying the kind of work others are most needed to do, and developing a projection of costs relative to increased revenue will establish a base to begin.

KNOW WHAT YOU HAVE TO OFFER

Personnel policies are used to establish employment standards. Among the most important policies are compensation practices, including salary and benefit provisions, work rules, matters involving work time and time off, performance appraisal, promotions, training and development arrangements, complaint procedures, and layoff provisions.

Personnel policies serve three functions: (1) they aid recruitment by conveying to prospective employees what you have to offer; (2) in the event several employees are hired, they ensure uniform, fair treatment; and (3) they serve as tools for managing the human element in business operations.

Before hiring even one person, know that you have a wide selection of personnel policies from which to choose. A small owner-operated business may be unable to pay the highest wages, but may offer other meaningful incentives. An employer willing to offer training and development opportunities; latitude to exercise responsibility and independence; and recognition through a bonus plan, profit sharing, or stock options may have a distinct advantage in attracting quality personnel.

Good employees, motivated by the informality and challenge of small business, are often willing to tie their futures to yours; they hire on with inspired enthusiasm because of potential. Recall how tiny start-ups in the computer industry hired secretaries, electronics assemblers, and other entry-level personnel with a combination of cash and stock payments. Thousands of people accepting everyday jobs became rich beyond their wildest dreams when the company they loyally served went public.

Worker-satisfaction studies consistently show that pay ranks below recognition in relative importance. Praise for good work by someone in authority builds self-esteem. The ability to participate in decisions concerning work goals and standards can make a job more interesting and build commitment. A sense of upward mobility and career progress can be achieved by incentive payments when goals are achieved.

Benefits Can Be Cost-Effective

As of this writing, most benefit programs continue to be treated as tax-deductible business expenses. Therefore, you can still offer a benefit incentive package at far less cost to you than employees might otherwise be required to pay on their own. Noncash benefits reduce the amount of taxes employees might otherwise pay and often represent incentives, such as flexible work schedules, that money can't buy. If you demonstrate a sense of caring for an employee "partner" by providing benefits most valued by that member of the team, you will win longstanding loyalty and commitment to your mission.

From your perspective as an employer, hiring workers involves substantial hidden costs that are both necessary and prudent if such hiring produces sufficient increased revenue. However, you should not forget that hiring even one employee mandates legally required payments for social security, workers' compensation, unemployment insurance, and state disability premiums that, when added to other benefit costs, can amount to 25 percent or more of payroll. This means that if you pay a salary of $400 a week, for example, hiring an employee may actually be costing you $500 a week.

Where you are able to offer benefits at a lower cost than the employee may otherwise be able to arrange, the value of total compensation to the employee may actually be as much as $600 a week. When offering employment, be sure to make the candidate aware of the value of your benefits program in dollar terms so salary level is understood to be only part of the total compensation package.

A sound business practice is to think about, then place the personnel policies you choose on paper before hiring anyone. This exercise will clarify what you have to offer and what a good employee can expect from you.

KNOW WHAT WORK NEEDS DOING

Once you have a clear idea of what will be offered to attract and retain a good employee, you must decide precisely what work you want a good employee to do. Planned selection begins by preparing a written description of the job to be filled.

The term duplication has received a bad reputation from budget-cost cutters in large organizations who seek to eliminate redundancies. But in the positive sense of hiring someone to relieve you of work already done well, duplication can yield a generous return. Hiring someone capable of learning from you, doubling your effort, or handling routine tasks expands your capacity.

TABLE 16-1. Job Specification Format.

XYZ CORPORATION

Job title:
Primary responsibilities:
Reporting relationships:
Main duties (list them in order of importance and estimate percentage of time spent on each):
Other duties (list duties performed on an irregular basis so there will be no surprises):
Formal education or training required:
Experience required:
Technical and/or administrative skills required:
Supervisory experience required:
Licenses or certificates required (including driver's license):
Quality of performance:
Production standards:
Effectiveness in working with others (customers, staff, regulatory agencies, or any one else):
Initiative:
Job knowledge and promotional readiness:
Dependability:

Think about what duties must be performed to meet business objectives. Then decide what skills and experience one must have to perform the work. When these are clearly known, you will be prepared to match an applicant's qualifications to the job's requirements.

TABLE 16-1 shows a handy format for preparing a job specification.

PAYING FAIR WAGES

Supply and demand in your local labor market determines prevailing rates of pay. In practice, pay for any given job will fall within a range of pay established by all employers in your community who hire the same kind of worker.

Salary surveys are the most reliable indicator of prevailing rates. The rate you actually pay will be tempered by what you can afford.

Employment agencies are a valuable source of information on prevailing rates for a wide variety of jobs. The nature of their business gives them daily exposure to actual rates offered by employers actively recruiting employees.

The U.S. Bureau of Labor Statistics (BLS) is another valuable source for prevailing-rate survey data. This federal agency publishes results from wage studies conducted in almost 150 geographic areas. Its findings are stated as an average of rates paid by employers in each survey area. BLS studies include almost every manufacturing and service class of employment.

You can get copies of these surveys at your library or by writing Area Wage Surveys, Bureau of Labor Statistics, Publications Sales Center, PO Box 2145, Chicago, IL 60690.

A convenient way to use BLS data is to find in the survey the average pay rate for the classification of employee you intend to hire. Consider this rate to be the midpoint of what all other employers in your area actually pay. Then take 85 percent of this midpoint rate and use it as a minimum of a reasonable salary range. Next take 115 percent of the midpoint rate and use it as a maximum of a reasonable salary range.

For example, if $400 a week is the average rate for the entry-level class of employee you intend to hire, use this formula:

$400 × 85% = $340 a week
$400 × 115% = $460 a week
Minimum of salary range: $340 a week
Midpoint of salary range: $400 a week
Maximum salary range: $460 a week

Using this salary range, over a period of several years you can increase earnings of a new employee by 35 percent at 5- to 8-percent intervals, based on merit and performance, without a job change.

This method establishes a planned pay structure, allowing you to match pay with performance and accomplishment of goals. It also provides flexibility to handle special situations.

When making employment offers, always remind the candidate that total earnings from your firm, over a period of years, can amount to hundreds of thousands of dollars. Over a period of 30 years, an employee's total earnings can approach or exceed $1 million.

FINDING THE RIGHT PEOPLE

Equipped with knowledge of what you have to offer and aware of precisely what you want an employee to do, you are ready to find the right person. While undertaking this task, be aware that recruiting and selecting the one right employee can cost $1,000 or more. Add to this the cost of training, which may require another $2,000 to $4,000, and you'll see that, as a small-business owner, you cannot afford many mistakes in hiring.

All employers take the same risk: your job is to mitigate it. The best way is to mirror the proven staffing techniques used by larger, established companies to the extent that you can. It is far more efficient to adhere to an unrushed, methodical selection process aimed at attracting a valued employee whom you want to work with for many years than to make a snap hiring decision.

RECRUITMENT SOURCES

You should not select a recruitment method that produces such a large number of applicants that you are unable to effectively screen and interview them. Neither do you want to use a method producing so few applicants that you are effectively deprived of comparative choice.

Source of qualified applicants are word-of-mouth, private employment agencies, state- or local-government employment development agencies, local schools or colleges, and newspaper advertising.

Word-of-Mouth

Small-business owners consistently report that word-of-mouth recruitment yields better employees, less turnover, is less costly, and is the most satisfactory source of personnel.

If you know your business, you probably already know associates, employees, and prospects who would consider a job offer from you. Many well-qualified individuals are not actively seeking a change of employer, but their interest could be kindled by the prospect of a new and potentially better opportunity.

Where a business already employs a few good workers, they are often most persuasive in letting others know they are happy on their jobs. This kind of ''advertising'' is apt to produce some exceptional applicants who will want to join them.

When combined with sound job design, interviewing, and experience verification methods, word-of-mouth can be an excellent source of talent.

Private Employment Agencies

Generally small-business owners find private employment agencies to be the next most satisfactory recruitment source. Agencies are paid a fee by the employer, the referred applicant, or some combination of the two; and in exchange, they can save you time and money.

Reliable employment agencies earn their fees by providing valuable recruitment, screening, and selection services. They perform work for you by advertising for employee applicants, screening responses, interviewing, testing, verifying references, and often training applicants, but final selection steps are left to you.

Temporary Personnel Employment Agencies

Temporary agencies go a step further by assigning trained people to your work location to perform work for which you contract or pay at an hourly or weekly rate. Rates of pay are generally higher than you might offer one of your own new hires, but they are negotiable.

When negotiating rates, keep in mind that the temporary person an agency assigns to you remains an employee of the agency during the contract period. This reduces your overhead because the agency takes care of all legally required payroll costs—social security, unemployment insurance, workers' compensation—and performs all payroll accounting, including deductions for income taxes, group insurance, and other benefits. You are not billed for services when work is not performed on holidays, vacations, or in cases of illness.

Let the agency representative know that if the employee assigned works out satisfactorily, you may have a need to hire that person as your own employee. Temporary-help agencies set minimum time requirements on such assignments before allowing you to hire the employee without a fee. Ask them for terms and conditions. Use the temporary time as a trial period to evaluate work performance with the clear understanding that neither party has a binding obligation of the employee's future service. It is surprising how often this method can introduce you to employees with top-notch talent.

Remember, too, that the employment agency is itself a small business and must bill at a sufficient rate to make a profit. Don't be such a tight negotiator that the agency is unable to afford to send you a qualified employee. It is not economical to try to fit a person to a job for which he or she is not suited even for temporary periods.

Government Employment Agencies

Every state has an employment development agency with branches in most local communities. Sometimes cities and counties also have specialized employee-training and placement agencies. Office locations can be found in your telephone directory.

These government employment agencies strive to provide recruitment and selection services of the same caliber as private employment agencies. In recent years, they have directed primary effort to test, train, and place lower-skilled employees in suitable jobs, thus providing a valuable service. Unfortunately, a great many qualified employees fail to register with these agencies, thus government agencies are not always able to provide comprehensive service.

The key to effective use of government employment agencies is presenting a specific job description to a placement coordinator and letting him or her know you can't afford hiring mistakes. A top-notch professional placement officer will often be able to produce a qualified employee anxious to prove experienced ability.

Public and Private Schools and Colleges

Schools and colleges, whether private or public, often provide placement services for their students. Some even develop specialized work-study programs in cooperation with selected businesses or industries to ensure that coordinated education and experience requirements are fully satisfied. Generally, students have a strong desire to offer everything they have in exchange for a chance to enter the labor force. They often seek mentors and demonstrate high loyalty when given an opportunity to combine forces with someone willing to take the time to show them the ropes.

The key to using this resource is to insist that referrals be screened to locate students willing to accept your conditions and standards of employment with enthusiasm. Let the placement coordinator know you are willing to coach, teach, and train the right student who is anxious to achieve reasonable expectations.

Newspaper Advertising

Newspaper recruiting is most commonly performed through classified advertisements. When using this recruitment tool, realize that you are committing yourself to perform the full range of tasks that employment agencies make a business of conducting. This means you will be substituting your time to perform work for money you could otherwise pay an employment agency.

The key to effective newspaper advertising is to draft the advertisement so it is highly appealing to *qualified* candidates but screens out unqualified job seekers.

Mindful of clarity and simplicity but also appeal, try to tailor your advertisement to reach the caliber of employee you seek. This is best accomplished by writing the advertisement from the applicant's viewpoint, and the question the applicant is asking is, "What's in it for me?" For example, "An exceptional opportunity offering salary increases with progressive responsibility for a qualified office assistant," has more appeal than, "Wanted, a high school graduate to do routine office work needed now."

If you don't want to be inundated by telephone calls, include only an address for mail response. If you don't want drop-ins, include only a post office box for reply.

You can get assistance in preparing your advertisement from your newspaper's classified advertising department; you will be advised on all key elements of the advertisement, including how to avoid discrimination pitfalls. Be sure to give a copy of the job specification to the paper's advertising representative.

Job Specification—Your Ultimate Recruiting Tool

Think of the job specification as your most fundamental recruitment tool. This is the instrument you must learn to depend on to match requirements of the job with education and experience of applicants. Your job specification is the measuring rod with which you recruit applicants having "can-do" abilities. Always provide representatives of recruitment sources with a copy of your job specifications and make sure to explain terms, phrases, and conditions contained in the document. Make them understand that it is a waste of your time and theirs to interview applicants lacking minimum qualifications.

When dealing with employment agencies or school and college placement offices, let them know you are counting on their professional judgment to view an applicant as a whole person rather than emphasizing any one isolated skill or ability. You would rather have applicants with balanced skills and abilities than a person most skilled in one area but seriously lacking in other significant areas.

SELECTING ONE FROM MANY

In the recruitment process, you found people with can-do qualities. In the selection process, you must find the one best person with "will-do" qualities.

The tools for selecting the person with the most promising will-do abilities are (1) the application form, (2) the employment interview, and (3) verifying information. With these tools, you will be able to screen out unqualified or lesser-qualified applicants and screen in applicants with greatest probability of success if hired. In its simplest form, effective screening is the process of matching the qualifications of each applicant against the predetermined standards contained in your job specification.

APPLICATION FORM

As with any tool used to do a job, the more skillfully you use the application form, the easier and better the job will be performed. The application form is much more than a written expression that someone needs a job. It is your stethoscope for studying a potential employee's education and work history.

Recent antidiscrimination and equal-opportunity laws compel use of modern application forms requesting only job-related information. Avoid any form that seeks data on age, physical disability (unless specific physical characteristics are required to do the job), race, religion, sex, or marital status.

Preprinted application forms and other forms needed to help accomplish personnel management tasks may be purchased from a variety of sources. Look in your telephone directory under the following subjects: Forms (Accounting, Business, Legal, Personnel, etc.), Business Forms and Systems, or Stationers.

Never interview or hire anyone until he or she has completed and submitted an employment application form, even if your recruitment sources have referred the candidate. There are both practical and legal reasons for doing so.

How to Review an Application Form

Always scrutinize the completed application form before conducting interviews. Here's what to look for:

1. Education qualifications
2. Experience qualifications
3. Recency of education and experience
4. Thoroughness in completing the application
5. Care in completing the application
6. Previous earnings and salary history
7. Any time gaps in employment history

In most cases, 10 to 30 percent of all candidates will be screened out by a careful analysis of the employment application.

Unless your recruitment sources have produced very few candidates, your time will be better spent carefully following the remaining steps in the selection process rather than in interviewing those not matching your standards.

Record the deficiency you found on the applications and send all screened-out applicants a courteous but brief letter thanking them for submitting the application, and saying that it will be kept on file but that they are not requested to attend an interview at this time. Do not give any specific reasons for your choice, and keep all applications on file for at least one year.

EMPLOYMENT INTERVIEW

The purpose of the employment interview is to make a specific evaluation of the applicant's qualifications and to determine his or her suitability to work specifically for you. Understand fully that your goal is to *select* the right person, not *reject* applicants out of hand. All applicants have strengths and weaknesses. Your job is to weigh both favorable and unfavorable characteristics to find the person with preferred balance. Any weaknesses must substantially be offset by paramount strengths.

Never make an employment offer until you have seen all whom you've determined to interview. Comparing and contrasting applicants will facilitate final selection.

An employment interview is serious business, not merely an occasion to have a friendly chat. Your time and money are on the line. Here's what you do: prepare, begin the interview, get the facts, and add it up.

Prepare

1. Set aside an hour for each interview and allow at least 15 minutes between interviews.
2. Arrange a comfortable, relaxed setting free from distractions, including telephone interruptions.
3. Notify the candidate of the date, time, and place for the interview and make sure someone will be available to greet the candidate at that time.
4. Arrange employment applications in the order of the interview schedule. Scrutinize each application again and note areas that require explanation and probing. Have only one candidate's application before you at the time of an interview.
5. Know what you are looking for; have copies of the job specifications available for both you and the candidate.

Begin the Interview

1. Start a small-talk conversation by making a general comment or two such as, "I hope you didn't have trouble getting here" or "Are you familiar with the area?"
2. Ease into briefly describing your firm and the job; talk about pay and advantages of your firm. From here on, limit yourself to questions—your goal is to interview the candidate, not be interviewed by the candidate. Don't talk too much.

Get the Facts

1. Refer to the application and ask, "I see that you worked for (previous firm) for (length of time), tell me about your job there?"
2. Questions to ask about experience include:
   What job(s) have you had that most qualify you for this position?
   What were your specific duties?
   How did your final responsibilities compare with initial responsibilities?
   Why do you feel you are fully qualified for this job?
   What sort of person was your supervisor?

What did you like most (least) about your supervisor?
What did you think about the people you worked with?
What areas of gratitude do you feel toward your previous employer?
Why do you consider yourself dependable?
What do you want most from a position with this firm?
What are your strengths (weaknesses)?
What will you contribute most to the success of this firm?
What are your salary, benefit, and working-condition expectations?
Why did you leave or want to leave previous employment?

3. Always ask questions to get clarification of ambiguous comments or items on the application. Whenever the candidate hedges a response, follow up with a probing question to get specifics. Never ask questions that are not job-related, particularly about marital status, philosophy, political preference, age, race, religion, and social habits.

4. Be completely objective; allow the candidate full opportunity to express meaning; don't interrupt. Listen, observe, and evaluate.

Add It Up

1. As the candidate responds to questions, make brief notes on strong points, weak points, and matters needing verification.

2. Make notes on personality traits, temperament, poise, attitudes, intelligence, motivation, initiative, ambition, preferences, and interests.

3. After thanking the candidate for the opportunity to get to know him or her, explain that you will make a final decision after interviewing all candidates and that final details on compensation will be discussed when you contact the successful candidate.

4. After the candidate has left and before the next interview, rate the candidate on a scale of 1 to 6 on each critical job requirement.

5. At the conclusion of all interviews, compare the candidates and rate them on a scale of 1 to 6.

VERIFYING INFORMATION

Up to this point, all information has come from the candidate. Objectivity requires that you get another point of view. Understand that you need to get reliable confirmation and expanded information; you are not looking for a snitch.

The many ways to verify information include mail and telephone inquiries; personal visits; and review of school transcripts, certificates, and police records.

The telephone is much preferred over mail inquiries because of speed, cost, ability to conduct dialog, and willingness of references to say more freely what may be difficult to put on paper.

When verifying information, look for:

1. Any inconsistencies with information on the employment application (confirm all dates and other objective statistical data)
2. Accuracy of names, places, education classes taken, jobs actually held, and reasons for leaving
3. Facts concerning job duties, attendance, dependability, quantity of work performed, quality of work performed, any disciplinary problems, attitude, ability to get along with others, acceptance of constructive criticism, strengths, weaknesses, significant accomplishments, ability to supervise, teamwork abilities, maturity, judgment, initiative, motivation, flexibility, and willingness to learn
4. Would the previous employer rehire the candidate? Would an existing employer recommend the candidate?

Compare these findings by again rating all interviewed candidates on a scale of 1 to 6.

FINAL SELECTION AND JOB OFFER

Equipped with information produced by skillful use of your selection tools, rank the candidates in the order of selection preference. Arrange for the top-ranked candidate to meet with you to discuss compensation terms and conditions and other hiring details. When agreement is reached, confirm starting date in writing.

Send all other candidates a courteous but brief letter informing them that another candidate was selected for the position and thanking them for their time and interest. Do not give any specific reasons for your choice, and keep all applications on file for at least one year.

When Hiring Close Friends or Relatives

Your brother-in-law needs a job. Your sister is putting on the pressure. What do you do?

You can bring efficiency and economy to your business operation by offering close friends and relatives equal opportunity to participate in your structured selection process, with no preferential treatment. If the close friend or relative is selected as the best qualified candidate, subsequent to hiring, always apply all employment standards, terms, and conditions impartially.

EFFECTIVE SUPERVISION

Once you've hired the right person for the right job, you must still strive to have that person do his or her best. The purpose of supervision is to direct activities of people so work gets done efficiently, effectively, and economically. The probability of this occurring is highest when people are trained, motivated, and recognized.

People-centered business owners are leaders who motivate employees to exceed expectations. They expand employee awareness that how they perform work articulates a dramatic statement about regard for excellence, productivity, imagination, pride, and success. In turn, rewards are shared.

Be cautious about trying to achieve perfection. Rather, be responsive to your employees and the working conditions you foster. Initiate action to meet your business and employee needs, yet evaluate and modify decisions if earlier judgments are not accomplishing the intended results.

PROGRESSIVE DISCIPLINE

The progressive discipline concept has evolved from countless court decisions and labor arbitration hearings. Its central premise is, depending on the seriousness of offense, employees must have forewarning of what constitutes a disciplinary offense; and if the offense continues, discipline shall become progressively severe.

When an employee's performance persists below standard or the employee violates a known work rule, you will meet legal requirements by following steps in the progressive discipline process.

1. *Oral reminders*. Discuss the offense and express confidence that the rule will not be violated again and that performance can be raised to standard.
2. *Written reminders*. Remind employee of prior warnings and reach agreement that the offense will not occur again. Write a memo to the employee summarizing the agreement and warn that continuation of the unacceptable behavior will result in further disciplinary action.
3. *Decision making—leave or suspension*. Discuss the offense; dismiss the employee from work for rest of the day with pay. Tell the employee that he or she is to decide whether or not there is a desire to continue working for you and a willingness to adhere to standards. Instruct employee to report his or her decision to you before work the next day. A suspension uses the

same process, but here the employee is released from work for one or more days without pay.

4. *Termination*. If the employee decides to continue working for you, he or she is required to sign a letter agreeing either to correct his or her behavior or to termination. If behavior is not corrected, the employee is terminated.

Tell employees clearly what is expected of them. When they understand this, they have a stunning propensity to want to respond. Be fair, be reasonable, share your expectations and rewards; your employees will be your strongest allies on the road to success.

17

Keeping Account of Your Business

We are all creatures of habit. As this fact applies to your business, good business habits generally result in success; bad business habits most often result in failure.

Studies show that of all the reasons businesses fail to succeed, the second most prevalent reason is poor record-keeping habits. The most prevalent reason is poor management, and this ties in with the ability, or lack of it, to keep accurate books of account and other business records.

WHY YOU NEED ACCURATE RECORDS

Records tell you how your business is scoring and thus keep you out of trouble. Trouble comes when your record keeping does not provide facts needed for making sound decisions.

Records can help carry on management activities, such as inventory control, buying, and selling; they can tell you your cash position, your daily business transactions, and spot established trends. They are essential in preparing taxes and planning, and much more.

It is practically impossible to get a business loan from a bank without good records and a properly prepared financial statement. it may even be difficult to secure credit in any form without some business records. Bankers and other credit granters need to study your balance sheet and other operating statements in order to decide whether credit should be extended. Your records must provide the basis for these statements.

Equally as important as the management and credit functions of good records is the requirement by federal- and local-government taxing agencies for adequate records. The responsibility for maintaining records and proving their accuracy falls on the taxpayer. Federal and local income taxes, payroll taxes, sales taxes, personal property taxes, and an increasing number of other laws and regulations require certain reports that are easier to prepare and substantiate if the figures are maintained in a good record-keeping system. If you are ever audited, records backing up tax returns must be available. How long you keep your records depends on the statute of limitations set forth by local and federal laws.

KEYS TO GOOD RECORD KEEPING

Maintaining accurate and up-to-date books of account need not be a burdensome chore. The real secret is to set up a simplified, but comprehensive record-keeping system; adopt a regimented procedure for making all entries; and set aside a definite period of time each day or each week, preferably at the same time of the day and same day each week, to keep your books current. No one business will use all the various types of records available. In fact, you may need only a few basic records for your particular business.

To have an effective record-keeping system, you should follow these four rules:

1. Any record-keeping system you use must be easy to set up, easy to use, and easy to understand.
2. The record-keeping system should be simple or convenient enough to allow maximum accuracy on matters directly related to your business. Don't keep records on things you don't need; keep precise records on things you do need.
3. You should have a systematic record-keeping method and system that is consistent from beginning to end.
4. Your record-keeping system should be up-to-date, which means your system must encourage timely, current entry of information.

CHOOSING THE SYSTEM THAT'S RIGHT FOR YOU

Your reason for keeping a record dictates the form your records will take. In the beginning, as a proprietor of a very small business, you are interested in keeping a set of books that can be maintained by persons with little or no experience or training in bookkeeping and accounting.

A number of "one-book" record-keeping systems and computer programs are available at low prices from local retail stores. Some come with instructions, forms, and spreadsheets designed for specific kinds of business, while others are for use in small businesses of a general nature. In addition, some trade associations, manufacturers, wholesalers, and tax-preparation firms offer their customers record-keeping systems—some specially designed for a particular type of business.

Which record-keeping and information system to use will depend on whether you desire to start out with a manual or an automated system. You should also consider whether you need a general system or will be better served by a system having special applications to your industry.

Some planning is necessary. You must determine if you want something just to get you started, that you will discard later, or if your future plans include expanding the system as you grow. The purpose of this planning is to get a clear fix on what you want your system to handle and produce, when you expect to change or replace your system, and the form and frequency of information you will want to maintain.

MANUAL RECORD-KEEPING SYSTEMS

Some well-known and readily available general bookkeeping systems, which are easy to use yet meet all basic record-keeping requirements, are described in this section.

Dome Simplified Monthly Bookkeeping Record 612 and *Dome Simplified Weekly Bookkeeping Record 600* are published by Dome Publishing Company, Dome Building, Providence, RI 02903, and are available in stationery stores and chain stores. They contain the following forms sufficient for recording the results of one year's business: monthly record of income and expenses, annual summary sheet of income and expenditures, weekly payroll records covering 15 employees, and individual employee compensation records. They also contain general instructions, specimen filled-in monthly record of income and expenses, and a list of 276 expenses that are legal deductions for federal income-tax purposes. The records were designed by a certified public accountant (CPA) and fit every type and kind of business.

Ideal System: General Bookkeeping and Tax Record 3611 and *Weekly Bookkeeping and Tax Record M2025* are published by Dymo Visual Systems Inc., PO Box 1568, Augusta, GA 30903. They are designed for every type of business, profession, trade, farm, or ranch operating primarily on a cash basis. They can be started any time, and there are sufficient forms for recording the results of one year's business.

Blackbourn's General Business Bookkeeping System by Blackbourn Systems, Inc., 1821 University Avenue, St. Paul, MN 55104, provides for accounting, inventory, and personnel records in quick, easy entries. It lists merchandise payments and record of sales and receipts on a left-hand page, and operating expenses on the opposite right-hand page. It shows monthly record of sales and monthly balance sheets with cash on hand, amounts owed, and amounts due. Other sections include accounts payable, complete with discount columns; inventory sheets; employee social-security and income-tax records; sales record by departments; notes receivable and payable; and depreciation schedule. It even includes a list of suggested, allowable tax deductions.

If you want a manual system that has special application to your business, contact the major trade association for your industry and ask for a description of any record-keeping system it offers. You'll be amazed to find this can cover everything from agriculture and pig farming to travel-agency and veterinary systems.

AUTOMATED RECORD-KEEPING SYSTEMS

Astute information and records management is absolutely vital to business success. And today you have access to inexpensive automation that was not available, at any price, to entrepreneurs starting businesses years ago.

The personal computer is one of the most important business management tools available to command operating success. This chief assistant, properly used, represents the most significant addition to small-business equipment in this century. It can give every business owner the power and competitive edge that used to be the exclusive preserve of big business. It can perform record keeping, billing, inventory control, product research, word processing, sales, and other information management tasks that previously took the work of a sizeable paid staff.

Choosing the Right Software

If you don't already own a personal computer but intend to use one for business, the importance of selecting software *before* buying a computer cannot be overemphasized. You should find the program that best suits your needs and then find the computer that is capable of running that program.

To locate suitable software, visit your library and ask to see the premier directory of available software—*Microcomputer Software Directory*—published by Computing Publications, Inc., Princeton, New Jersey. This valuable resource describes more than 3,500 computer software packages designed to have maximum application to small-business operations. The directory is a quick reference guide divided into six main sections so you have a variety of ways to find the software right for you. Most important, the directory groups software packages by type of business and industry it is designed to serve and gives salient information about hardware requirements. The directory also details names and addresses of manufacturers and suppliers, so you can get names of local dealers who will give you maximum after-sales support.

Before buying a software package, always be sure you receive a comprehensive demonstration, including hands-on experience, preferably using hardware you intend to purchase. If you have an immediate need for a simplified, inexpensive, automated bookkeeping system, just to get started, the publishers of the Dome manual bookkeeping system also produce a software version: *Accounting by Computer—Dome Simplified Bookkeeping System Software*, Great American Software, Inc., PO Box 910, Amherst, NH 03031.

It uses the precise format of the Dome ledger-book system. It allows entry of receipts and expenses on each *page* on the computer screen and produces income, expense, payroll, and other financial reports. It has pop-up accessories, such as a calculator, notepad, list of accounts, perpetual calendar, analysis by payee, and account or type of expense for the past year, month, or day. It runs on IBM, Apple, Commodore, and Tandy computers.

OTHER RECORD-KEEPING ASSISTANCE

You don't need a degree in accounting to maintain useful records. But if you get impatient working with numbers, you may want to farm out this function to a business bookkeeping service. You can find such services in your telephone directory under the heading "Bookkeeping Services." Two such bookkeeping service firms are described below.

Binex Automated Business Systems, Binex Corp., 4441 Auburn Blvd., Sacramento, CA 95841, is a complete computer-based report system capable of providing an income statement, balance sheet, cash flow analysis, vendor analysis, and a variety of other information. BINEX also produces Withholding Tax Statements (W-2 forms), data for federal and state employment taxes, sales taxes, and complete employee payroll history. Because the family of computer programs is so complete and flexible, local BINEX outlets or franchisers can provide you with the exact information you need in your small business.

General Business Services, Inc., 51 Monroe Street, Rockville, MD 20850, has locally authorized business counselors who provide complete, easy-to-maintain, preprinted, manual one-write or computerized record-keeping systems, custom designed for sole proprietors, partnerships, and corporations. The system includes a monthly profit-and-loss statement and proof of accuracy in meeting IRS requirements. It also offers, on an optional basis, accounts receivable, computerized monthly billings, collection system for delinquent accounts, and a tax-preparation service for employed individuals.

ADDITIONAL BUSINESS RECORDS AND WHAT THEY TELL YOU

In addition to general bookkeeping records, you should maintain the following records as needed: sales, cash, inventory and purchase, fixed asset, credit, employee, and operating plan.

Sales Records

Sales records provide facts that you can use to determine sales trends.

Record of Individual Sales Transactions. Helps you to account for outward flow of goods. You should have a sales slip or a cash-register-tape record for all merchandise leaving your inventory. Sales slips should be prenumbered and each number accounted for.

Accountability Records. Shows how your firm is making or losing money. By subtracting the cost of sales (the cost of the items sold) from your sales for that month, you get your gross profit. From this gross, you subtract other expenses to get your net profit before taxes. By breaking down your profit-and-loss statement by departments or by significant types of merchandise, you can determine whether a department or a type of goods is paying its way in terms of space occupied, work involved, and other costs. Some firms go a step further and make up a profit-and-loss statement on each salesperson.

Summary of Daily Sales. This summary (by salesperson or type of merchandise) is helpful in figuring trends in sales (seasonal, weekly, and so on). It makes up the record of sales for accounting purposes.

Cash Records

Cash records alert you to what is happening to your cash.

Daily Cash Reconciliation. Provides data (in summary form) for entry in the cash-receipts journal. These data are picked up from cash-register tapes (or other sources of cash-receipts information) and are reconciled according to beginning-of-day and end-of-day balance changes and bank deposits.

Cash Receipts Journal. Lists all the cash coming into your business and its source. The amounts entered in this journal should be deposited *intact* in the bank. Never use cash receipts for paying small bills. Pay them by check or with money from your petty-cash fund.

Bank Reconciliation. Necessary for determining whether your firm's checkbook agrees with the bank's records. You or some trusted person who does not have access to your cash receipts or checks should receive the monthly bank statement and prepare the reconciliation. The reconciled bank balance should be checked against both your bank book and your general ledger account for cash in bank.

Inventory and Purchase Records

Inventory and purchase records provide facts needed for buying and selling.

Inventory Control Record. Essential for making buying-and-selling decisions. Some firms control their stock by frequently taking physical-unit inventories. Others use dollar-inventory records, which give a rough idea of what their inventory (based on gross-profit margins) may be from day-to-day in terms of dollars. Firms with thousands of different items (drugstores, for example) find dollar-inventory records easier to use than physical-inventory control. Such records give them their total inventory in dollars.

Item Perpetual Inventory Record. Provides a ready balance of stock on hand. Some firms selling big-ticket items use an inventory card or computer entry for each class of item. They post details of merchandise received and sold on them. They check the accuracy of the balance shown on the entries by making periodic spot checks on the number of units in the stockroom.

Model Stock Plan. Provides a record of basic stock in sizes, colors, types, price, and amounts. It is sometimes called the *never-out list.*

Out-of-Stock Sheet. Sometimes called a *want* sheet. It notifies a buyer that certain items need to be reordered. Items in low supply should be listed early enough to allow time for delivery before the stock is exhausted.

Open-to-Buy Record. Helps you prevent overstocking by adjusting purchases to sales. It is a running account of the dollar amount that can be bought without jeopardizing the inventory position that you try to maintain.

Purchase-Order File. Tells what has been ordered and its status (for example, in transit, expected in 15 days, and so on). Some firms keep this file by making a copy of each purchase order and jotting down the expected delivery dates, changes, and so on.

Open-Purchase Order File. Helps you to tell whether shipments are coming through on time. It is particularly helpful for merchandising fashion items and replacement parts and for merchandise involving timing. Some merchants make an extra copy of their purchase orders to use for this file.

Supplier File. Provides a handy reference on your suppliers. It is helpful when negotiating with a supplier because you can quickly figure the annual amount of business you do with each. You can set up this file by using extra copies of your purchase orders and filing them under suppliers' names.

Return Goods File. Provides a record of merchandise returned to supplier by dates, amounts, and reasons. It helps to facilitate payments and control quality.

Price Change Book. Records markdowns and markups by dates, amounts, and percentages.

Fixed-asset Records

Fixed-asset records help you keep track of business assets, equipment, and insurance coverage.

Fixture and Personal Property Records. Needed for recording the purchase, the date, and the price of all fixtures, display and personal property items, and for computing depreciation allowances. They are also useful to record which items may be in the possession of employees or sold for salvage.

Equipment Record. Essential for preparing income tax returns if you wish to take advantage of depreciation deductions. It shows the nature of each piece of equipment, the date you acquired it, its costs, estimated life, and method of depreciation.

Insurance Register. Helpful when filing claims for losses and during annual review of insurance coverage with a qualified insurance adviser. This register shows policy numbers, companies, kinds and amounts of coverage, expiration dates, and premiums.

Credit Records

Credit records help keep track of who owes you and whether they are paying on schedule.

Charge Account Application. Helps you decide whether to extend credit to a customer. This form shows the customer's place of employment, bank, and other pertinent information. It should also indicate credit limits.

Accounts Receivable Aging List. Shows length of time that customers are delinquent and helps you to tell which ones may become bad debts. This sheet lists in one column the receivables dating from the past month to the current month and shows total balance for each customer. The portions of the total that are from the previous month, the month before that, and so on, are shown in appropriate columns. These are your potential bad debts.

Employee Records

Employee records are necessary to control costs related to hiring employees and paying wages.

Record of Employee Earnings and Amounts Withheld. By months, quarters, and each year. It is essential in preparing payroll tax returns and furnishing employees with required W-2 forms and corresponding state forms. This record should also show the amounts withheld for social security.

Employee's Withholding Exemption Certificate (Form W-4). Supporting record for the withholding exemptions taken by your employees. The law requires employees to file new exemption certificates once a year if there has been a change in their exemption status.

Employment Eligibility Verification (Form I-8). Used to verify the identity and individual's eligibility for employment in the United States to prevent hiring of illegal aliens.

Record of Hours Worked. Shows hours worked each day by each nonexecutive employee. It proves your compliance with the law on minimum wages and overtime and is also useful in keeping track of payroll costs and absences caused by illness, vacation time, and tardiness.

Record of Expense Allowances (and reimbursements paid yourself and employees who incur expenses in connection with their jobs). Helps in budgeting and controlling personnel expense allowance and supports income-tax deduction.

Employment Applications. Provide a permanent record on each applicant hired. They can be used also to prove good faith when employment of underage persons is alleged.

Record of Changes in Rate of Pay. This record shows the nature of the change, authorization, and reason for rates of pay.

Record of Reasons for Termination of Employment. Helps in contesting unwarranted claims for unemployment compensation and for answering personal reference checks by future employers. Some firms include this record on the employment application form, which they file as "inactive" when the person is no longer employed.

Record of Employee Benefits. Helps in reviewing what you spend for benefits on each employee, such as group hospitalization, life insurance, retirement, paid holidays, paid vacations, and so on.

Job Descriptions (for each job). Provides a list of the qualifications you need in an employee. It is useful in training new employees and can help prevent confusion by spelling out what is done by whom.

Crucial Incidents Record (for each employee). Helpful in reviewing the employee's progress, or when considering pay changes or promotions. This record describes briefly the unusual (good or bad) things that the employee has done on the job.

Operating Plan Records

Operating plan records help you establish your overall operating plan and keep you on track in carrying out your plan.

Operating Plan. Provides goals for your operation during a certain period of time: week, month, or season. You project what you plan to do during the coming period (before the period starts) in terms of sales (broken down into classes that are significant for your operation) and what expenses (fixed, controllable, and discretionary) will be. By these forecasts, you can estimate your financial position in terms of cash, receivables, inventory, and payables at the end of the period.

Operating Summary. Provides a basis for determining whether your operating plan was successful. It compares what actually happened during the period with the goals you set before the period started. The summary should include the same items as those in your operating plan.

Sales Promotion Plan. Helps you plan, coordinate, and control sales promotion activities, such as advertising, display, and special events.

ANALYZING YOUR RECORDS

Having a solid set of records available when you need them can be a godsend. Taking time to plan your system for "at-will" information entry, storage, and retrieval is precisely the technique used by other successful businesses to win handsome profits. Organizing your records allows you to operate at peak efficiency when it comes time to analyze your business.

Are You Handling Your Records Efficiently?

The following questions are designed to help check your methods for handling records. As you study these questions, they may suggest others that could be helpful in finding and eliminating any wasted motion that might have crept into your record keeping.

In preparing monthly statements to send to customers, do you use antiquated methods such as copying from a ledger card? Some businesses save time and work by preparing statements and ledger cards at the same time, one being a carbon copy of the other, or computerizing this process. Others attach copies of sales tickets to the statement, which show only the total charges for the month and the customer's balance. This saves time and effort.

Are you handling payroll data more than once? Do you, for example, record payroll data in a payroll journal, then write it on a payroll check stub, and finally write it again on an individual employee record? The use of an inexpensive one-write or computer system will enable you to handle the payroll journal, check stub, and employee ledger in one operation.

Do you maintain unnecessary ledger records of your accounts payable? Many small businesses have found that a file of unpaid bills works as well and requires less clerical effort than maintaining duplicate records. Check with your accountant on the advantages of the voucher system for handling payables.

Are you missing the boat by not using small-business computers for record keeping and analysis? Electronic calculators and relatively inexpensive business computers provide great record-keeping assistance to small-business owners. Programs have been written specifically to account for cash receipts, inventory control, and a host of other record-keeping needs. Such programs will produce electronic tabulations and printouts for record purposes.

Are old records cluttering up your storage space? Not all records need to be saved forever. Work out a record retention program with the help of your accountant and attorney, and then destroy records in accordance with that program. You may want to check out the possibilities of putting some records— ones that the law requires—on microfilm or computer disc.

What Are Your Records Telling You?

You don't have to be a financial wizard to review and analyze your business records to see how they point the way to bigger profits. All you really have to do is ask yourself some basic questions as you look at the figures. Here are some essential questions you should ask as you perform this task:

■ How much business (cash and credit) am I doing? How much is tied up in receivables?

■ How are my collections? What are my losses from credit sales? Who owes me money? Who is delinquent? Should I continue to extend credit to delinquent accounts? How soon can I anticipate realizing a return on my accounts receivable?

■ How much cash do I have on hand and in the bank? Does this amount agree with what records tell me I should have or is there a shortage? How much is my investment in merchandise? How often do I turn over my inventory? Have I allowed my inventory to become obsolete?

■ How much merchandise did I take out of my business for personal or family use that affects my gross profit calculations?

■ How much do I owe my suppliers and other creditors? Have I received all of my outstanding credits for returned merchandise?

■ How much gross profit (margin) did I earn?

■ What were my expenses, including those not requiring cash outlays?

■ What is my weekly payroll? Do I have adequate payroll records to meet the requirements of workers' compensation, wage-hour laws, social security, unemployment insurance, and withholding taxes?

■ How much net profit did I earn (and how much resultant income taxes will I owe)?

■ What is my capital; that is, of my total assets, how much would be left for me after paying my creditors in full?

■ Are my sales, expenses, profits, and capital showing improvement or did I do better last year? How do I stand as compared with two periods ago? Is my position about the same, improving, or deteriorating?

■ On what lines of goods or in what departments am I making a profit, breaking even, or losing money?

■ Am I taking full advantage of cash discounts for prompt payments? How do my discounts taken compare with my discounts lost?

■ How do the financial facts of my business compare with those of similar businesses?

When you are just going into business, an adequate record-keeping system builds a necessary foundation, provides assistance to help your business grow, and enhances your opportunity to earn large profits.

18
Make the
U.S. Government
Your Silent Partner

To be most effective when approaching tax matters, you must have a positive attitude. You have a distinct advantage when you treat the U.S. government and the various state or local taxing agencies as business partners rather than oppressive tyrants.

While you have a duty to pay taxes to support the tremendous variety of services and protections the government provides, you certainly have no obligation to carry a greater personal tax burden than the government actually requires.

The U.S. Supreme Court has made repeated pronouncements of this fact. In the case of *Gregory* v. *Helvering*, 293 U.S. 465 (Jan. 7, 1935), the Court stated: ''The legal right of a taxpayer to decrease the amount of what otherwise would be taxes, or altogether avoid them, by means which the law permits, cannot be doubted.'' And it was Acting U.S. Supreme Court Justice Oliver Wendell Holmes, Jr., who wrote the famous decision stating: ''To avoid is legal but to evade is illegal. We may admit that this case is near the line. The very meaning of a line in the law is that you intentionally may go as close to it as you can if you do not pass it,'' *Superior Oil Co.* v. *Mississippi*, 280 U.S. 390 (Feb. 24, 1930).

Every important aspect of running a successful business requires that you either know or seek the advice of experts who know how to use business-related information to your best advantage. Dealing with constantly changing tax laws should be treated in the same way as dealing with any other important business matter.

This chapter is intended to provide information about federal taxes; however, tax policies do change because of revised IRS interpretation, judicial interpretation, or newly enacted tax law and regulations. While information presented here is correct at the time of writing, all questions of interpretation should be addressed by your own competent tax advisor.

Tax law changes aimed at reform, tax equity, and simplification may significantly impact every individual and business in America. Efforts to repeal special tax rules, known as "loopholes," which appear to benefit some taxpayers more than others, may remove methods Americans have long used to build financial assets by lowering tax liability. But if your sincere intention is to operate a successful small business, if you have chosen this method to accumulate wealth, the U.S. Government continues to offer you more ways to reduce tax liability than may be available in any other income-earning activity.

The assistance your federal-government partner makes available is represented in the form of deductions from gross income and tax credits. Today, small business represents perhaps the only significant remaining avenue to reduce taxable income from one source by applying losses generated by another activity.

HOW TO DISTINGUISH YOUR BUSINESS FROM A FAVORITE HOBBY, SPORT, OR PASTIME

Characteristics of a hobby, particularly if it produces income, are quite similar to a business. Devotion of time, interest, and investment are common to both; however, tax treatment is quite different.

Tax laws define a business as an activity carried on for profit. For an activity to be considered a business, therefore, a profit motive must be present and some type of economic activity must be involved. Unlike a business activity, a hobby is generally considered to be engaged in purely for personal satisfaction even though it may produce money. Actually, federal tax law does not use the word "hobby"; instead, it makes mention of an activity *not* engaged in for profit.

With few exceptions, the IRS will presume a profit motive if any activity results in a profit in three out of five consecutive years. As such, income from the activity engaged in for profit (a business) is considered self-employment income. Any losses resulting from such a business can be deducted from other forms of income. In contrast, any losses resulting from hobby deductions are classified as miscellaneous itemized deductions, and all such deductions must exceed 2 percent of adjusted gross income (AGI).

What all this means is that while you can deduct full losses from a business regardless of your AGI, if the activity is a hobby, you must include all earnings as income but can only claim deductions if they exceed the 2-percent floor. Thus, hobby deductions are not given equal weight to business deductions.

The IRS considers a business activity under two specific rules: subjective facts and circumstances and objective time and profit.

Subjective Facts and Circumstances

Under the subjective facts and circumstances rule, the IRS considers whether you operate your business in a businesslike way; the knowledge and experience you have in the particular area of business; the time and effort you devote to the business; and the degree of purely personal pleasure that most people would derive from engaging in the business.

The Manner in Which You Carry On the Activity. In other words, have you taken all necessary steps to establish your business image? Have you acquired all necessary permits or licenses, obtained a product or identified a service to offer, and is your pursuit producing sales? Do you keep business records; are they accurate and complete? Are you depositing all business receipts in a separate bank account? In short, are you conducting your activity in a business-like way?

Your Expertise or the Expertise of Advisors Who May Be Assisting in the Conduct of Your Business. Are you demonstrating skill in operating your business? Do you use sound business practices? Have you had previous business experience; or if not, are you seeking qualified advice or have you enrolled in business-education courses? Are you making the proper kind of decisions and engaging in those fundamental activities that could reasonably be expected in connection with your business?

The Time and Effort You Expend in Carrying On the Business. A business usually carries on its activities with a certain degree of regularity. If business activities are not performed daily, does some business-related activity occur weekly and monthly according to an established procedure? How diligently and in earnest is the business effort being pursued? How much time, proportional to your other activities, is being spent with the objective of producing income? Are efforts to make the business a success conducted continuously and in a pattern most likely to produce beneficial results leading eventually to a profit?

Expectations That Assets Used in the Activity May Appreciate in Value. Is any investment, such as an expenditure of funds to buy inventory, materials, equipment, supplies, or other property, likely to be worth more next week, next month, next year, or at any other time in the future?

The Previous Success You Have Had Carrying On Other Similar Activities. In other words, is the activity engaged in for profit actually in a field of endeavor for which you have knowledge, experience, skill, education, or abilities, or do you have some other basis for a reasonable expectation that your business objective will be satisfied? You need not have been in business previously to meet this criterion; it's sufficient that you possess the interest, inclination or have been exposed and have devoted time to the field of endeavor.

Elements of Personal Pleasure or Recreation. You may deduct 80 percent of legitimate entertainment expenses if they are incurred in connection with your business. Similarly, combining recreation with business is allowable if you have legitimate business reasons for doing so, and if the recreation is ancillary to your primary business purpose. This subject is discussed at greater length in the following section. The important point is that you not try to conduct a business merely for the purpose of writing off all pleasure and recreation expenses. Actually, there is no need to do so. You can take full advantage of all available tax breaks involving recreation or pleasure by demonstrating a solid profit motive in conducting your business.

Objective Time and Profit

Your History of Income or Losses with Respect to the Activity. Consider the history of the business; the period of time you have actually conducted the activity as a business distinguishes a business from a hobby, sport, or other favorite pastime. Consider the extent to which you have made accomplishments in the business. It can be expected that losses may occur in the early years of a business, but eventually the business should produce a profit or may not meet all criteria for being a business.

The Amount of Occasional Profit, if Any, Earned From the Business. It's OK with the IRS to have a couple of years of losses then suddenly make an embarrassingly large profit. Or quite the opposite, you may make a bundle in your first business year then be forced to use losses from an activity engaged in for profit to offset income from other sources. The IRS will take all facts into consideration when determining whether erratic income is from a hobby or a business. Expenses of a business may be tax deductible from other forms of earned income when there are occasional losses. Likewise, profits are to be included with other income and subject to the same provisions as other taxable earned income. Hobby income and expenses are treated differently.

As a reminder, there is no tax effect if you take money out of your business. However, all such transactions must be accounted for in determining whether your business made a profit for the entire business year. You can do this easily by writing checks payable to yourself when making appropriate withdrawals of income from your business. Avoid writing checks payable to cash. This will help you to know which disbursements are for business and which are for personal reasons.

The Financial Status of Your Business. It is not necessary that your business be your sole means of livelihood to be considered a business for tax purposes. Rather, you may hold other employment; be a homemaker, a student, a retiree; or your financial status may depend on a combination of hundreds of factors. However, if you are to apply tax laws to your best advantage, you must be able to show annually, by facts and circumstances, that you were in business during the tax year.

LET GOVERNMENT TAX POLICIES HELP YOU

Because of the truly large number of business expenses that may be deducted and losses that can be used to offset other income, detailed explanation and treatment of all of them would take more space than can be accommodated in this book. What follows is an explanation of some of the beneficial interpretations in effect at the time of this writing.

If you have doubts concerning the proper treatment of particular expense deductions or business losses, consult a qualified tax advisor. However, in order for a tax advisor to be properly prepared in the event of a requested visit by the IRS, it is fundamental that you keep good records, including all receipts, cancelled checks, everything you intend to use to substantiate a business expense or loss. Remember that keeping account of your business with clear records bestows many important advantages on you as a business person; favorable tax treatment of business expenses or losses is certainly among the chief of them.

Transportation/Automobile Expenses

A likely major expense of a great number of small businesses comes under the heading Transportation/Auto Expenses. Particularly if your business is established as a sole proprietorship, transportation/auto expenses may be proportionately larger than any other expense you have in the early years of doing business.

Transportation expenses include such items as air, train, bus, and cab fares connected with transacting your business. Travel expenses, when you are away from home on business, may also be deductible; but they differ from transportation expenses and are treated under a separate tax regulation, which will be discussed.

Expenses to drive and maintain your car for business purposes are deductible. If your car is used only partly for business, you must divide your expenses between business and personal use. However, if you use your car entirely for business purposes, you may deduct the full cost of its operation, including a reasonable allowance for depreciation.

IRS allows you to use either of two methods for deducting all business auto expenses. The first method is based on all your actual expenses plus depreciation. It requires that you keep actual receipts for proving your expenses. The second method is based instead on a standard mileage rate, and you must keep adequate mileage records, rather than receipts, to verify you drove your car on business—mere estimates are not acceptable. Which method is best for you depends on many factors, but the result can make a substantial difference in the amount of the total auto deductions you may claim.

If you are just starting your business, be sure to check with IRS or a qualified tax advisor on which method is best for your circumstances. Depending on which method you choose, actual receipts or the standard mileage rate allowable at the time, the intent is that you get the benefit of deducting, in addition to depreciation, cost of gas, oil, lubrication, repairs, maintenance, tires, supplies, garage rental, tools, parking, auto service club membership, insurance, state and local taxes, licensing, tune-ups, antifreeze, interest paid on auto loans, and any other expenses you incur.

If you lease a car used for business, you may deduct your lease payments to the extent the car is actually used for business.

You cannot claim a deduction for commuting expenses between your home and usual place of business, nor for auto fines, penalties, or traffic tickets.

Travel, Entertainment, and Gift Expenses

Under specified conditions, you may deduct travel, entertainment, and gift expenses, but you must be able to prove they are for the sole intent of increasing the taxable income your business is earning.

Travel. Travel expenses are defined as the ordinary and necessary expenses of domestic and foreign travel "away from home" for the purpose of your business. You are considered to be away from home if your business activities require you to be away from the general area of your "tax home" substantially longer than for an ordinary day's work. While away, you will, of course, need to get sleep or rest during nonworking time.

Travel expenses include lodging when you are away from home on business; air, rail, and bus fares; cost of transporting sample cases or other materials; baggage and transportation expenses to and from airports or stations; cost of transportation while at the point of destination; cleaning and laundry, telephone, telegraph, and public stenographer's fees; and tips. Also included are the cost of operating a housetrailer while on business, 80 percent of meal expenses, and other similar expenses related to qualifying travel.

For tax purposes, different treatment applies to expenses, depending on whether travel was entirely for business, primarily for business, or primarily personal, so be sure to check out the differences with IRS or your tax advisor. Depending on the primary purpose of your travel, you may be able to deduct all travel expenses or only business-related travel expenses to and from your destination, but not to extend your stay for vacation or a nonbusiness side trip. You may deduct travel expenses you have for yourself, not your family, to attend a convention if you can show that your attendance benefits your own business and is not for political or social purposes unrelated to it.

You should keep good records of all business-related travel expenses. You can do so easily by entering information in an account book, diary, or similar record and keeping receipts. Information in your record should include:

1. Each separate amount spent, except for small items that can be placed in a reasonable category, such as phone calls or other incidentals, totaled on a daily basis
2. The dates you left and returned home for each trip and the number of days spent on business away from home
3. The destination or location of your travel
4. The business reason for your travel or the nature of the business benefit derived or expected to be derived as a result of your travel

Entertainment. Business entertainment expenses are deductible if they are ordinary and necessary, and amounts spent are directly related to or associated with the active conduct of your business. Expenses that are lavish or extravagant are not allowed; but those that are allowed are generally considered to provide entertainment, amusement, or recreation for your customers in order to generate business income. This covers entertaining business guests at night clubs, social and athletic events, theaters, sporting clubs; entertaining your legitimate business customers while conducting business on yachts, on hunting or fishing vacations, or on similar trips; furnishing food and beverages or a car to your business guests or customers, and 80 percent of business meal expenses.

For tax purposes, different treatment of entertainment expenses may apply, depending on what the entertainment was intended to accomplish and its nature and setting. IRS has rules to help you decide these matters. Briefly, they fall into three categories:

1. The directly related entertainment rule, i.e., entertainment was conducted in a clear business setting and you had more than a general expectation of acquiring income or some other specific benefit

2. The associated entertainment rule, i.e., entertainment was associated with the active conduct of your business and directly preceded or followed a substantial business discussion
3. The business meal rule, i.e., circumstances were conducive to a business discussion

One of these three categories may apply and have a bearing on the kind and amount of entertainment expenses eligible to be deducted. Just as with travel expenses, you should keep an account book, diary, or similar record showing:

1. Amount of each business entertainment expenditure, except for small items that may be aggregated on a daily basis
2. Date the entertainment took place
3. Name, address or location, and type of entertainment, such as dinner, theater, and so on
4. Reason that you entertained, the expected gain or benefit, and the nature of the business discussion
5. Name, title, and business affiliation of the person entertained

Gifts. The cost of business gifts or flowers may be deducted; however, the total amount deductible during the tax year cannot exceed $25 per person. Information you will need to document business gifts include:

1. Cost of gift
2. Date the gift was given
3. Reason you gave the gift and expected benefit to be derived
4. Name, title, and business affiliation or relationship of the person receiving the gift
5. Description of the gift

BUSINESS-AT-HOME DEDUCTIONS

If you are self-employed or salaried and conducting a sideline business from your home, you have an advantage over an employee who happens to do work at home for an employer. Tax law makes a clear distinction between at-home-run businesses and employees working at home. Information provided here pertains only to a business that you conduct from home.

In general, there are two categories of deductions you may claim when conducting a business from your home: regular business deductions and home-office deductions.

Regular Business Deductions

You may claim deductions from gross business income, legitimate amounts expended on items or service necessary to conduct your day-to-day business. These expenditures include telephone, postage and shipping costs, office or workshop supplies, tools and equipment, printing, duplicating, advertising and promotion expenses, newspapers, magazines, books, furniture, bookshelves, file cabinets, audio and video recorders, bank charges, trash collection, cleaning, laundry and delivery charges, business insurance, licenses, selling expenses, trade dues, typewriters, clocks, personal computers, fees for professional services, and many more everyday items used in the home exclusively for business.

IRS has special rules for tax treatment of business equipment such as personal computers (PCs) when they are not used exclusively for business. The general rule is that the PC or other equipment must be used more than 50 percent of the time for business in order for a deduction to be claimed. That portion of the item's cost attributable to personal use cannot be written off as a business deduction. However, do not confuse time limits for business-equipment usage with the amount of time you need to spend conducting your business. The two are as different as apples and oranges.

When considering income and losses attributable to your business, IRS looks at the degree of your personal involvement in the business and then classifies it as either "active" or "passive." You receive more favorable tax treatment when involvement in your business is classified as active. Tax rules specify that you are a "material participant" and therefore active when you meet either of two tests:

1. You put more than 500 hours a year in a single income-producing business activity regardless of how many hours others put into that activity
2. You put in "substantially all" the hours and effort required of the business (even if it is a sideline or part-time business) or you put in at least 100 hours a year and that number of hours is at least as much as anyone else puts into the business.

When meeting either of these two tests, income and losses are considered active, and you get the benefit of more favorable treatment.

When calculating amounts of time necessary for business equipment to meet the more-than-50-percent test, compare the actual usage time to the amount of time you and others "actively" put into your business. For example, assume you have a sideline business that you put 300 hours a year into and that is substantially all the hours and effort required of the business for that year. You buy a PC exclusively for business and use it 52 hours a year. The purchase of the computer saves considerable time, labor, or professional service expense and, therefore, has great value to your business. In addition, you anticipate the number of hours you will be devoting to the business and using the computer will greatly increase in future years as your business grows. Therefore, you have met all required tests and purchase of the computer may be considered a legitimate business deduction.

So long as your income-producing activity meets the definition of a business as measured by the facts-and-circumstances and time-and-profit criteria previously discussed, you may claim legitimate expenditures as regular business deductions.

You may run your business full time or as a sideline part-time business and claim deductions. Remember though, you must be able to prove with records and documents that you are conducting an income-producing activity with systematic regularity in a diligent businesslike way with the intention of making a profit.

Home-Office Deductions

The cost of space in your home or apartment used exclusively to conduct your business may be deducted as a legitimate business deduction. You may also deduct pro-rata expenditures for electricity, gas, water, insurance premiums, cleaning, mortgage insurance, rent, and repairs directly attributable to business-use space. While homeowners may deduct a portion of their mortgage payments and even claim depreciation on the part of the residence used for business purposes, doing so could complicate the tax-free rollover provision normally available when you sell your house and purchase another. Therefore, seek qualified tax advice and take a careful look at all implications before taking this deduction.

If you decide to claim a home-office deduction, remember that you may be required to demonstrate that your home office is used exclusively, and on a regular basis, as your principal place of business or as a place in which clients or customers meet or deal with you in the normal course of your business. IRS uses two key tests when considering the legitimacy of a home-office deduction: exclusive use and regular basis.

Exclusive Use. You are required to set aside a specific section, portion, room, or rooms (or separate structure) of your residence for the exclusive purpose of carrying on business. With the exception of use as a day-care center, the area cannot serve both business and personal purposes. That means it cannot double as a television room for the kids, even outside of regular business hours. It must be kept for business, and its business use must be substantiated by physical evidence—a desk, chair, filing cabinet, and so on.

An exception is provided if you are a retail seller and your home is the sole location of your business, for example, if you are a cosmetics distributor or if you are involved in any other type of home-sales, part-time enterprise. If this is the case, the ordinary and necessary expenses allowable for storage of inventory are deductible if such space is used on a regular basis and is a separately identifiable space suitable for storage.

Regular Basis. To support your claim for a deduction, you must be able to show that the space reserved in your residence for business purposes is used in a businesslike way with regularity. You can do so by maintaining a log of the hours the space is used or by showing you conform to a normal pattern in using the space. Various documentation will assist you in doing this, such as writing out the procedures you follow to use the space, keeping a diary, or maintaining a visitor's record of customers and service deliveries. In addition, you should keep a record of telephone calls made from your home and retain business mail addressed to your home.

If you meet these reasonable standards and if you keep careful records, the home-office deduction can effect a sizeable reduction in your tax bill. Remember, however, your deductible expenses for the home office may not exceed the gross income derived from the business conducted from that office.

Record-keeping Tips

Keeping good records is the key to claiming tax deductions in a business run out of your home. If you follow IRS procedures precisely, you should have very little difficulty proving your claim in the event of an audit.

Always remember to batch expenses incurred in your home-office business in three categories—direct expenses, indirect expenses, and unrelated expenses.

Direct Expenses. Regular business expenses such as cost of inventory, equipment, office furniture, supplies, licenses, labor, advertising, and telephone are direct expenses. These are day-to-day cost items without which you could not conduct business regardless of location. All such expenses are fully deductible so long as you meet all other IRS criteria of engaging in a business for profit.

Indirect Expenses. Indirect expenses have as their source the cost of keeping up and running your place of business, which happens to be your home. These expenses are partially deductible, depending on the pro-rata portions used directly for business. If you are a homeowner, you may deduct part of the real property taxes, mortgage interest, and casualty losses you pay on your home as a business expense. The remaining personal portion of these expenses may be deductible on your Form 1040, Schedule A tax return if you itemize deductions. If you rent, rather than own your home, a portion of the rent payment may be deducted if the space is used exclusively and regularly for business.

Utility expenses, such as electricity, gas, water, and garbage removal, and other services such as cleaning and insurance may also be deductible if all other requirements are met and you have calculated the percentage amount used for business.

The business percentage of the cost of repairs including labor—other than your own—and supplies may be deductible. For example, a repair to your furnace maintains your entire home and if 20 percent of the area in your home is used for business, 20 percent of the cost of furnace repair may be deducted.

The thing to keep in mind is repairs keep your place of business, which happens to be your home, in good working order and extend its useful life. Other types of qualifying common repairs include patching walls and floors, painting, wall papering, repairing roofs and gutters, mending leaks, electric wiring, plumbing, and fixing broken windows proportionate to direct business use.

Repairs of this sort must be carefully distinguished from a general plan to make permanent improvements that the IRS calls a capital expenditure. A *capital expenditure* is intended not merely to repair something broken; rather, it is designed to fund a general plan to alter, remodel, increase the value of the property, or give it a new or different use. Some work that may be classified as repair, when standing alone, might actually be a capital expenditure when part of a general plan to make major modifications or alter your house to make it suitable for business use.

For example, you buy an older home and fix up two rooms to use as a hairdressing shop. You patch the plaster on the ceilings and walls, paint the place, replace deteriorated flooring, put in an outside door, and install new wiring and plumbing. If the plaster patching, painting, and floor repair were performed standing alone, they would be classified as repairs. However, since this work is done as part of a general plan to alter the house for business use, the amount you pay for this work is actually a capital expenditure.

Tax treatment for each is different. Repairs are fully deductible as expenses during the year they are incurred. Capital expenditures may only be deductible as depreciation over a longer period of cost recovery.

If you make a point of keeping good records, canceled checks, receipts, and related documents, you will greatly assist your accountant to figure all the benefits you deserve and also please IRS with your keen business ability.

Unrelated Expenses. IRS treats expenses that benefit only the parts of your home that are not used for business as unrelated expenses. Generally, lawn care, landscaping, and other work not performed in or on space used regularly and exclusively for business is classified as unrelated to your business. You cannot deduct any unrelated expenses.

Expenses regularly and exclusively incurred in a home-run business must be deducted in this order:

1. Mortgage interest, real estate taxes, and deductible casualty losses, if any, figured on a pro-rata percentage of the amount of space used for business. For example, assume business-use space is 300 square feet out of a 1,500 square-foot home, condominium, or apartment; 300 sq. ft. ÷ 1,500 sq. ft. = 20%. That amount is deductible and claimed first.
2. Your direct business expenses not related to the home unit itself; in other words, expenses that are the regular cost of doing business. These were described in the section on Regular Business Deductions.
3. Your cost to pay for the home unit itself, figured on a pro-rata percentage of business use. These were described in the section on Home-Office Deduction and include maintenance, utilities, insurance, and rent. Depreciation is claimed last.

DEDUCTION AS EXPENSE VERSUS DEPRECIATION

Tax law allows you to write off business-equipment expenditures either by directly taking a deduction (a method known as expensing) or by taking a portion of the expenditure each year figured as depreciation.

Direct Deduction

If you choose to take a direct deduction for business-equipment expenditures, there are some limitations. The total cost you may elect to deduct for a tax year, under section 179 of the Tax Code, may not exceed $10,000 and cannot exceed the taxable income generated by your business. However, if your gross business income is less than $10,000 and the business-equipment expenditure exceeds your gross business income but is not more than $10,000, you may carry over to the next tax year that portion of the unused deduction.

For example, you buy a computer that costs $8,000. You use it more than 50 percent of the time for business. However, the gross income from your business is only $6,000 in that same tax year. Under section 179 you may deduct only $6,000 as a business-equipment expenditure in that same tax year. The remaining $2,000 cost may be carried over to the next tax year and added to the cost of other qualifying equipment purchased in the new tax year.

Automobile Purchase

Purchase of a passenger automobile for business purposes is treated differently from other business equipment. Your total section 179 deduction and depreciation for an auto cannot exceed $2,560 in one tax year. See IRS Publication 534, *Depreciation*, for more information.

Figuring Depreciation

Depreciation is a term used for the method of recovering business-equipment and capital-improvement expenditures over a period of years of the "class life" of an item. A portion of the expenditure is deductible as a business expense during each year the item is used in your business.

To figure depreciation, you must determine three things about the property: its actual and complete cost (otherwise known as its basis); the date you first used the property for business purposes (otherwise known as placing it in service); and the method of depreciation you are permitted to use.

As of this writing, the 1986 Tax Reform Act requires you to use the modified accelerated cost recovery system (MACRS) for newly acquired tangible property. Property with characteristics that exclude it from MACRS because of date of acquisition or other technical reasons must be depreciated in one of three other ways: accelerated cost recovery system (ACRS), straight-line method, or declining-balance method.

Be sure to consult with your qualified tax advisor on these depreciation particulars. Discussion of the MACRS method is presented here to demonstrate how the new practice applies to most tangible property used in small business.

Under the MACRS method, property is classed as being in a 3-, 5-, 7-, 10-, 15-, or 20-year, class-life category. Much of the business equipment you will depreciate in a small business will fall in the 5-year, class-life category. This includes computers and peripheral equipment, typewriters, calculators, etc. Other office items, such as office furniture and fixtures, desks, files, etc., will fall mainly in the 7-year, class-life category. This means you may write off as a deduction a portion of the business-equipment expenditure in each of the 5-year or 7-year periods, whichever applies.

Take This Year's Excess Deductions Next Year

One drawback to home-office deductions is that IRS rules don't let you create a business loss or increase a net loss by claiming them. However, the rules permit you to carry forward to the next tax year those deductions that would have resulted in such losses had you used them in the current tax year. Deductions carried to a later tax year retain their character (TABLE 18-1).

TABLE 18-1. Handling of Excess Deductions.

Assume gross income from business
use of your home...$12,000

TOTAL EXPENSES:

1. Business percentage (say 20%) of mortgage interest, property taxes,
and casualty losses.......................................$2,000
2. Regular business deductions............................$9,000
3. Remaining expenses:
    a. Maintenance, insurance, utilities, etc. (20%)........... $800
    b. Depreciation or rent (20%).........................$1,600

GROSS INCOME LIMITATION:

Total of 1 and 2 (above)	..........$11,000	$11,000
Limit on further deductions	....	$1,000
Minus expenses in 3(a) above	..............$800	($800)
Limit on further deductions	....	$200
Depreciation or rent 3(b) above	...........$1,600	$1,600
Minus depreciation allowable	....	($200)

Carryover expenses (subject to income limitations in
  current tax year) to future tax year $1,400

TAX CREDITS

As a business owner earning income from a profitable business, you may take advantage of some important tax-liability reduction methods known as tax credits. The value of tax credits is they may be used to offset tax payments that would otherwise be due. They are different from tax deductions, which are used to reduce taxable income on which taxes are based. Nevertheless, tax credits may result in big tax savings.

As of this writing, tax law lumps various tax credits into a catch-all category known as general business credit. For the most part, this may consist of a combination of two or more of the following: allowable unused investment credit from earlier tax years, jobs credit, alcohol-fuel credit, research credit, and low-income housing credit.

Tax law limits the amount of general-business credit you may take in any one tax year. However, if your general-business-credit entitlement for the year is greater than this limit, you may carry the excess to a following tax year and subtract it from your income tax for that year.

To take full advantage of tax credits handed to you by your friendly U.S.-government partner, get a copy of IRS Publication 572, *General Business Credit*, and get help from your qualified tax advisor.

PERSONAL PENSION PLANS FOR THE SELF-EMPLOYED

Tax law allows individuals to take enormous tax deductions to improve retirement by plowing funds into their personal pension programs. This is particularly true if you are not otherwise covered by an employer-sponsored retirement plan even though you are covered by social security. It is also partially true even if you are otherwise covered by an employer-sponsored retirement plan and also covered by social security, depending on the amount of your AGI.

Individual Retirement Account

At the time of this writing, if neither you nor your spouse are "active participants" in an employer-sponsored retirement plan, you may contribute and deduct from earned income up to $2,000 each year before figuring your taxes. However, if you or your spouse *is* an active participant in an employer-sponsored retirement plan, you may contribute up to $2,000 each year, but the amount you are allowed to deduct is determined by your AGI and marital status.

Regardless of whether you are eligible to take a tax deduction for individual retirement account (IRA) contributions, depositing what you can afford into an IRA makes good business sense. The reason is that your IRA offers the benefit of tax-deferred growth. That is, your savings contributions grow much faster in an IRA because the earnings are sheltered from taxes until withdrawn. FIGURE 18-1 illustrates the value of tax-deferred appreciation.

Keogh Accounts

As a full- or part-time owner of your sideline business who is earning income from your for-profit activity, the U.S. government offers another lucrative way to feather your retirement nest.

If you meet all tax-law requirements, you may set up another retirement plan, known as a Keogh HR-10 plan, in addition to your IRA. At the time of this writing, contributions to the plan cannot exceed $30,000 or 15 percent of "compensation" (generally, earned income from the business), whichever is less. Amounts contributed are deductible from gross income *before* figuring taxes, and investment earnings in the plan are sheltered from taxes until withdrawn.

To set up your own Keogh plan, you must have self-employment net earnings, even if from a sideline business, and you can have a Keogh even if you are otherwise covered by another employer-sponsored retirement plan.

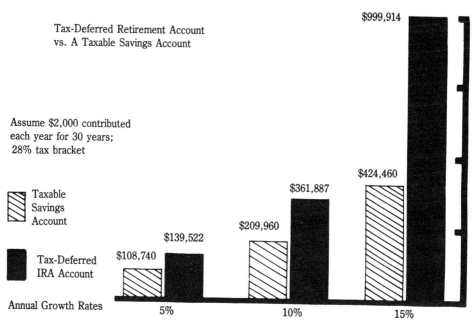

FIG. 18-1. *Tax-deferred retirement account versus taxable savings account.*

The Keogh plan must be approved by IRS (a "qualified" plan), and you must figure the amount that you can deduct based on whether you have a "defined-benefit" or a "defined-contribution" plan. Be sure to get advice from a qualified tax expert to understand these terms and help set up your Keogh plan.

The juiciest advantage of establishing your qualified Keogh plan may be the big tax break you can receive. On your tax return 1040 form, Keogh contributions are reported as an adjustment to income; they are subtracted before you compute your tax, and therefore your liability to IRS is considerably reduced. Perhaps just as important, taxes on the accruing interest are deferred until you finally begin to tap the account at age 59½ or older. Money that would ordinarily go for taxes remains in the account compounding and earning additional interest until mandatory withdrawal at age 70½.

Accumulate Wealth with IRAs and Keoghs

For a person in business, the terrific advantages of using both a Keogh account and IRAs are:

1. They may allow gigantic tax deductions that may not be available to you if you are not in business. While IRAs are available to all wage earners, the

added tax benefit of a Keogh account in combination with an IRA can produce unusually large tax savings and investment growth.

2. Because of penalties involved in early withdrawal of funds, Keoghs and IRAs encourage a disciplined savings program to benefit you in later years. Without such incentives, the average person seems to spend all that is earned, including paying a significant amount in taxes that might be saved if placed in Keoghs and IRAs. Depending on your tax bracket, it is not uncommon to find that the U.S. government is, in effect, handing you $500 or more in tax savings for every $2,000 you place in your own personal retirement account.

3. The powerful cumulative effect of annual savings combined with compounded interest or other investment return over a period of years can build an immense fortune with almost insignificant risk. Few other tax-sheltered programs can match both aspects of astonishing rewards and secure money as the combined Keogh and IRA system, all with blessing and encouragement from the U.S. government.

When you reach retirement age, you will be required to pay taxes on the money you withdraw from your IRAs and Keoghs. But at that stage in your life, you will probably be earning less than you are now, might be in a correspondingly lower tax bracket, and might qualify for favorable, one-time, income-averaging treatment available only to retirement-plan distributions. Thus you may pay far less in taxes than otherwise had you reported your Keogh contributions as income during your peak earning years.

There's one catch: you must leave your money in the account until age 59½ unless you are willing to accept a 10 percent penalty, and then withdrawals are taxed as regular income. Moreover, early withdrawals may make you ineligible to make additional contributions to the account for a period of five tax years.

A FINAL WORD

Tax deductions allowable if you are engaged in business number in the hundreds. As described in Chapter 17, Dome Publishing Co., Inc., produces an inexpensive, simplified bookkeeping system that contains a comprehensive listing of allowable tax deductions. Actually, you may be able to take advantage of many more. For more information on beneficial tax deductions of every variety, obtain a copy of IRS Publication 334, *Tax Guide for Small Business*.

In short, you can generate large tax savings, depending on your tax status and bracket, if you are incurring expenses related to your legitimate business. Business losses still may be used to offset other forms of income. The general rule of thumb is that any expense or any loss incurred in connection with your business should be used to lock in all tax savings permitted by law.

19

How to
Succeed in Business

All the seemingly complicated talk about taxes and long-range pension planning that appeared in the previous chapter might seem overwhelming. It shouldn't be. Taking care of business means simplifying complications; anything worth doing in business *can* be managed. Succeeding means confronting problems one at a time and finding solutions. If you do this, a progression of accomplishments will unfold before you.

Realize there is virtually no limit to your ability to solve business problems when you apply intelligent thought. At one time or another, everybody in business experiences frustration and disappointment; it comes with the territory. But knowledge of this fact is an important step in the journey to business success. Knowledge that you are in the midst of frustration is an important signpost. It tells you there may be impending danger. Frustration warns you to step back from the seemingly overwhelming problems that confront you.

Properly used, frustration should stimulate your creativity and imagination so that you will find the means to overcome temporary setbacks and go on to build a happier, healthier, more prosperous life for yourself and your loved ones.

ACRES OF DIAMONDS

The key to turning back frustration is to look about you for potentials previously unnoticed, possibilities heretofore overlooked.

When you confront what seems to be a major problem, know that somewhere about you is a larger opportunity. Years ago this concept was labeled "acres of diamonds" by Russell Conwell, founder of Temple University. The true story he told as he appeared before American audiences in the late 1800s was of a farmer who had settled in Africa but then sold his farm in order to prospect for diamonds. His search was unsuccessful; and utterly despondent, the farmer brought his life to an untimely end. About the time of this event, the new owner of the farm found a large stone in a stream running through the property. The discovery proved to be a large diamond of great value. Further exploration revealed that the farm contained literally acres of diamonds.

Dr. Conwell used this story to remind his audiences that opportunity is often within immediate reach if you have the wisdom and foresight to see it. Often you can find the solution you seek merely by thinking of new and better ways to be of service. Understand that no unfortunate experience need be a permanent liability.

Perhaps you have known past failures, made some poor judgments, or suffered a recent defeat. Then congratulations are in order, for you have joined the privileged elite who understand despair. Knowing this condition, you are hereby invited to join a new club. The password permitting entry is, "There is no such reality as permanent defeat."

KEYS TO BUSINESS SUCCESS

If you get into trouble or if you want to know the secrets to others' business success, the 10 keys are presented here for your advantage:

Positive Mental Attitude

A positive mental attitude is the first essential key. At the beginning of a large task, such as starting a business, a positive receptive attitude, more than anything else, will contribute to a successful outcome. Keeping an open mind when engaging in business transactions provides power to choose a most appropriate direction. If your circumstances are not what you desire, you may change them by modifying your mental attitude.

When an unexpected problem seems to obstruct your path, a positive mindset provides the open space you need to find within yourself, or around you, the necessary solution. Cultivating the habit of forming a positive attitude at will takes time; but once mastered, it becomes the wellspring of great power. And the most marvelous feature of this discovery is that by controlling your attitude, you regulate the consequences of unforeseen events.

You own your own mind, and you are the only one who controls it. You cannot control all the actions of others nor prevent occurrence of countless unfortunate events touching your life. But by taking conscious ownership of your mind, you can control how you react to events and to people.

The capacity to understand and deal with difficult people is nurtured by self-discipline and tolerance. An important insight is that all people are inspired by common motives and threatened by common fears. Basic motives consist of desire for self-preservation, material possessions, self-expression, immortality, freedom of thought and actions, self-esteem, and recognition. These motives are driven by emotions of happiness, fear, love, sex, ego, pleasure, envy, and anger. Basic fears consist of loss of dignity, health, material possessions, love, and liberty and fear of criticism, old age, and death.

Acquiring techniques for effective application of this knowledge ranks among the most important skills you can command.

Controlling your attitude allows you to channel actions of others and circumstances through the conscious awareness of your own reaction and the kinds of behavior you exhibit. This facility bestows mastery over any situation.

The ability to acknowledge where you stand relative to others eliminates sources of friction. It also forms the basis of friendship, harmony, and cooperation. It is essential in the display of leadership. The ability to command your mind and your attitude is the greatest source of power you possess.

Preparation

Preparation is the second essential key to business success. Using the power of the first key, a positive mental attitude, you acquire knowledge, experience, skills, and abilities. You achieve breakthroughs by locating and learning to use sources of information. You acquire respect for educational institutions, libraries, knowledgeable people, and work experience. You form disciplined business habits, and you increase your value.

Now you are equipped to take advantage of a propitious occasion when it arises because you know that such an occasion is worth no more and no less than the amount of preparation enabling you to make the most of it. You realize that you are today the sum of what you prepared to be yesterday; tomorrow, you will become what you are preparing to be today. You have learned how to avoid procrastination and achieve what you set out to accomplish. Being fully prepared, you are ready to tap the infinite, immense potential within you.

Imagination

Applying imagination to what you know and do is the third key to business success. Equipped with what you already know, begin to imagine how what you do can be done better, easier, cheaper, faster, or otherwise generate inspired new appeal.

There is nothing mysterious or magical about this process. By merely forming the habit of visualizing improvement, your mind will become an action center of exquisite sensitivity. Go about your activities in a state of receptive attention. Over time, your imagination will operate automatically and continuously, all the while uncovering ideas from your new awareness.

When telling others of your ideas for improvement, be careful that the form your expression takes cannot be construed as criticism of what they are doing. Convey your expression in positive terms, placing emphasis on beneficial results. This approach facilitates greater acceptance of new ideas.

Be open to the comments and suggestions of others. Allow your great mind to explore alternative possibilities. Think in terms of expanded horizons. Create new categories. Record on paper each new idea and review this list every day.

Setting Goals

Setting goals is the fourth essential key. Envelop your goals within a plan of action. Prepare a list of tasks to accomplish goals and specify a timetable for their accomplishment.

Studies have shown that only about 5 percent of people in all walks of life consciously establish definite goals and then strive to attain them. The vast majority merely drift along, depending mainly on circumstances to control their lives. Most fail to chart their own destinations and therefore rarely experience the satisfaction of achievement.

People with goals succeed because they know where they are going. A person with goals is analogous to a ship leaving a harbor on a thoroughly planned and mapped voyage. With rare exception, a visionary captain outfitted with a quality-constructed ship, supplied with a highly talented and trained crew will arrive at his or her destination. But another ship with no captain and crew, no aiming point, goal, or destination, its only asset being that its engines are running, can hardly be expected to get out of the harbor at all. The ship will not have a successful journey because it has no guidance, no destination; and it is generally the same with a human being.

Business success is nothing more than achievement through a logical application of this same goal-oriented approach through the vehicle of a moneymaking enterprise. Success comes about by pursuing a conscious plan channeled by a predetermined course in a knowing direction.

Conditions of life desired by most people—peace of mind, happiness, more money, and so on—are not really goals but states of being. On the other hand, goals have a quality of definiteness about them. They have a precise end, and progress toward that end can be measured and recognized with exactness.

Achieving the condition that you want occurs by setting and achieving one goal after another. The sum total brings about that condition of life you prefer, but it is the process of setting goals that gives you direction and purpose.

Thinking about only one goal at a time, forcing it into your subconscious mind, and recalling it regularly helps minimize distractions. Making your mind the conscious gatekeeper of your goal allows it to consider and produce answers to problems as they are encountered. Frustration and confusion are eliminated because you have a clear objective; and your mind is the one powerful resource that provides guidance on your journey.

Contented people are those who are using achievement of goals to bridge the gap between what they have and what they want. It is this process that gives their lives purpose and meaning; satisfaction is their great reward.

Nagging worries, baseless imaginings, confusion, and groundless fears are all products of inactivity, purposeless behavior patterns, and uncharitable thought. They can be driven away by setting goals; they will vanish with the attainment of achievement. Fixing in your mind a definite goal, pursuing that goal with conviction, and energizing to your optimum so that your cherished goals are realized provides strength, power, and determination to overcome all difficulties.

Timing

Timing is the fifth essential key to success. Business success is not just a chance occurrence, coming because of fate or blind luck to some but not to others. Rather, it occurs by using each key progressively to unlock opportunity. Some people appear to proceed almost automatically in a successful business direction. More likely, upon uncovering all facts, you would find their opportunity occurred only after they proceeded through the steps and had become ready for it. When the grand occasion could no longer be withheld, their progress took on the appearance of an unstoppable dynamo.

It is not merely by coincidence that when you are ready to receive something, it most often seems to appear. With near certainty, preparation has preceded the event. The principle of cause and effect may be unseen, but be sure that it is at work.

You can make the most of timing by having a clear understanding of prevailing conditions. You should be aware of economic cycles, know if your market or industry is experiencing rapid growth, determine sufficiency of your financial resources, and assess other important conditions.

Once equipped with sustained preparation, the opportunity you seek will present itself. Skillful timing will permit that opportunity to be used to your best advantage.

Desire

Desire is the sixth important key. Intense desire is the stimulation that transforms an intangible dream to surging, dynamic reality. The strength of this emotion has been the forerunner of all human progress. Seeking an outlet for display of your talents is the highest form of human desire. It is the vehicle by which visualization becomes a tangible expression.

Planting intense desire for what you want at the deepest levels of consciousness induces you to go in the direction of your own will. When you identify that item or aspect of life deemed to be most rewarding to you, desire for it increases energy levels; you feel more alive mentally and physically.

Desire is harnessed by clearly visualizing what you want. Going after what you want brings meaning to your life. You are able to tap unknown levels of creativity and skill to satisfy your desire.

Desire for attainment of financial independence often intensifies attention on a business of your own. You see yourself in possession of tangible rewards through the process of conducting the business of your dreams. Thoughts of the fruits of business bring to consciousness images of what you have the potential to be. These thoughts have the powerful ability to galvanize your commitment to carry out your business plan.

Desire produces resourcefulness and creativity. When your mind is not mobilized by desire, think of it as a blank computer screen. Introducing desire is analogous to inserting a program into the computer, causing it to function as the manufacturer intended. So equipped, effective use of the computer produces a marvelous printout of your own creation. So, too, does your mind produce marvelous creations when stimulated by desire.

When you are convinced that you deserve abundant prosperity and self-expression through the medium of your own business, when this becomes your most cherished desire, you have mobilized a most powerful force for gaining that achievement.

Initiating Action

Initiating action is the seventh important key to business success. All the other keys to business success are worthless unless you activate them. ''Do the thing and you shall have the power,'' said Ralph Waldo Emerson.

You have the absolute right and the power to initiate action in whatever direction you choose. When you do so as a regular part of your business-building routine, results will accumulate, producing major accomplishments.

An important element of initiating action is doing so according to a definite, predetermined plan. Knowing your major purpose and pursuing it with a daily regimen according to plan will remove obstacles as a stream of lava clears a track to its destination.

Think about your own experiences. Have you ever wondered why some people always seem to produce results, while others with equal talent and education just seem to get by? A comparison of actions provides the answer. Successful people initiate action because they want more for themselves and their families, *now*. These are people who know what they want, get moving on a plan of action, find success in a business of their own, enjoy what they are doing, and look forward to an exciting future.

Others, equally smart, lack commitment to action. Often they are unchallenged and without career satisfaction, they are bored or frustrated working for others, and they don't seem to know how to get moving. The only reason they remain stymied is they don't take action to move on to the next opportunity.

If you are genuinely motivated to have your own business, to conduct it successfully, you need to initiate action. You must commit to a campaign philosophy with all-out effort. This approach is reserved for people who are serious about being in business for lifetime rewards. It is an approach that takes commitment but is extremely exciting.

Maintaining Faith and Belief

Maintaining faith and belief is the eighth important key to business success. The credo, what the mind can conceive and believe can be achieved, is a simple but powerful truth. It is the formula by which every great advance in the world around us has been made. It is the very definition of success. Every person who sets out to do something and then accomplishes it is successful. And the beauty is each of us has the freedom to decide what it is we want to do.

There is no reason in the world why you should ever deny yourself faith and belief. Instead, you should gain strength from the quiet, firm, inner knowledge that using fully these keys to success is the essential requirement to accomplishing your goals. You must know that the answers you seek will come to you in your own time—if you fully prepare and keep looking for them.

Many people yearning to be in business lack confidence. They tend to underestimate both their ability to succeed and their earnings potential. They view themselves entirely by what they have grown accustomed to doing, and they can't break the habit. They are unable to proceed to new opportunities because they have never commanded the belief that they can; they lack the courage to try.

Yet every day, thousands do make the bold move to activate their own business in the belief that they can become the persons they would like to be. They have conviction that they are fully qualified to attain the object of their yet unattained desire. They demonstrate an immense capacity for faith and transmute ordinary energy into significant financial reward. You, too, can stand out from the others and accomplish what you want at a higher level by believing that you can.

Joining with Others

Joining with others in a spirit of harmony to achieve a major purpose is the ninth important key to business success. This key is supported by the fundamental principle that no greater power for achievement occurs than when two or more people coordinate efforts in a spirit of harmony for the attainment of a mutual purpose. It is as though the process of two minds, sharing dreams and working in harmony, produces a third force—an infinitely more powerful force than either could produce working alone.

Harmony in human relationships fosters high energy, abundant creativity, deep resourcefulness, motivated activity, inspired effort, dynamic achievement, and profuse satisfaction. Harmonious participation with others to accomplish a mutually sincere purpose can accomplish more in a shorter period of time and do a far better job with less strain than several individuals working in isolation. This doesn't mean that each person in the alliance will duplicate or intrude on the responsibility of another; quite the opposite. It means the work will be divided along lines of expertise to accomplish a mutually desired end, and each member of the alliance will profit from the reward.

When encountering obstacles or problems, answers can often be found by joining with others in a cooperative alliance, thus benefiting from the contribution of each to produce solutions.

Persistence

Persistence is the tenth key to business success. Even after repeated attempts that failed, unwavering persistence will ultimately determine the degree of success you will achieve.

Every adult of average intelligence has the capacity to be successful at what he or she does. You have the right to attain economic security by marketing a sufficient quantity of a quality product or service. You have the opportunity to have the better things in life, to command the source of greater income by operating your own business in whatever area of life you choose.

If you didn't know how to do so before, you now have the keys to business success, which, when used as a guide, can lead to improved circumstances at will. They have been stated to precisely parallel the powerful formula used by successful people in business today. Properly applied, they can bring you, without false hope, the conditions of life you desire while providing immunity from unnecessary risk and wasted time.

You have the privilege to use these keys under certain prescribed conditions. The human urge to gain income and satisfaction from your own business cannot be extinguished. Until you try a business avenue to what you feel you deserve, you will remain unfulfilled. You cannot put aside the burning desire to locate a satisfying outlet for displaying your talents. You are obsessed with the thought that life is giving more to others than to you. You cannot remove the compulsion to command your own direction and create your own destiny. Finally, you have a clear vision of a dominant purpose that can produce income by implementing a precise action plan for its achievement. If you meet these conditions, you are authorized to use these keys to business success and apply them persistently.

No past defeat, mistake in judgment, or unfortunate experience will prevent you from seeking success again. You are inspired and empowered to reverse any previous failure, to take ownership of your life, and to realize your full share of this world's abundance. You have decided to apply the keys to business success because doing so requires no higher degree of superiority than what you possess. You are prepared to seek success with commitment and persistence.

PUTTING IT ALL TOGETHER

The tools you use to do any job at hand are your mind, your abilities, your unique and individual talents, and your time. You use these tools to carry out a plan, a road map if you will; and fueled by the courage of your convictions, you set out to reach your destination. You know in advance there will be problems and setbacks, but you also know that nothing on earth can stand in the way of your using these tools to carry out a plan backed by persistence and determination.

It is left to you to decide on the plan you will follow and which tools you will use. Some make a very narrow choice. Others use each tool to the maximum and receive an abundant return in the form of purposeful living and tangible rewards, ranging over the entire span of their lives.

You are true to yourself when you take each of these tools and use them to their fullest. It is then you achieve a satisfying return. Using the tools available to you is largely a matter of forming sound habits—habits that expand your opportunity. As these habits produce achievement, you can take comfort, relish the feeling of well-being, and enjoy your leisure time because you have so deservedly earned it.

Contented people have no reason to disparage hard work or long hours devoted to business, for their rewards will take the form of both tangible and intangible accomplishments. Sacrifice brings little if any resentment because the larger purpose leading to fulfillment is being served. Persistence, even after repeated attempts that failed, will ultimately determine the degree of greatness and success you will achieve. Personal fulfillment will make all temporary hardships worthwhile.

With the tools available to us all, you can achieve riches and build security lasting a lifetime; you can know the wonderful feeling of immense self-worth and being of value, and the pure joy of peace of mind that comes from accomplishment.

EPILOGUE: COMING TO TERMS WITH THE FUTURE

Being in business is a powerful tool to facilitate a sense of achievement and acquire personal wealth. Even so, it is not realistic to assume that all who desire these rewards will find business to be a preferred way of life.

Being in business is a process, not a panacea. In logical progression, each facet of business builds on that which preceded it. The process begins when you create from a dream the kind of business you want to occupy your life.

Inspired by strong preferences on how you want to affect the world and how you expect the world to affect you, the process evolves until it becomes the mature expression of the kind, quality, and size of business you desire to conduct.

TAKE TIME TO REFLECT

After you have started a business, shepherded it through the early years, and arrived at a point of proven success, it is healthy to stop long enough to consider the future. Do you want your business to continue to grow? Are you prepared for the risks inherent in expansion? What are your plans for expansion? Will you need to move to larger quarters? Is it necessary to relocate to better reach your market or to maximize production efficiencies and economies?

Other Alternatives

Should you consider other growth channels? Is it feasible to expand by acquiring or merging with another business? Should you pursue expansion by seeking venture capital, eventually leading to a publicly held corporation? Can you duplicate your initial business success by franchising operations? After years of building the business, do you find it to be at the apex of its life cycle and is now the time to sell?

Whether because you are nearing retirement age or simply want to do other things, is it timely for you, the entrepreneur, to step aside and delegate to managers the day-to-day responsibility to plan, direct, and coordinate activities of the company?

MAKING A CHOICE

When you consider all the alternatives for the future, a decision on where you want to be next year, in five years, or in ten years takes on the power of a self-fulfilling prophesy. What you envision the future to hold is most probably what you will get.

Depending on a wide assortment of personal and business considerations, your future may be fully immersed in business, partially active in business, or retired from a business way of life. Each of these choices presents a different set of opportunities, problems, and life styles. Whatever your choice, the state of being you create for yourself can be an exciting adventure.

Selecting the path of business growth will generally mean continuing a total commitment to business for at least another five to seven years. Taking the path of partial business involvement requires giving permission to others to conduct business using their own management styles and without undue intrusion of your authority.

Choosing the path to retire from a business of your own requires planning other satisfying activities to occupy your interest and time. After a long, fast-paced career running a business, inactivity can lead to a life so boring that suddenly you find yourself living with anxiety, tension, irritability, or chronic fatigue. This can be prevented by planning your future. Just as you learned in business, any worthwhile pursuit or life style requires a positive mental attitude, setting goals, and engaging in preparation to achieve them. A more relaxed life style, greater enjoyment of recreation activities, or acquiring new hobby interests will require a conscious mental adjustment.

Which direction is best for you? What are your goals for the future?

Appendix A

Checklist for Converting Your Favorite Hobby, Sport, Pastime, or Idea to Cash

✔ Have you compiled and prioritized a list of the activities and interests you enjoy most?

✔ Do you review this list several times daily?

✔ Have you used sources of information readily available to acquire and organize specialized knowledge in your priority field of activity or interest?

✔ Have you applied imagination to your primary interest field and area of specialized knowledge in order to identify an unmet need?

✔ Are you able to establish a mental condition whereby your subconscious mind may freely transform thought impulses into tangible product or service purposes to fill this need?

✔ Have you created intense desire for the things you want in life?

✔ Have you identified the things you want in life with specificity, not just as general conditions of living?

✔ Do you daily visualize yourself already in possession of the things you desire?

✔ Do you daily visualize yourself in a position to produce these things through a practical plan of accomplishment?

✔ Are you taking action with persistence to carry out at least one priority task each day to fulfill your practical plan of accomplishment?

✔ Do you use mental exercises (autosuggestion) to reinforce faith and belief in yourself and your plans?

✔ Are you willing to work with consistency at what you do?

✔ When you encounter obstacles, are you able to look for alternatives or new approaches to overcome them?

✔ When you are unable to find solutions to problems, are you inclined to seek additional specialized information on the subject?

✔ When you feel discouraged, do you go back to your master plan and redouble your efforts to accomplish goals toward its accomplishment?

✔ Are you honest with yourself and ethical in all of your transactions?

✔ When forming and carrying out your plans, do you frame issues and needs in specifics and pay attention to details?

✔ Is the time you are willing to devote to your enterprise in line with time requirements demanded of the activity?

✔ Do you reduce the number of competing interests to which you devote your time?

✔ Have you reduced your plan of accomplishment to specific tasks and do you go about accomplishing each task systematically in order of priority?

✔ Do you make a daily evaluation of the tasks you have accomplished?

✔ Have you objectively identified and evaluated all risks and have you determined a bottom line at which point the risks are beyond what you can afford or outweigh realistically obtainable results?

✔ Do you associate yourself with others who have purposes in common with your own and do you share experiences and evaluate progress with them regularly?

✔ Do you surround yourself with those who have expert knowledge in areas of importance to you?

✔ Do you recognize when you are involved in an area beyond your expertise; do you seek expert assistance and additional specialized knowledge when this occurs?

✔ Do you reciprocate for the services others have rendered you?

✔ Are you receiving satisfaction from the efforts you are expending?

✔ Can you objectively measure the progress toward accomplishment of your tasks and goals in relation to the efforts you are making?

✔ Are your sacrifices out of proportion to your intended rewards?

✔ Are you beginning to recognize that you are approaching those short-term points where progress is in line with your expectations?

Appendix B

Inventory of Low-cost Businesses

SERVICE BUSINESSES

Advertising Agency
Amateur Team Sponsoring Service
Answer Letters from Children Service (Santa Claus, Easter Bunny, etc.)
Audiovisual, Photography Service—Unusual/Unique
Baby-Sitting Agency
Computer Equipment Repair
Convention Planning Service
Dating Service
Demonstrators of Products for Business Service
Digital Watch Repair
Dog and Other Pet Training Service
Drapery-Making Service
Employment Services Agency—Specialized
Energy-Loss Prevention Service
Entertainment Agency
Errand Service for Businesses, Attorneys, etc.
Escort Service
Family Hair Salon
Flat-Fee Real Estate Service
Furniture Stripping
Guard Dog Service
Handyman at Large

Homemaking Advisory Service
Home Remodeling, Specialized (such as kitchens, closets, garages, etc.)
Home Repair Advisory Service
Local Guide Service
Maid Employment Agency
Mobile Shoe Repair
Mobile Surface Stripping and Painting Service
Motel Sitting (Vacation Relief)
Office Personnel Referral Club (services available only to members)
Party and Event Planning Service
Party Entertainment Bureau
Party Movie Bureau
Pay and Co-op Television Service
Pet Adoption Agency
Pet ID Tag Service
Pet Sitting/Grooming Service
Promote the Goat Service—Roasts
Publicity, Raffle, and Stunt Promotion Service
Rent-a-Plant Business
Roommate-Finding Service
Secretarial Service
Security Patrol Service
Signboard Advertising Bureau
Solar Sales and Installation Service
Stop Smoking Clinic
Teen Dance Planning Service
Telephone Answering Service
Temporary Help Bureau
Travel Agency—Local Tours and Events
Tutoring Agency
Video Production Bureau—Local Publicity Events
Wake-Up Service
Walk-the-Dog Service
Wallpapering/Painting Service
Window and Home Care Service

MANUFACTURING BUSINESSES
Burlwood Table Manufacturing
Create Personalized Jigsaw Puzzles

Crafts—Home Manufacturing
Customized Basket, Rug, and Handicraft Making
Sculptured Candle Manufacturing
Specialty Manufacturing—You Name It
Stained Glass Manufacturing
Stuffed-Toy/Animal Manufacturing
Unique Wind-Chime Making
Weather-Vane Making

SPORTS/RECREATION BUSINESSES

Aerobic Dance Studio
Athletic- or Sports-Equipment Rental or Repair
Athletic Teaching and Sports Lessons
Backpacking and Hiking Tours
Camping Equipment Rental and Repair
Candid Photos, Unique Shots or Kids-on-a-Pony-Type Photos
Electronic Game Programming
Exercise Studio
Fishing or Hunting Guide
Game or Fish Farm
Hobby Teaching—Skills Shop
Recreational Planning Service for Local Groups
Singles Clubs/Travel Tours
Singles Dance Clubs
Sports Clubs

TOURIST BUSINESSES

Antique Photo Shop
Balloon Vending
Flower Vending
Gifts from or for Folks Back Home Service
Handicraft Co-op or Consignment Shop

RETAIL BUSINESSES

Advertising Specialty Items
Antique Rentals
Appliance Repair
Art-Show Promoting

Bicycle Shop
Bronze-Plating Service
Children's Apparel/Secondhand Shop
Computer-Related Sales and Service
Convenience Services—You Name It
Costume Rental Shop
Day Care/Tot Tutoring
Discount Fabric/Sewing Instruction Shop
Do-It-Yourself Electronic Repair Shop
Energy Store
Gift Shop Boutique
Gourmet Cookware or Any One of Thousands of Other Specialty Shops
Intimate Apparel Shop
Mobile Gift Shop
Obtain Any Wanted Unique or Odd Item for-a-Customer Shop
One-Hour Photo
Optical Accessory Shop
Paint and Wallcovering Shop
Pet Portraits
Pipe Shop
Plant Store/Advisory Shop
Religious Gift Shop
Sign Painting Shop
Survival Store
Taxidermy Shop
T-Shirt or Other Specialty Clothing Store
Telephone Store
Used Book Store
Used Carpet Store
Used Furniture Store

PUBLISHING BUSINESSES

Free Classified Newspaper
Make-Prints-from-Anything Shop
Newsletter Publishing
Rental List Publishing
Who's Who Publishing (Local)

FOOD BUSINESSES

Afternoon Tearoom/Tea Dancing
Barbecue Party Cook
Catering Specialty Items Service—You Name It
Cookbook/Mail-Order Recipes
Dehydrating Food for Others Service
Diners Club Service
Food Broker/Specialty Foods Locator
Freelance Bartender Bureau
Gourmet Shop—Use Your Imagination
Health/Low-Calorie Bakery
Homemade Cake/Pie Shop
Hors d'oeuvres Service
Ice Sculpturing
Low-Cost Box Lunch Service
Make Any Recipe and Bring It to Your Home Service
Mobile Restaurant—Gourmet/Specialty
No-Alcohol Bar
Party Cook/Catering Service
Pasta, Meat, and Cheese Shop
Recipe Club
Reducer's Restaurant
Smoked Food for Others (Fish, Sausage, etc.) Service
Teach Others to Cook Service
Wedding Cakes at Home Business

AUTOMOBILE BUSINESSES

Automobile Detailing
Auto Painting or Repair Shop
Do-It-Yourself Auto Repair Shop
Mobile Auto Repair
Sheepskin or Exotic Seat-Cover Shop
Vinyl/Glass Repair

UNUSUAL BUSINESSES

Apparel-Making for Special Personal Needs
Art Rental Agency
Art-Show Promoting

Bartering Club
Bonsai Gallery
Ceremony for Any Occasion Service
Charter Boats for Others or Locate Mountain Cabins, etc.
Chimney Sweep
Christmas Shopping for Others Service
Comedian for Fun and Profit Bureau
Consulting Service—You Name It
Contest Promoting
Firewood Dealer
Franchise Analysis/Consulting
Fund Raising
Furniture Rental Store
Gift for Any Occasion Service
Gold Mining
House Sitting (While on Vacation, etc.)
Import/Export Consulting
Liquidated Goods Dealer/Broker
Mail Order
Mobile Locksmithing
Multilevel Marketing Businesses
Paper Recycling
Personal Shopping Service Bureau
Pet Cemetery
Plastics and Glass Recycling Center
Private Mailbox Service
Psychic/Consulting Services
Raise Unique/Unusual Foods, Herbs, Spices, or Seasonings
Rent-a-Tent (or hundreds of other unusual items)
Reunion Promotion Service
Special Ceremonies or Gifts for College Students from Parents Services Bureau
Specialty Teaching Service Bureau
Swap Meet Promoting
Weight Control Clinic

Appendix C

Personal Financial Statement

I Own

Cash _ $
    Bank Accounts _ _ _ _ _ _ $_____
    Other _ _ _ _ _ _ _ _ _ _ _ _____
Securities—quick-sale value _ _ _ _ _ _ _ _
Real estate—quick-sale value _ _ _ _ _ _ _
Furniture—quick-sale value _ _ _ _ _ _ _ _
Car—quick-sale value _ _ _ _ _ _ _ _ _ _ _
Cash-value life insurance _ _ _ _ _ _ _ _ _
Savings bonds _ _ _ _ _ _ _ _ _ _ _ _ _
Other assets _ _ _ _ _ _ _ _ _ _ _ _ _ _
Receivables _ _ _ _ _ _ _ _ _ _ _ _ _ _ _
    Total _ _ _ _ _ _ _ _ _ _ _ _ _ $

I own _ _ _ _ _ _ _ _ _ _ _ $
I owe _ _ _ _ _ _ _ _ _ _ _ $
My net worth is _ _ _ _ _ _ _ $

I Owe

Current household bills _ _ _ _ _ _ _ _ _ _ _ $
Installment contracts _ _ _ _ _ _ _ _ _ _ _
    Car _ _ _ _ _ _ _ _ _ _ _ $_____
    Appliances _ _ _ _ _ _ _ _ _____
    Personal loan _ _ _ _ _ _ _ _____
    Other _ _ _ _ _ _ _ _ _ _ _____
Real estate mortgage _ _ _ _ _ _ _ _ _ _ _
    (describe _____

_____)

Other loans _ _ _ _ _ _ _ _ _ _ _ _ _ _
    (describe _____

_____)

    Total _ _ _ _ _ _ _ _ _ _ _ _ _ $

Family Cost-of-Living Budget

DETAILED BUDGET

Regular monthly payments:

House payments or rent _ _ _ _ _ _ _ _ _ _	$
Car payments (including insurance) _ _ _ _.	
Appliance-TV payments _ _ _ _ _ _ _ _ _	
Home improvement loan payments _ _ _ _	
Personal loan payments _ _ _ _ _ _ _ _ .	
Health plan payments _ _ _ _ _ _ _ _ _	
Life insurance premiums _ _ _ _ _ _ _ _ .	
Other insurance premiums _ _ _ _ _ _ _ _ .	
Miscellaneous payments _ _ _ _ _ _ _ _ _	
Total _ _ _ _ _ _ _ _ _ _ _ _ _ _ _	$

Household operating expense:

Telephone _ _ _ _ _ _ _ _ _ _ _ _ _ _ _ .	$
Gas and electricity _ _ _ _ _ _ _ _ _ _ _ _ .	
Water _ _ _ _ _ _ _ _ _ _ _ _ _ _ _ _ _	
Other household expense, repairs, mainte-	
nance _ _ _ _ _ _ _ _ _ _ _ _ _ _ _ _	
Total _ _ _ _ _ _ _ _ _ _ _ _ _ _ _ _	$

Family expense:

Clothing, cleaning, laundry _ _ _ _ _ _ _ _ _ $

Drugs _ _ _ _ _ _ _ _ _ _ _ _ _ _ _ _

Doctors and dentists _ _ _ _ _ _ _ _ _

Education _ _ _ _ _ _ _ _ _ _ _ _ _

Dues _ _ _ _ _ _ _ _ _ _ _ _ _ _ _

Gifts and contributions _ _ _ _ _ _ _ _

Travel _ _ _ _ _ _ _ _ _ _ _ _ _

Newspapers, magazines, books _ _ _ _ _ _

Auto upkeep and gas _ _ _ _ _ _ _ _

Spending money and allowances _ _ _ _ _

Total _ _ _ _ _ _ _ _ _ _ _ _ _ $

Food expense:

Food—at home _ _ _ _ _ _ _ _ _ _ $

Food—away from home _ _ _ _ _ _ _ _

Total _ _ _ _ _ _ _ _ _ _ _ _ _ $

Tax expense:

Federal and state income taxes _ _ _ _ _

Other taxes not included above _ _ _ _ _

Total _ _ _ _ _ _ _ _ _ _ _ _ $

Budget Summary

Regular monthly payments _ _ _ _ _ _ _ _ $

Household operating expense _ _ _ _ _ _ _

Family expense _ _ _ _ _ _ _ _ _ _ _

Food expense _ _ _ _ _ _ _ _ _ _ _ _

Tax expense _ _ _ _ _ _ _ _ _ _ _ _

Total _ _ _ _ _ _ _ _ _ _ _ _

Balance Sheet

—————— ———, 19————

	YEAR I	YEAR II
Current Assets		
Cash	$ _____	$ _____
Accounts receivable	_____	_____
Inventory	_____	_____
Fixed Assets		
Real estate	_____	_____
Fixtures and equipment	_____	_____
Vehicles	_____	_____
Other Assets		
License	_____	_____
Goodwill	_____	_____
TOTAL ASSETS	$ _____	$ _____
Current Liabilities		
Notes payable (due within 1 year)	$ _____	$ _____
Accounts payable	_____	_____
Accrued expenses	_____	_____
Taxes owed	_____	_____
Long-Term Liabilities		
Notes payable (due after 1 year)	_____	_____
Other	_____	_____
TOTAL LIABILITIES	$ _____	$ _____
NET WORTH (ASSETS minus LIABILITIES)	$ _____	$ _____

TOTAL LIABILITIES plus NET WORTH should equal ASSETS

Appendix F

Projected Profit-and-Loss Statement

	Month 1	Month 2	Month 3	Month 4	Month 5	Month 6	Month 7	Month 8	Month 9	Month 10	Month 11	Month 12
Total Net Sales												
Cost of Sales												
GROSS PROFIT												
Controllable Expenses												
Salaries												
Payroll taxes												
Security												
Advertising												
Automobile												
Dues and subscriptions												
Legal and accounting												
Office supplies												
Telephone												
Utilities												
Miscellaneous												
Total Controllable Expenses												
Fixed Expenses												
Depreciation												
Insurance												
Rent												
Taxes and licenses												
Loan Payments												
Total Fixed Expenses												
TOTAL EXPENSES												
NET PROFIT (LOSS) (before taxes)												

Cash Flow Projections

			Cash (beginning of month) Cash on hand	Cash in bank	Cash in investments	Total Cash	Income (during month) Cash sales	Credit sales payments	Investment income	Loans	Other cash income	Total Income	TOTAL CASH AND INCOME	Expenses (during month) Inventory or new material	Wages (including owner's)	Taxes	Equipment expense	Overhead	Selling expense	Transportation	Loan repayment	Other cash expenses	TOTAL EXPENSES	CASH FLOW EXCESS (end of month)	CASH FLOW CUMULATIVE (monthly)

Appendix H

Schedule of Furniture, Fixtures and Equipment

Item (Suggested list - omit or add items as required. Use separate sheets to list details under each main heading)	If cash purchase (new or used) enter full amount below and in the last column	If installment purchase (new or used) enter in the last column down payment plus at least one installment			Estimate of your initial cash requirements for furniture, fixtures and equipment
		Price	Down payment	Amount of each installment	
Display refrigerators					
Supplemental storage case					
Display stands, shelves, tables					
Window display fixtures					
Wrapping counter					
Cash register					
Lighting					
Workroom tables					
Delivery equipment					
Safe					
Outside sign					
Miscellaneous equipment					
Total furniture, fixtures and equipment					$

No Disclosure, No Profit without Consent Form

I, _____ , agree to review the product or idea, the general name of which is
(Name of Reviewer)
_____ and presented by _____ merely for purposes of determining
(General Name of Product)   (Name of Presenter)
manufacturing or production feasibility.

In doing so, I assume no responsibility for and am, therefore, released of any liability involving any information you provide to me about the product or idea.

In return, I agree to not knowingly or intentionally disclose, sell, assign, lease, or in any other way profit or attempt to profit from information, manufacture, production, or sale of the product or idea without written consent of the presenter.

_____
(Signature of Reviewer)

_____
(Signature of Presenter)

_____
(Signature of Witness)

_____
(Date)

Index

Edited by Lonnie W. Dalrymple

Other Bestsellers From TAB

☐ **BECOMING SELF-EMPLOYED: HOW TO CREATE AN INDEPENDENT LIVELIHOOD—Susan Elliott**

If you've ever felt the urge to leave the corporate world to become your own boss, you'll want this book. It reveals what it's like to become successful, and what mistakes to avoid. Includes case studies of twenty successful entrepreneurs—what they did right, what they did wrong, and what they plan for the future and why. 160 pp., 19 illus.
Paper $7.95   **Book No. 30149**

☐ **HOW TO WRITE YOUR OWN WILL—John C. Howell**

Written by a nationally respected trial lawyer and corporate attorney with over 25 years experience, this invaluable book defines all the necessary terms, offers precise explanations for each type of will, and even relates the circumstances under which consultation with a lawyer is advisable. The necessary forms are clearly illustrated and easy to follow. Also presented are the methods of completely avoiding or minimizing the effect of probate. The instructions and documents discussed are in accordance with the statutes of all 50 states. 192 pp.
Paper $9.95   **Book No. 30137**

☐ **THE ENTREPRENEUR'S GUIDE TO STARTING A SUCCESSFUL BUSINESS—James W. Halloran**

Here's a realistic approach to what it takes to start a small business, written by a successful entrepreneur and business owner. You'll learn step-by-step every phase of a business start-up from getting the initial idea to realizing a profit. Included is advice on: designing a store layout, pricing formulas and strategies, advertising and promotion, and more. 256 pp.
Paper $15.95   **Book No. 30049**

☐ **UNDERSTANDING WALL STREET—2nd Edition—Jeffrey B. Little and Lucien Rhodes**

This bestselling guide to understanding and investing on Wall Street has been completely updated to reflect the most current developments in the stock market. The substantial growth of mutual funds, the emergence of index options, the sweeping new tax bill, and how to keep making money even after the market reaches record highs and lows are a few of the things explained in this long-awaited revision. 240 pp., illustrated.
Paper $9.95   **Hard $19.95**
Book No. 30020

☐ **FORMING CORPORATIONS AND PARTNERSHIPS—John C. Howell**

If you're considering offering a service out of your home, buying a franchise, incorporating your present business, or starting a business venture of any type, you need this time- and money-saving guide. It explains the process of creating a corporation, gives information on franchising, the laws of partnership, and more. 192 pp., 5 1/2″ × 8″.
Paper $9.95   **Book No. 30143**

☐ **WINNING AT WORK: THE ROAD TO CAREER SUCCESS—Kenneth E. Norris**

The employee who knows the secret of "doing the little things well" gets ahead! Norris gives you important tips on: working with the boss toward making the company successful . . . mastering the art of making friends with other employees, especially those in important positions . . . developing a winning work philosophy . . . accomplishing work tasks without getting involved in administrative games . . . managing subordinates . . . and more. 126 pp.
Hard $14.95   **Book No. 30077**

☐ **THE SMALL BUSINESS TAX ADVISOR: UNDERSTANDING THE NEW TAX LAW—Cliff Roberson, LLM, Ph.D**

The passage of the Tax Reform Act presented business and corporations with the most dramatic changes in tax laws and liabilities ever. Now, this thorough, easy-to-follow sourcebook provides the information you need to reduce your tax liability—while staying within the recently tightened guidelines! Writing especially for the small business, corporation, and stockholder, business law and tax expert Cliff Roberson gives you a practical overview of: All the new income tax rates. 176 pp., 6″ × 9″.
Paper $12.95   **Book No. 30024**

☐ **EVERYDAY LAW FOR EVERYONE—John C. Howell**

Everyday Law for Everyone explains everything the average citizen needs to know to confidently handle a variety of common legal problems. By following this guide you will be able to: write your own will, change your name, win landlord/tenant disputes, set up partnerships, avoid a probate, adopt a child, form your own corporation, and draw up business contracts—without the expense of complications of hiring a lawyer! *Everyday Law for Everyone* presents the facts about our legal system. A number of legal forms and documents that you can use in specific situations, or refer to when writing your own are included. By doing some of the work yourself, you can save on costly legal fees. Knowledge is your greatest defense! With this laymen's guide, you can be in a controlling position when the unexpected happens. 238 pp.
Paper $9.95   **Book No. 30011**

Other Bestsellers From TAB

☐ **THE PERSONAL TAX ADVISOR: UNDERSTANDING THE NEW TAX LAW**—Cliff Roberson, LLM, Ph.D

If the new federal tax law has left you puzzled as to how it will affect your taxes, this sourcebook will make it all amazingly clear. It simplifies the massive three-volume, 2800-page tax law into language the average taxpayer can understand. There's a personal tax calendar listing important tax dates, a deductions checklist, and advice on preparing for a tax audit. Major areas examined include: permissible deductions, non-real estate investments, fringe benefits, record keeping requirements, real estate, tax shelters, pensions, and tax audits. 176 pp., 6″ × 9″, Paperback.
Paper $12.95   **Book No. 3013**

☐ **THE BUSINESSPERSON'S LEGAL ADVISOR**—Cliff Roberson

Avoid legal problems and get the best legal advice when needed, at the least possible cost! This invaluable business guide covers: how and where to obtain licenses and permits; collecting accounts receivable, business insurance, protect warranties, and disclaimers; hiring and dealing with attorneys; actions to take if your business is failing; and more. 240 pp., 19 illus.
Paper $14.95   **Book No. 2624**